Of special interest to students of contemporary history will be Woods's discussion of the careers and views of Juan Peron and Nelson Rockefeller—for American policy contributed in no small way to Peron's rise, and Rockefeller was the man chiefly responsible for the U.S. rapprochement with Argentina in 1944-45. Woods also gives special attention to the impact of the Wilsonian tradition—especially its contradictions—on policy formation. The last chapter, dealing with Argentina's admission to the U.N., sheds some light on the origins of the Cold War.

Wood's investigation of the Argentine problem makes a significant contribution toward the understanding of U.S.-Latin American relations in the era of the Good Neighbor Policy, and provides new insights into the evolution of hemispheric policy as a whole during World War II. It reflects the growing emphasis on bureaucratic politics as a principal determinant of U.S. diplomacy.

Randall Bennett Woods is associate professor of history at the University of Arkansas. He received the B.A., M.A., and Ph.D. from the University of Texas at Austin. He has published articles in the *Pacific Historical Review*, *Social Science Quarterly*, and *Journal of Inter-American Studies*.

THE ROOSEVELT
FOREIGN-POLICY ESTABLISHMENT
AND THE "GOOD NEIGHBOR"

THE ROOSEVELT
FOREIGN-POLICY
ESTABLISHMENT
AND THE
"GOOD NEIGHBOR"

The United States and Argentina
1941-1945

RANDALL BENNETT WOODS

THE REGENTS PRESS OF KANSAS
Lawrence

© Copyright 1979 by The Regents Press of Kansas
Printed in the United States of America

Library of Congress Cataloging in Publication Data
Woods, Randall Bennett, 1944-
The Roosevelt foreign-policy establishment and
the good neighbor.

Bibliography: p.
Includes index.
1. United States—Foreign relations—Argentine
Republic. 2. Argentine Republic—Foreign relations
—United States. 3. United States—Foreign
relations—1933–1945. I. Title.
E183.8.A7W66   327.73′082   78-10435
ISBN 0-7006-0188-0

FOR RHODA

CONTENTS

PREFACE

Writing in 1961, Bryce Wood penned what has become the standard interpretation of that elusive historical phenomenon known as the Good Neighbor Policy. Between 1933 and 1939 United States policy toward the rest of the hemisphere was based on the "anticipation of reciprocity"; that is, in response to the policies of nonintervention and noninterference, the United States expected the Latin American governments to make friendly compromises with the policy concerns of the United States. With the outbreak of war in Europe in 1939, Washington moved beyond the anticipation to the "evocation" of reciprocity. In an attempt to construct an inter-American collective-security organization capable of defending the hemisphere from Axis subversion and aggression, the United States made specific economic and political concessions to various Latin American nations. The Good Neighbor Policy was more than a system of reciprocity; it comprised, according to Wood, a series of relationships built up during the 1930s between the other American republics and the United States. While each was unique, all of these bilateral dialogues were characterized by trust and mutual respect.[1]

Wood maintained that the durability of the Good Neighbor Policy depended on three things: "continuity in the policy of the United States; moderation in the policy of the Latin American states toward United States investors; and mutual resistance to certain types of incursion from outside."[2] In *The Containment of Latin America*, David Green argues that existing inter-American ties were altered during World War II because United States policy-makers were convinced that the trend toward "revolutionary nationalism" in Latin America posed a threat to North American markets and investments. With a view toward preventing the emergence of state-controlled economies, the United States worked assiduously from 1941 through 1947 to expand its power and presence in Latin America.[3] Undoubtedly, Washington's desire to maintain an economic open door in Latin America played a significant role in the deliberations of United States officials and did affect the continuity of the Good Neighbor Policy. Even more important to the special relationships built up between the United States and the American republics during the 1930s, however, were the two other factors envisioned by Wood: disruption of the diplomatic community that had formulated and implemented the Good Neighbor Policy, and the refusal of one republic to join with the United States in combating extrahemispheric intervention.

From 1939 through 1944 various Argentine governments rejected North America's insistent demand for hemispheric solidarity and collective security. Instead of severing relations with the Axis, they attempted to form a neutralist bloc in southern South America and permitted German agents to use Argentina as a base for Axis espionage and subversion in the Western Hemisphere. Argentine neutrality, if not tolerance of foreign intelligence activities, was a natural outgrowth of the republic's physical location, economic situation, and diplomatic tradition and was not, as so many North Americans believed, a sudden anti–United States aberration. Though German espionage activities did pose a threat to the Allied war effort until late 1943, it may be argued that Argentine nonalignment represented no greater menace to United States interests than the neutralist policies of Ireland, Switzerland, and Spain. Yet, Washington's posture toward those nations differed widely from its hard-line stance toward Buenos Aires. Despite the fact that Argentina was a major supplier of meat, wheat, hides, tungsten, and other vital raw materials to the Allies throughout the war, the American foreign-affairs establishment, from 1942 through 1944, used virtually every tactic known to the international community short of military assault to destabilize three Argentine governments and to force the nation to accept unconditionally North American leadership in extrahemispheric affairs. To say the least, the Roosevelt administration's coercive tactics ran counter to the principles of nonintervention and noninterference that underlay the Good Neighbor Policy.

Washington's reaction to the Argentine problem, seen by *latinos* everywhere as a major test of the Good Neighbor Policy, was not determined solely or even primarily by strategic considerations, as E. O. Guerrant and other historians of the "traditional" school argue,[4] or by a desire to preserve an economic open door in Latin America, as David Green and the revisionists maintain. Washington's response was shaped, above all, by the ever-changing balance of power within the United States foreign-policy establishment. As Wood points out, inter-American relations during the period from 1933 to 1941 never left the hands of a few dedicated, well-informed State Department officials. As they built and serviced each of the unique relationships that emerged during the era of the Good Neighbor, they suffered no significant challenge to their control over policy. With the outbreak of World War II, however, this situation changed dramatically. To deal with the immense problems caused by American participation in the struggle against the Axis, President Roosevelt called into being a score of new agencies and brought into the policy-making process organizations and bureaucrats that had virtually no experience in foreign affairs.[5] Further complicating the diplomatic equation was Roosevelt's tendency to let decisions emerge from bureaucratic conflict and organizational proliferation. This administrative characteristic, so apparent in the president's attempts to deal with the Depression, carried over into foreign policy after 1941.[6] As a result, Argentine-American relations were dramatically affected by the struggle between groups within the State Department and by struggles between the State Department, the Treasury Deparment, the Caribbean Defense Command, and other agencies.

The rapid wartime expansion of the foreign-policy establishment, when coupled with application of the competitive principle, meant that hemispheric affairs and, especially, Argentine-American relations were influenced by men and organizations that not only differed over interpretation of the Good Neighbor Policy but that were responding to needs and drives wholly unrelated to any concept of hemispheric community. In turn, the diplomats who were traditionally charged with responsibility for hemispheric affairs devoted increasingly more effort to protecting their policy-making prerogatives and less to cultivating the bilateral bonds engendered by the Good Neighbor Policy. In making recommendations to the State Department, for example, the American embassy in Buenos Aires acted to prevent encroachment upon its authority by agents of the Board of Economic Warfare, the Foreign Economic Administration, and other agencies operating in Buenos Aires, as well as to further a particular concept of the national interest. The substance of Cordell Hull's policy toward Argentina, the timing of his decisions, and the manner in which he framed options for the White House were determined as much by his rivalry with Sumner Welles, Henry Morgenthau, and Henry Wallace as with his perception of where America's long-range interest lay south of the Rio Grande. Rapprochement with Argentina in 1944–45 came about in part because, as World War II neared its close and the Roosevelt administration prepared for the coming peace, the struggle for control of hemispheric policy momentarily came to a halt and two new bureaucratic coalitions—one concerned primarily with the resurrection of the principles of nonintervention and noninterference in hemispheric affairs and the other preoccupied with international cooperation within the context of a world organization—decided to cooperate in the restoration of hemispheric solidarity.[7]

thesis

In brief, the contention of this book will be that during World War II the Good Neighbor Policy was undermined by, first, Argentina's refusal to make an all-out commitment to the war against the Axis and, second, bureaucratic proliferation and competition within the Roosevelt foreign-policy establishment and their dramatic effect on the way Washington responded to Argentine neutrality. By 1944 various governments of Central and South America were in open rebellion against Washington's response to Argentine neutrality, seeing in it a threat to the policies of nonintervention and noninterference, as well as an alarming indicator of the future course of inter-American relations. This rebellion, coupled with pressure from various interest groups in the United States, the refusal of Great Britain to join in the coercion of Argentina, President Roosevelt's decision to streamline the State Department, and the emergence of a clique of policy-makers just as devoted to the precepts of the Good Neighbor Policy as were its original architects, produced an Argentine-American rapprochement and a temporary restoration of Latin-American faith in the United States.

The research upon which this book is based is a product not only of my efforts but of those of the dedicated staffs of the following libraries and manuscript collections: the National Archives and the Library of Congress, Washington, D.C.; the libraries of the University of Texas, the University of Virginia, the University of Iowa, and the University of Arkansas; Sterling Library at Yale University; the Rockefeller Family Archives in New York

City; the Franklin D. Roosevelt Library, Hyde Park, New York; and the Harry S. Truman Library, Independence, Missouri.

For financial assistance in connection with preparation of the manuscript, I am indebted to the Research Reserve Fund of the University of Arkansas and to the Eleanor Roosevelt Institute.

Numerous colleagues and former teachers read all or part of the manuscript at various stages of its preparation and furnished many helpful insights and constructive criticisms. The former teachers include Clarence Lasby, Nancy Barker, and Thomas McGann, all of the University of Texas at Austin. The colleagues include Willard Gatewood, Timothy Donovan, and James Chase, all of the University of Arkansas. I am also indebted to William R. Emerson of the Franklin D. Roosevelt Library, Norris Hundley of the University of California at Los Angeles, John Harrison of the University of Miami, and William Griffith of the University of Kansas for the valuable aid and advice they have given me during the course of the project. Michael Grady Woods typed the manuscript and made numerous editorial suggestions.

The individual who more than any other is responsible for my career and for matching me with this topic is Robert Divine of the University of Texas. No mentor could have done more for a student. Without the love and support furnished by my wife, Rhoda, and my children, Nicole and Jeffrey, I would most certainly have abandoned this project years ago. Needless to say, any errors of form, style, and judgment in this work are solely mine.

1

THE GOOD NEIGHBOR POLICY
AND ARGENTINE NEUTRALISM

The basic objectives of United States diplomacy in regard to Latin America have remained virtually unchanged since the promulgation of the Monroe Doctrine in 1823. Throughout the nineteenth century and the first three-quarters of the twentieth, American diplomats labored to prevent foreign intervention in Latin America, to protect United States economic interests south of the Rio Grande, and to guard the strategic approaches to the Western Hemisphere.[1] The way in which Washington has pursued these goals, however, has varied tremendously under the impact of domestic political warfare, the ever-changing international situation, and the public's conception of America's role in world affairs.

The United States emerged from the Spanish-American War determined to play an active role abroad. Adherents of the New Manifest Destiny won an ever-increasing number of Americans to the idea that it was the nation's duty to spread the blessings of freedom, democracy, and capitalism to every region of the world.[2] Social Darwinists argued that human society was but a jungle where the laws of natural selection and survival of the fittest operated at every level. Nations, like organisms, competed for living space and natural resources. Those that did not expand died. The social scientists who developed the biological rationale for expansion were joined by captains of industry who proclaimed that the answer to the cyclical depressions that plagued the American economy was the establishment of new markets capable of absorbing the nation's surplus production. Missionaries, who in the 1890s had "sworn to evangelize the world in this decade," demanded that Washington protect them and that the public support them as they brought Christianity to millions of heathens

1

around the world. Convinced of the superiority of American political institutions, social imperialists maintained that the United States had a duty to bring the blessings of liberty and democracy to those living under the oppressive rule of tyrants and dictators. The mechanism for the new expansionism was supplied by Alfred Thayer Mahan and his disciples. Invoking the British imperial model, he persuaded many Americans that United States foreign policy should focus on the acquisition of a series of bases along the major trading routes of the world, construction of an isthmian canal in Central America, and establishment of a large navy to protect American merchants and missionaries as they opened up underdeveloped areas.[3]

Even when diplomats such as John Quincy Adams and James K. Polk were laboring to round out the nation's continental frontiers, Latin America had figured in the long-term plans of United States expansionists. With the advent of the New Manifest Destiny, the area south of the Rio Grande took center stage in the eyes of American policy-makers. Central and South America abounded with undeveloped natural resources, potential consumers, souls waiting to be saved, and governments in need of tutelage. Although the Monroe Doctrine laid claim to the area for North American exploitation, post-1900 expansionists were afraid, almost to the point of paranoia, that a major European power would preempt the United States in the palaces, churches, and marketplaces of Latin American society. Washington was particularly concerned about protecting the approaches to the projected isthmian canal, so vital to America's proposed transoceanic empire. The three presidents who controlled the Latin-American policy of the United States between the Spanish American War and World War I all shared these fears and goals, but each supplied his own interpretation of the New Manifest Destiny, and each brought to inter-American affairs his own unique variety of imperialism.

Never questioning either America's right to exploit Latin America economically or its duty to instruct it in the precepts of "civilization," Theodore Roosevelt, a devoted disciple of Mahan, directed his efforts to the construction of an isthmian canal and to forestalling European penetration of the New World. In pursuit of these and other goals, he coerced various Latin American republics and then defended his activities by articulating in 1904 the definitive rationale for United States intervention—the Roosevelt Corollary to the Monroe Doctrine.[4] Latin Americans felt threatened enough by Roosevelt's intervention into Cuban affairs and by his treatment of Colombia in regard to the Panama Canal, but they were even more alarmed by the president's overall attitude toward the hemispheric community, an attitude that was characterized by obsession with power and insensitivity to the rights of weaker nations.[5]

Responsibility for Roosevelt's empire in the Caribbean fell to his hand-picked successor, William Howard Taft. Even more than Roosevelt, Taft and his secretary of state, Philander Knox, believed that in order to preserve Latin America as a reliable field for investment and to protect United States strategic interests in the area, they would have to restrict European influence to an absolute minimum. Taft and Knox perceived, however, that the Roosevelt Corollary, if interpreted literally, would impose an awesome burden on the United States and would lead to frequent armed intervention, something they ardently hoped to avoid. Knox's solution to the problem of how to protect American interests south of the Rio Grande without maintaining permanent marine garrisons throughout the hemisphere was a curious blend of corporate finance and strong-arm imperialism. The secretary of state persuaded Taft that if the United States could displace Latin American indebtedness from Europe to the United States, the threat of foreign meddling would vanish, along with the need for American intervention. Unfortunately, United States financiers proved to be just as anxious about the security of their investments as were their European counterparts. Once they had been persuaded to invest in Latin American stocks and bonds, they demanded that Washington use whatever force was necessary to ensure stability and regularity of interest payments. Thus, while dollar diplomacy was designed to facilitate United States control of the Western Hemisphere and while it perhaps reduced the threat of nonhemispheric interference, the policy also led to massive military intervention and so to mounting alienation in Latin America.[6]

In 1912 Theodore Roosevelt, enraged by his successor's handling of America's Caribbean and Far Eastern empires as well as his neglect of the Rooseveltian domestic programs, challenged Taft for the presidency and, in so doing, hopelessly split the Republican party. As a result, Woodrow Wilson became the second Democrat to enter the White House since the Civil War. Wilson brought a new style to foreign affairs and new objectives to the Latin American policy of the United States. This former academician believed that the basic drive behind American foreign policy should not be material self-interest or power for power's sake, but rather a desire to serve mankind through the propagation of freedom and democracy. This is not to say that he ignored either the existence of powerful economic interests in international life or the necessity of defending the nation's strategic interests. Indeed, he looked after United States economic and strategic concerns in Latin America quite conscientiously. Nevertheless, he felt that American policy ought to go beyond these concerns. Reflecting his Calvinist upbringing, Woodrow Wilson viewed the nation as God's chosen instrument for bringing the blessings of civilization, peace, Christianity, and democracy to all mankind. The president saw democracy as the most humane and Christian form of government; and transcending the doctrine of predestination, he repeatedly asserted that all men were capable of being trained in the political techniques of representative government.[7] Moral imperialism—as Arthur Link has labeled Wilson's Latin American policy —was as interventionist as Roosevelt's big stick or dollar diplomacy.[8] Wilson's tactics were all the more offensive to Latin Americans because, in addition to producing armed intervention in Haiti and Mexico, they revealed both a total disregard for the unique political and economic conditions that existed in the various republics and an aggressive unwillingness to allow the South and Central American peoples to work out their own destiny.

Latin Americans were hopeful that Wilson's World War I pronouncements about self-determination and the juridical equality of all states signaled a new era in the inter-American policy of the United States. Indeed, a number of *latino* statesmen, led by Argentina's Carlos Saavedra Lamas, enthusiastically embraced the League of Nations concept, hoping that Geneva would act as a brake on United States imperialism south of the Rio Grande. After the United States Senate rejected membership in the league and the American people repudiated Wilsonian idealism by returning the GOP to power, many *latinos* readied themselves for a new version of the big stick.

Despite Sen. Henry Cabot Lodge's statement, on the hundredth anniversary of the Monroe Doctrine in 1923, that the historic proclamation "is no more to be disturbed or questioned or interpreted by other nations than [is] the independence of the United States,"[9] forces built after World War I for a change in the tactics if not the basic goals of America's hemispheric policy. In the postwar decade, American investments south of the Rio Grande grew to almost $6 billion. The rising tide of revolutionary national-

4

ism, generated in part by remembrances of past North American exploitation, became of increasing concern to Wall Street and to the business-oriented Harding, Coolidge, and Hoover administrations. Too, the war had destroyed in Britain, France, and Germany much of their capability for economic expansion abroad and, with it, the need for intervention to prevent extrahemispheric financial penetration. The strategic imperative for intervention had evaporated as well: after 1921 no naval power threatened the security of the canal. A concomitant of America's global retreat from responsibility was the desire at home to shed the task of policing the Western Hemisphere. Anti-imperialists, spearheaded by LaFollette Progressives, demanded a repudiation of the Roosevelt Corollary to the Monroe Doctrine and denounced United States economic imperialism for relegating most Latin Americans to perpetual peonage.[10]

As a result of these diverse factors, Republican diplomats acted from 1921 to 1933 to eliminate some of the grosser aspects of United States hegemony in the Western Hemisphere.[11] The Republican phase of the Good Neighbor Policy culminated in 1928 with publication of the Clark Memorandum. That document, while reserving to the United States the right of intervention under international law, did renounce the Roosevelt Corollary and declared that the Monroe Doctrine was intended to be, not a cover for United States imperialism, but a shield protecting the Western Hemisphere from European interference.[12]

With the advent of the New Deal the concept of the Good Neighbor began to take more definite shape. The reasons that had prompted a change in tactics for dealing with Latin America after 1921 were still valid in 1933. But there were also compelling new factors pushing the Roosevelt administration to adopt nonintervention and cooperation, rather than the principles of the New Manifest Destiny, in its dealings with Latin America. There was certainly no threat of a foreign power menacing the approaches of the Panama Canal through construction of military bases in the Caribbean. Moreover, the Depression had further lessened the threat of extrahemispheric economic exploitation. After Roosevelt torpedoed the London Economic Conference and the New Deal passed through its brief period of economic nationalism, the president and the secretary of state, Cordell Hull (a fervent believer in the ability of free trade to solve the world's economic problems), began to view improved commercial relations with the New World as a means to pull the United States out of the Depression.

5

Out of a belief that hemispheric cooperation would facilitate a return to prosperity, as well as the conviction that continued military and diplomatic intervention constituted a threat rather than a shield for American lives and property in Latin America, the Roosevelt administration launched a concerted drive to convince the American republics of Washington's respect for their national sovereignty and its solicitude for their economic well-being. After ostentatiously repudiating intervention at the inter-American conference held in Montevideo in 1933, the United States and the Cuban government in May 1934 signed a treaty abrogating the Platt Amendment, which had transformed the "ever-faithful isle" into an American protectorate following the Spanish-American War. In August the last contingent of Marines left Haiti, and that black republic was at last free to pursue its political destiny in its own way. The dismantling of America's network of protectorates was accompanied by reciprocal tariff agreements and, in 1934, by the establishment of the new Export-Import Bank to foster trade with Cuba and other Latin American countries. The bank, established to provide Latin American nations with capital that would enable them to purchase United States exports, earned far less good will, however, than did the bilateral trade agreements eventually negotiated between Washington and ten other American republics. The United States relinquished its last formal New World protectorate in 1936, when the State Department negotiated a new treaty with Panama that deprived Washington of the "right" to intervene militarily.[13]

Latin America welcomed the Good Neighbor Policy as much for its apparent spirit as for its substance. It seemed to many that at last the United States intended to treat the American republics as a community of nations, each with a unique culture and political heritage and each possessed of the right to formulate domestic and foreign policies absolutely free from outside interference.[14] One of the principal factors behind America's renunciation of the big stick, dollar diplomacy, and moral imperialism after World War I was the absence of any real threat to the security of the Western Hemisphere. As Japan, Italy, and Germany moved to implement their expansionist schemes, this sense of well-being evaporated, and as a result the Good Neighbor Policy experienced its first major test.

As Bryce Wood has pointed out, America's renunciation of the right to dominate was based on the anticipation of reciprocity: in response to Washington's promise to abjure intervention and to implement free trade, it was expected that Central and South American governments would make concessions to the major policy concerns of the United States. Initially Washington launched the Good Neighbor Policy in order to safeguard American lives and property south of the Rio Grande and to promote trade between the United States and the rest of the hemisphere. With the increased aggressiveness of Germany, Italy, and Japan after 1936, however, the objectives of the Good Neighbor Policy changed radically. The State Department became, for the first time since World War I, truly apprehensive about the security of the Western Hemisphere.[15] There thus developed a second phase of the Good Neighbor Policy, in which the Roosevelt administration expected that in return for the renunciation of intervention, the American republics would join with the United States to transform the Pan-American system into a collective-security organization. From 1936 through 1941 Washington attempted to persuade the governments of Latin America to view their interests in foreign affairs as identical with that of the United States and to pledge to regard an attack on one as an attack on all.[16]

Latin America was well aware that one of the primary justifications for American imperialism prior to World War I was the threat of foreign intervention in the Western Hemisphere. Consequently, the gathering war clouds in Europe and the Far East alarmed the American republics both because they genuinely feared the imperial ambitions of the aggressor nations and because they suspected that the international crisis might drive the United States to abandon nonintervention and noncoercion. Many of the American republics believed that the United States would be able to forge the Western Hemisphere into a collective-security organization and then convert the resulting hemisphere alliance system into a vehicle for traditional American imperialism.[17] One nation was particularly fearful that United States diplomats would react to the global crisis by violating and circumscribing the freedom of action of the several states.

During the second phase of the Good Neighbor Policy, Argentina vigorously resisted the attempted conversion of a Pan-American association into a military alliance. Pan-Americanism was nothing more than a spirit of cooperativeness, argued Argentine diplomats, and inter-American meetings were simply voluntary conferences held for the purpose of consultation.[18] The United States–Argentine debate over the nature of the Inter-American System became particularly animated after Hitler invaded Poland in the fall of 1939, thus plunging Europe into World War II. As the United States was drawn irresistably toward war with the Axis, moving from neutrality to belligerency to a state of undeclared war between 1939 and 1941, the Roosevelt administration stepped up its efforts to mobilize the hemisphere for a possible all-out war effort. In sharp contrast, Argentina maintained a strict neutrality toward both sets of belligerents and derided Washington's arguments that the hemisphere must regard an attack on one nation as an attack on all.

Argentina's challenge to the second phase of the Good Neighbor Policy, like her determination to remain nonaligned during World War II, was not, as many Americans were to believe, the result of Axis infiltration and domination; nor was it a sudden aberration caused by transitory events. Rather, both Argentina's position toward World War II generally and its reaction to the Roosevelt administration's drive to merge Latin American and United States foreign policies were the products of geography, economics, immigration patterns, the Depression, and the military's historical involvement in Argentine political life. In short, Argentina's neutralist posture toward World War II and its resistance to the United States campaign for a collective-security organization reflected Argentina's national experience.

The Argentineans are a proud, independent, and cosmopolitan people who historically have viewed themselves as a community set apart from the rest of Latin America. On the eve of World War II, Argentina possessed the whitest and most Europeanized population in all of South America. Spaniards, Italians, and, to a lesser extent, Germans innundated Argentina between 1880 and 1930.[19] One result of this influx was that Argentine culture became and remained heavily influenced by European standards and tastes. For example, France has always played a leading role in Argentine social and literary circles; Germany, in scientific and military affairs; and Great Britain, in business and political matters.[20]

Due partly to the relatively high educational level of twentieth-century immigrants and partly to the highest per capita income in Latin America prior to 1943, the literacy rate in Argentina at mid century was an astounding 90 percent. The nation's educational system ranked among the best in the Western Hemisphere. The Argentine press was the strongest and most independent in Latin America. Educational opportunity and prosperity produced one of the oldest and largest middle classes in the New World.[21]

Argentina's economy, while very strong, was still hobbled in the 1930s by having to depend on foreign sources for certain vital manufactured goods.

Nevertheless, because it relied on Europe rather than the United States for these products, Argentina's economic structure was a plus in its struggle with North America for leadership of the Western Hemisphere. Argentina possesses one of the most productive pastoral-agricultural systems in the world. The broad plain of central Argentina, known as the Pampas, is an extremely fertile area with a mild climate and adequate rainfall. The tremendous quantities of meat, wheat, hides, quebracho (a substance essential to the tanning process), and linseed oil produced by this South American Caucasus made Argentina one of the most important producers of raw material in the world. That nation's abundance of foodstuffs was matched, however, by its dearth of the mineral and power resources needed for industrialization. An abundance of specialized natural resources and a need for manufactured products, particularly heavy machinery, meant that Argentine prosperity depended upon foreign trade. Her economic lifeline ran quite literally from the huge port of Buenos Aires to the entrepôts of Western Europe.[22] This situation freed Argentina from economic dependence on the United States and other American states and, much to the distress of American diplomats who were trying to weld the hemisphere into a military and economic unit, infused her foreign policy with an internationalist hue.

Geography, no less than economics, has had a major impact on Argentine diplomacy. The nation's location at the southeastern tip of South America has historically isolated it from the great power coalitions and international currents of the nineteenth and twentieth centuries. This remoteness has allowed Argentina the freedom to develop her own approach to world affairs.[23]

Foremost among the "traits" produced by Argentina's national experience is an ebullient patriotism accompanied by excessive sensitivity to criticism. Whether they are urban laborers, white-collar workers, or provincial gauchos living in a world of "machismo," Argentineans have bitterly resented any implication that they are inferior and have strenuously resisted political tutelage by the United States or any other state. Noted for their intensity and national energy, Argentineans have distinguished themselves in almost every field of endeavor, and they have regarded their country as the equal of any other nation in every respect.[24]

From the interrelationships between immigration patterns, economic trends, geography, and mass psychological characteristics, two recurrent themes in Argentine foreign policy emerged: neutralism and nationalism.

During the course of her national experience there has been no economic or military need for foreign alliances, and thus Argentina, relishing its independence, has shunned entangling connections with Europe, North America, and even other Latin American states. For example, when James G. Blaine, United States secretary of state, sought in the late nineteenth century to promote hemispheric prosperity—and, not coincidentally, to aid United States economic penetration of Central and South America—by establishing a Pan-American organization, Argentina vigorously resisted.[25] After the outbreak of World War I, Pres. Hipólito Irigoyen refused to support either the Central Powers or the Allies. His policy of nonalignment enjoyed broad popular support because it brought peace and unparalleled prosperity.[26] It is safe to say that neutrality in the face of world conflict had become by 1942 an accepted tradition among foreign-policy-makers in Buenos Aires.

Neutrality did not mean isolation, however. Argentina has attempted throughout the nineteenth and twentieth centuries to assume the role of spokesman and protector for all Latin America. Increasingly, Argentine diplomats perceived that the key to hemispheric leadership lay with their nation's ability to spearhead Latin opposition to North American encroachments.[27] When the first Pan-American Conference met in 1889, Argentine representatives pointed out the possibilities for political and economic exploitation in Secretary Blaine's proposed inter-American organization and boldly asked the United States to state its intentions. To their Latin colleagues the Argentine delegates insisted that the real hope for the Latin American community was to be found in a Pan-Latinism from which the United States would be excluded. So successful was Argentina in challenging North America's first real attempt to establish hemispheric hegemony that by 1890 Buenos Aires, not Washington, stood as champion of the New World in the eyes of many *latinos*.[28] The passage of time would only confirm Argentina's conviction that the best method for augmenting the nation's influence in Central and South America was to oppose United States attempts to give form and structure to the principle of inter-American solidarity.

The Depression and the breakdown of the Versailles peace structure in the 1930s spawned a particularly virulent strain of nationalism in Argentina which further whetted the republic's desire for hemispheric leadership and simultaneously fostered a determination to remain aloof from the conflicts developing in Europe and the Far East. Within Argentina the Depression

10

created new demands for order and stability—unfortunately at the expense of democracy. Tariff barriers and quota systems established by the United States and the sterling-bloc nations had a particularly unsettling effect on this trade-oriented nation, depending as it did on free access to the grain and beef markets of the world. Reflecting the frustrations and tensions bred by the economic crisis, Argentine politics entered a period that José Romero has referred to as the era of fraudulent democracy. During these years a series of military strong men, supported by the conservative oligarchy, governed by manipulating Argentine's democratic processes and institutions.[29]

Between 1890 and 1920 Argentina produced one of the better-defined party systems in South America. The National Democratic, or Conservative, party dominated Argentine political life throughout the nineteenth and early twentieth centuries. The party of the landed aristocracy, or *estanciero*, it stood for free trade abroad and maintenance of the status quo at home. The name Conservative was traditionally linked with foreign economic exploitation and political corruption. Although the twentieth century witnessed a steady expansion of the party organization so as to accommodate businessmen and financiers, the heart of the National Democrats continued to be the great landowners of the Pampas. The Radical party, middle-class to the core, was economically and socially conservative but was plagued by internal disputes and an inability to focus its energies. Although Radical candidates were often able to challenge the Conservatives effectively by clamoring for political reform and electoral honesty, the Radicals' early history was characterized by intransigence—refusal to vote or participate in public life until free elections were guaranteed—and its later activities were characterized by its inability to appeal to the lower classes.[30] The Socialist party, formed in 1894, was small and generally evolutionary rather than revolutionary, but among its members were some of the nation's most eminent intellectual and political figures. Socialists in Argentina, as elsewhere, were divided by issues such as international anarchism, utopianism, and nationalism and, in general, were torn between the demands of theory and the practical need to organize unions and strikes.[31] The Conservatives and Radicals, much more than the Socialists, shifted and side-stepped, moving deftly to straddle issues and to capture (or purchase) a plurality.

To many Argentineans after 1929, democracy and the traditional parties seemed to be bankrupt. As the Depression and popular frustration at the government's inability to deal with it mounted, an increasing number of

11

citizens decided that the fatherland was being crippled by a weak executive; by a sterile Congress, devoted to petty bickering; and by municipalities which were feeding on jobbery and corruption. Fundamental problems—such as a poorly balanced economy, vast inequities between rural and urban society, and illiteracy and poverty among the lower classes—cried out for solutions. Argentine foreign policy seemed stagnant; national momentum seemed at a standstill. Many of the discontented turned to those in Argentina who, wishing to purify Argentine national life through massive doses of totalitarianism, looked to Benito Mussolini and Charles Maurras for inspiration.[32]

The various groups that gathered under the nationalist umbrella brought their own specific grievances and unique panaceas to the movement. First came the impoverished sons of ruined *estancieros,* whose naturally reactionary ideals were accentuated by a gradual loss of the power and prestige that they felt to be their birthright.[33] The movement also included a large segment of the German- and Italian-trained officer corps, who looked to the corporate state (or some version of it) and to expansion into southern South America as remedies for Argentina's social and economic ills. Equally important to the Argentine Right was the intensely anti-Communist and pro-Spanish Catholic clergy, whose political views were a cross between those of Francisco Franco and Philip II. These groups sought, quite simply, to transform Argentina into an authoritarian society that would be controlled by the army and the Church.[34] According to such groups as Alianza de la Nacionalista, the precepts of nineteenth-century liberalism, democracy, and constitutional government had never been applicable to South America.[35] Propagandists for the totalitarian movement constantly advocated a return to discipline, order, and authority in order to deal with the Communist specter threatening the fatherland.[36] According to nationalist spokesmen, emulation of the traditions of Catholic and imperial Spain would revitalize Argentine society and enhance her position as champion of Latin America.[37]

The nationalist movement in Argentina was able to take advantage of the fact that economists and *descamisados* alike blamed the Depression on the nation's dependence on foreign capital, particularly British and American. Nationalist spokesmen denounced British interests in utilities, the meat-packing industry, and railroads as a gross violation of the national sovereignty. The New Deal was depicted as a reactionary movement designed to save North American capitalism; the Good Neighbor Policy, as a cover for American businessmen who were busily sucking the blood out of every American republic from Mexico to Argentina.[38]

Historians such as Arthur Whitaker (*Argentina*) and Marvin Goldwert (*Democracy, Militarism, and Nationalism in Argentina, 1930–1966*) refer to the phenomenon described above as "integral nationalism" and contrast it with "liberal nationalism." Generally, liberal nationalists believed in a strong, unified Argentina which would be able to play a vigorous role in hemispheric and world affairs. They supported military preparedness and resented European and North American economic penetration of Argentina. Nonetheless, they refused to embrace fascism in order to accomplish their goals. They were, in Goldwert's words, "constitutionalist, neocivilianist, and [after 1939] proally."[39] Integral nationalism prevailed in Argentina during the 1940s because (1) a large segment of the population supported its diplomatic objectives—namely, resistance to United States leadership in the Western Hemisphere, neutrality in World War II, and Argentine domination of southern South America—and (2) one of the movement's principal components, the Argentine officer corps, controlled national politics throughout the 1930s and 1940s.

In the name of eliminating electoral fraud, restoring order, and purging the state of foreign influences, the military actively intervened in Argentine political life from 1928 through 1945 by forming alliances with various civilian groups, putting up candidates for office, and occasionally seizing control of the government by force. The various chief executives of the era, whether members of the officer corps or not, ruled only so long as they worked to achieve the goals and meet the needs of the nation's warrior class.[40]

As the United States responded to Japanese, German, and Italian aggression by attempting to convert the Western Hemisphere into a collective-security system, the military in Argentina concluded that it was in the interest of their country to preserve its freedom of action and to maintain a policy of strict neutrality toward the conflicts developing in the Far East and Europe. Indeed, nonalignment was attractive to the officer corps not only because it conformed to their concept of the national interest but also because it promised to fulfill a number of organizational goals, not the least of which was self-preservation. Military planners were well aware that in the event of hostilities with the Axis, Argentina would be on her own and could expect no help whatsoever from the United States Caribbean Defense

13

Command. Should some provocative act such as breaking relations with the Axis be committed by Argentina, its remote location and extended coastline would make it impossible to defend against German retaliation. A majority of the officer corps was convinced that on military grounds alone the risk of open conflict with the Axis had to be avoided at all costs.[41]

Contributing to the military's desire to resist the North American drive for a hemispheric collective-security organization and to avoid participating in World War II were its historic ties with the German Army. The intimate relationship between the two officer corps began in 1899, when the Wehrmacht was invited to organize the Argentine War Academy, the Colegio Militar. Germans holding Argentine commissions rotated on the staff of the institution for the next fifteen years. A decree of 1905, which provided that only graduates of the Colegio Militar could receive commissions, created an officer corps that had a uniform educational background and one that was strongly influenced by German ideals and standards. In 1935 Berlin dispatched a six-man commission to advise the Argentine general staff, and Buenos Aires responded by sending some twenty officers each year to study in Germany.[42] This is not to say that the rapport that existed between the two organizations led to a desire within the Argentine officer corps for Nazi domination of the Western Hemisphere, or even for an Axis victory in World War II.[43] Nevertheless, respect for German professional standards and achievements did impel the army, and thus the nation, toward noninvolvement. And of course, as German-American relations deteriorated after 1939, the Wehrmacht encouraged their Argentine comrades to resist United States pressure to join in converting the Western Hemisphere into an anti-Axis bloc.

But neutrality for the military was more than just a defensive tactic; it was a stratagem that promised to satisfy the basic organizational drive for self-aggrandizement—that is, the tendency of every bureaucratic agency to grow in budget, personnel, and influence. The officer corps understood that nonalignment would enable Argentina to play the contending power blocs off against each other and to extract, as the price for continued neutrality, the armaments, technology, and industrial equipment that would make Argentina's war machine the most powerful in South America.[44]

Thus, a variety of forces, events, personalities, and organizations combined to foster a determination within Argentina's foreign-policy establishment to remain aloof from all extrahemispheric clashes and to play as

14

influential a role as possible in South America. After 1936 Buenos Aires was prepared to resist Washington's attempts to weld the hemisphere into an anti-Axis block, while using the international crisis to enhance Argentina's power and prestige within the Latin American community.

The first of the Argentine-American encounters over the nature of the Inter-American System after the breakdown of the Versailles peace structure came in 1936, when President Roosevelt and Secretary Hull convened a special Inter-American Conference for the Maintenance of Peace. The American delegation came determined to have the conferees endorse the Monroe Doctrine and establish a continent-wide collective-security organization that could deal with the threat of armed aggression or subversion from abroad. At this juncture the North American initiative for a regional security system had definite isolationist overtones. The State Department was aware that whatever happened in Europe and the Far East vitally affected United States interests, but American diplomats had been unable to do anything to halt Fascist aggression in those areas because of the strength of isolationist opinion in the United States. The work of the Nye Committee, revisionist historians, student pacifist organizations, and other groups convinced most Americans that European conflicts had no bearing on the national interest. The man in the street was determined at this point that the United States would not be drawn into another superfluous war through participation in the League of Nations or other "European" collective-security schemes. Isolationists and interventionists could agree, however, on the necessity of preparing the defenses of "Fortress America" to deal with any threat to the Western Hemisphere from across the Atlantic or Pacific. As a result, at Buenos Aires, Secretary Hull urged the other republics to sign an obligatory pledge of reciprocal assistance in case of an attack by a non-American power on any nation of the Western Hemisphere, to create a permanent consultative organ, and to enact for themselves the neutrality legislation recently passed by Congress.[45]

The Argentine delegation was adamantly opposed to the American plan because it contravened virtually every hallowed principle of Argentine foreign policy. Led by Carlos Saavedra Lamas, who had recently received the Nobel Peace Prize and was president-elect of the League of Nations, the Argentine delegation adopted a specious internationalism for the purpose of obstructing Washington's plans. Saavedra Lamas and his colleagues proclaimed that mandatory collaboration and the establishment of a regional organization not only would destroy Latin America's freedom of action but would also subvert the League of Nations. Moreover, adoption of an automatic arms embargo upon the outbreak of war (as provided in the neutrality laws of the United States) would violate provisions of the League of Nations Charter. More importantly, perhaps, the Argentineans were able to convince a majority of their Latin American colleagues that the United States would be able, by virtue of its military power alone, to dominate any security organization. The key issue in inter-American affairs, declared Saavedra Lamas, was not that a non-American power might intervene in the New World, but that one American state might intervene in the affairs of another.[46] As a result of Argentina's very effective counteroffensive, the United States had to settle for a nonobligatory resolution providing for inter-American consultation in case of an attack on any hemispheric republic by a non-American state. In return, Hull and his colleagues signed a pledge which Latin America hoped would put United States imperialism to rest once and for all. It declared inadmissable the right of any state to intervene "directly or indirectly, and for whatever reason, in the internal or external affairs of any other of the Parties."[47]

During the interlude between the Buenos Aires meeting and the next Pan-American Conference in 1938, the League of Nations and the doctrine of collective security were severely discredited by the league's failure to deal with Japan's encroachments in China and Hitler's subversion first of Austria and then of Czechoslovakia. Meanwhile, German and Italian propagandists, cultural emissaries, and commercial agents accelerated their drive to secure an ideological, financial, and, if possible, political foothold in South America. Washington assumed that covert activities by the aggressor nations in the Western Hemisphere, together with the deteriorating situation abroad, would make the republics of Latin America more receptive to United States arguments in behalf of a regional security arrangement.[48]

The International Conference of American States that was held in Lima in December 1938 was, like the Buenos Aires meeting, dominated by an Argentine-American conflict over the structure of the inter-American consultative system and the right of one or more American states to pass judgment on domestic developments in another. With the Spanish Civil War still raging and the Munich Conference barely over, Washington was particularly sensitive to the threat of German and Italian subversion in the Western Hemisphere. The United States delegation therefore proposed joint action to prevent the subversion of "unstable governments" by Fascist-oriented systems and suggested the establishment of regular as well as emergency meetings of foreign ministers to delineate hemispheric policy toward the rest of the world. Again, Argentina, joined by Uruguay, Paraguay, Chile, and several other states situated far from the protective arm of the Caribbean Defense Command, led the opposition to the United States. The Ortiz administration, which had swept into power in 1938, was outwardly more friendly to the United States, but, like its predecessor, it was determined to resist the creation of a regional security system and to profit from Washington's attempts to control Latin American foreign policy. Saavedra Lamas's successor in the Foreign Office, José M. Cantilo, first sought to have the conference called off. Failing in that, he delivered a few perfunctory remarks to the opening session and then sailed off on a protracted vacation cruise. He left behind a weak delegation which had been carefully instructed to make no binding commitments.[49]

As a result, American diplomats were compelled to accept the innocuous Declaration of Lima, which weakly reaffirmed the principle of continental solidarity in the face of an extrahemispheric threat; proclaimed that if the general "peace, security or territorial integrity" were threatened from any source, the signatories would consult; and provided that the foreign ministers of the several states could be called into conference at the behest of any one member. As if these resolutions were not sufficiently vague, the Argentineans secured the inclusion of a formal proviso that reserved complete freedom of action to each member of the Pan-American Union under all circumstances. In the future the freedom-of-action clause would hobble Washington's attempts to portray the Declaration of Lima as a binding collective-security pact.[50]

When Germany invaded Poland in 1939, the public mood in Argentina was not greatly different from that in the United States. True, there was the flourishing nationalist movement and, in some quarters, even frank admiration for Hitler and Mussolini, but the vast majority of the public and the press sympathized with the victims of Axis aggression and their tardy champions.[51] The United States ambassador, Norman Armour, reported from Buenos Aires that the city was shocked by the blitzkreig and was enthusiastic in its support of the democracies. Nevertheless, these prejudiced reactions in no way altered the nation's sense of where its national interest lay. The economic realities, geographical imperatives, and cultural factors behind

17

Argentine foreign policy remained relatively unaffected by the outbreak of war in Europe. Above all else, the Argentineans wanted peace; they foresaw nothing but economic distress and diminished power if their nation became involved in an extrahemispheric war. Thus, while Argentina joined whole-heartedly with the United States and six other American republics in calling the First Consultative Meeting of Foreign Ministers at Panama, Buenos Aires was determined to block any action that might possibly involve Argentina in a war with the Axis.[52] When the United States contingent proposed to keep Axis submarines and other naval vessels out of American waters by establishing a three-hundred-mile neutrality zone around North and South America, Buenos Aires protested that such a move would needlessly disrupt relations between the New World and the Old. The Declaration of Panama proclaimed hemispheric neutrality toward the European phase of World War II and established the neutrality belt, but it satisfied Argentina by leaving up to each individual state the question of whether or not to patrol.[53]

In the spring of 1940, the "phony war" in Europe came to an abrupt close as German panzer units smashed through Belgium and the Nether-lands and into the heart of France. Fearful that Hitler would force France and Holland to allow their New World colonies to be used as staging areas for the subversion or invasion of the rest of the Western Hemisphere, the Roosevelt administration shepherded through Congress, on 18 June 1940, a joint resolution declaring that the United States would not recognize the transfer of American real estate from one nonhemispheric nation to another. Immediately thereafter, the State Department called the Second Consultative Meeting of American Foreign Ministers in order to commit the republics of Central and South America to the "no transfer principle."[54]

At the Havana Conference, which opened in July 1940, North American diplomats encountered stiff Argentine opposition as they sought to push through a comprehensive resolution prohibiting the forceable transfer of hemispheric territory and providing for intervention by the American states in the event that such a transfer was attempted. While questioning both the necessity and the justice of America's attempt to sit in judgment on political shifts in Europe, the Argentineans opposed the United States formula, pri-marily on the grounds that it would lead to the assumption of sovereignty by one American nation or group of nations over another. Assuming its role as protector of the weak and oppressed, the Argentine delegation

denounced Washington's plan as a threat to hemispheric neutrality and
gross violation of the principle of nonintervention.[55]

The logjam was broken only when Hull decided to go over the
of the Argentine representatives and to appeal directly to the Chief E
tive. Hull was able to convince Ortiz that in the North American pro
there was relatively little danger to Argentina's diplomatic objectives.
result, from the presidential palace, the Casa Rosada, came the directiv
the Argentine contingent was to sign the Act of Havana and the Conv
on the Provisional Administration of European Colonies and Possessi
the Americas. The first asserted that an outside attack on any Am
state "shall be considered as an act of aggression against the states
sign this declaration." The second strictly prohibited the transfer from
power to another of European-held territory in the New World, and
vided machinery for collective American administration of affected pro
in case such an attempt was made. Significantly, the Act of Havana
no farther in defining the specific obligations of the parties involved, i
war erupted between one of the American republics and a nonhemis
state. Argentina was well aware that inter-American solidarity wa
subject to interpretation by each American government.[56]

Prior to Pearl Harbor, the Havana Conference marked the final at
by the Roosevelt administration to awaken the hemisphere to the d
that lurked beyond both oceans and to convince the Americas that
spheric solidarity was the only true safeguard against attack from th
natories of the Tripartite Pact. Havana also represented the zenith of A
tine cooperation with the United States. Convinced that Washingto
trying to drag Argentina into a war that was manifestly not in the l
national interest, various Argentine governments from 1940 through
hewed carefully to a neutral course and attempted to utilize the v
enhance Buenos Aires's power and prestige within the Latin Am
community. Not only Argentina's challenge to Washington's crusa
hemispheric security but also Argentina's determination to stand
from a war that so vitally affected the interests of her northern nei
posed an apparently irreconcilable dilemma for American policy-m
Simply stated, their problem was how to compel an American state to
its diplomatic position without violating the principle of noninterve
Although many Latin American states made a wholehearted commitm
the Allied cause, a number continued to support Argentina's right, sh

armed aggression against its neighbors, to pursue its own foreign policies in its own way. To a sizable number of *latinos*, especially after 1943, Washington's response to Argentina's independent stance during World War II constituted a true test of the Good Neighbor Policy and an indication of the direction that inter-American affairs would take in the postwar period. That response was, in turn, largely a product of the characteristics and priorities of various bureaucratic entities within the Roosevelt administration that were struggling for control of the Latin American policy of the United States.

2

LATIN AMERICANIST VS. INTERNATIONALIST: THE RIO CONFERENCE OF 1942

Pearl Harbor and the subsequent declarations of war on the United States by Germany and Italy set in motion the inter-American machinery for consultation on joint action against the enemies of the hemisphere. On 9 December 1941, Secretary of State Cordell Hull invoked Article Fifteen of the Havana Resolutions, which declared that any attempt by a nonhemispheric state to violate the territorial integrity, political independence, or national sovereignty of any American nation would be considered an act of aggression against all and would result in consultation among the signatory powers. In response, the Governing Board of the Pan-American Union scheduled a meeting for 15 January 1942, to be held in Rio de Janeiro.[1] The conference, like the two preceding inter-American conclaves, was highlighted by a clash between Argentina and the United States over two issues: hemispheric policy toward World War II and the nature of the inter-American consultative system established during the 1930s. As in the past, Argentina demanded the right to remain neutral and insisted that the Inter-American System should be nothing more than a forum for discussion. The United States sought to have all American states sever relations with the Axis and urged that the consultative system be converted into a collective-security organization. Despite this basic divergence and the crisis atmosphere created by the United States' sudden entry into the war, hemispheric unity was preserved as Argentine and American diplomats agreed to a resolution that merely recommended to each American republic that it sever relations with the Axis nations. Both Washington's decision to acquiesce in Argentina's insistence on a nonbinding pact and its refusal to isolate Argentina within the hemispheric community were the outgrowth of a power struggle within the Roosevelt foreign-policy establishment between two rival coalitions of diplomats.

In his search for new ideas with which to combat the Depression, Franklin Roosevelt stimulated rather than eliminated bureaucratic conflict and personal rivalries within his administration. Thinking that out of conflict and compromise would come the best possible solution, he deliberately assigned two advisors or groups of advisors with diametrically opposed views to work on the same problem.[2] In practice, however, the president's techniques often blurred the lines of authority and responsibility, and led to bitter rivalries that distorted the decision-making process. Contributing to the confusion that characterized the Roosevelt administration was FDR's well-known inability to say no to a subordinate who was reaching for more power and authority. Moreover, an in-depth look at Roosevelt's personal relations with his official family indicates that he actually enjoyed the maneuverings and Byzantine intrigues of the hundreds of powerful men who flocked into Washington during the 1930s and 1940s. Confident that his charm and personal magnetism would be sufficient to keep department and agency heads loyal to him, he saw no reason to interfere with the bureaucratic bloodletting. Only if an intergovernmental power struggle threatened either his political position or, after 1941, the war effort, did he force a resolution.[3] The State Department and the Good Neighbor Policy were not exempt from Roosevelt's penchant for policy-making by bureaucratic conflict.[4]

On the eve of the Japanese attack on Pearl Harbor, formulation of inter-American policy within the federal bureaucracy was the responsibility of two "organizations" which were highly competitive but virtually invisible to outsiders. Each had its own goals, programs, and priorities; each had a quite definite view of the place the Pan-American community should occupy in United States foreign policy; and each was characterized by its own particular brand of parochialism. Although both groups functioned within the State Department, communication between the two was virtually nonexistent. In their determination to control the Latin American field, both bureaucratic coalitions presented policy alternatives to the president in ways designed to gain his approval and to discredit each other. One organization triumphed over the other because of its special relationship to the White House, exclusive access to certain intelligence data, and control over the actual implementation of policy.

The first group, which will be referred to as the Latin Americanists, was composed of career diplomats who had for years been concerned almost exclusively with the development of hemispheric policy. Its leaders—Undersecretary Sumner Welles; Laurence Duggan, assistant secretary for political affairs; Philip Bonsal, chief of the Division of American Republic Affairs; and Emilio Collado, special assistant to the undersecretary—sprang from similar backgrounds and shared a common view of inter-American affairs. Harvard-educated and reform-oriented, these individuals, most of whom were ardent New Dealers, regarded Latin America as their area of expertise and their private policy-making domain. As bureaucrats who had long been responsible for a particular area, they were intensely parochial and thus tended to view the entire panorama of international affairs from the perspective of the hemispheric community.[5] According to Welles:

> The inter-American system . . . has its roots in the common recognition of the sovereign equality of all the American states, and in their joint belief that they find individual advantage in co-operation. . . . Continued participation by the United States in this system should become the permanent cornerstone of American foreign policy. Hemispheric unity, and the security and welfare of the United States itself depend on it.[6]

Believing that the United States should develop a long-term nonpartisan policy toward Latin America, this coalition of officials had devoted its efforts during the 1930s to eradicating the anti-Americanism created by years of United States intervention and, after 1936, to establishing an inter-American consultative system that could act to protect the hemisphere in the event of an external threat. The Latin Americanists regarded the association as their own creation and hence were determined to protect its integrity amidst the stresses and strains generated by global war. In an address to the American Political Science Association delivered shortly after Pearl Harbor, Laurence Duggan assured the hemispheric republics of Washington's belief that

> the strength of the inter-American structure results from strict abstinence from intermeddling or interference in the internal or external concerns of the other countries. . . . The most precious asset the United States now has in the Western Hemisphere is the confidence and respect that one man of good-will has in another. This

could be lost overnight by a hasty, ill-considered step of apparent urgent necessity.[7]

The organization's willingness to trust in the consultative system and the Good Neighbor Policy in order to right all wrongs is well illustrated by its attitude toward Argentina. Although they were acutely aware that Argentina had effectively blocked Washington's plans for the creation of a hemispheric alliance, the Latin Americanists still believed that if a non-hemispheric power were to attack the Americas, pressure on Buenos Aires from the other republics would be sufficient to compel participation in common defense measures. Washington could not take unilateral coercive action to force a change in Argentine policy without undercutting the entire Good Neighbor Policy and obscuring the fact of inter-American mutuality of interest.[8] As Welles later wrote:

> The very foundation of the inter-American system was the United States' acceptance of the juridical equality of all the American republics. From that standpoint, particularly since no inter-American conference could yet take action except by unanimous agreement, it was illogical to regard Argentina as hostile to the United States merely because her policy differed diametrically from our own.[9]

By January 1942, reliance on the inter-American association of nations to solve problems between republics and to formulate hemispheric policy toward the rest of the world had become standard operating procedure within this organization.

There was in the State Department, however, a second set of diplomats who were concerned with the formulation of Latin American policy but who operated quite apart from the Latin American establishment. This group, led by Secretary of State Cordell Hull and Assistant Secretary Breckinridge Long, adhered to a much different view of inter-American affairs.

In the first place, their backgrounds were vastly dissimilar to those of the Latin Americanists. Hull and Long were old Wilsonians. The secretary first entered public life as a Democratic congressman in 1907 and was inevitably drawn to Woodrow Wilson when the Princeton academician turned to national politics in 1911.[10] After Wilson captured the presidency the following year, Hull not only became a staunch supporter of the administration's domestic programs but took the Wilsonian philosophy toward foreign affairs as his own. That the United States ought to be the "supreme moral factor in the World's progress," that American political institutions were superior to all others, and that the concept of collective security held the key to the future peace of the world—all seemed as self-evident to the young Tennessee politician as to the Calvinist in the White House.[11] Long, a former student of Wilson's at Princeton, equaled Hull in his ardor for the New Freedom and his devotion to the principles of Wilsonian diplomacy. At the 1916 Democratic Convention he authored the plank advocating the creation of a world organization, and he was on intimate terms with Wilson until the latter's death in 1924.[12]

In the second place, both because of their backgrounds and because of their positions within the department, members of this group were less regionally oriented than the Latin Americanists and, as a result, tended to view United States relations with Latin America as part of a much larger whole. Thus, although Hull, Long, and their colleagues had participated in the formulation and implementation of the Good Neighbor Policy,[13] they generally regarded it as only a means to a larger end. In return for Washington's renunciation of intervention and for its virtual abandonment of United States business interests south of the Rio Grande, the internationalists anticipated that the other American states would trust Washington to determine hemispheric policy toward the rest of the world.[14] The Inter-American System was to act first as a collective-security organization, a sort of New-World League of Nations to prevent the forces of fascism from spreading to the Western Hemisphere, and second as a device to mobilize Latin American support for United States policies toward the rest of the world.

A sometimes member of this group was Adolf Berle, who had joined the State Department in 1938 as assistant secretary of state for Latin American affairs. Although always interested in hemispheric matters and in preserving the sanctity of the Inter-American System, Berle, a former brain truster and general counsel to the Reconstruction Finance Corporation from 1933 to 1938, had not participated in establishing the "special relationships" between the American republics and the United States that characterized the Good Neighbor Era. He, along with Assistant Secretary of State Dean Acheson, attempted to remain in the good graces of both the Welles group and the internationalists.[15] Nevertheless, when forced to choose, Berle generally sided with the internationalists. As assistant secretary from 1938 to

1944 and as ambassador to Brazil during 1944 and 1945, Berle was in a position to influence both inter-American relations and the bureaucratic situation, and he sometimes did assert himself, particularly from 1944 on. He was more important, however, as a conduit of information to the White House. Berle continued to enjoy independent access to the Oval Office throughout his career, and Roosevelt valued him as a relatively impartial witness to events within the State Department and the hemisphere.[16]

The internationalists were at once less and more parochial than the Latin American group: less, in that they saw Washington's relations with Latin America as only one side of a multifaceted global problem; more, in that their knowledge of hemispheric affairs was, in places, quite superficial. Ignorance of indigenous political conditions and regional rivalries was an inevitable by-product of Hull's, Long's, and Berle's being formulators of general policy. Not surprisingly, then, the internationalists evaluated the American republics primarily on the basis of the latter's attitude toward World War II.[17] Preservation of the consultative system and hemispheric unity based on "the juridical equality of all the American republics" certainly did not top their list of diplomatic priorities.

After the attack on Pearl Harbor the internationalists clearly expected each New World nation to sever all ties with the Axis and even to participate actively in the war effort. From their perspective, World War II "was a life-and-death struggle, the result of which could only mean freedom and advancement for Latin America or domination and probably occupation by the Axis."[18] In the epic battle about to be waged against fascism, one was either for the forces of freedom and humanity or against them: nonalignment by a hemispheric state after 7 December 1941 was nothing less than treachery.[19]

The internationalists' tendency to take an oversimplified view of Latin American affairs and their overriding determination to obtain hemispheric support for the war against the Axis powers are perhaps best exemplified by their attitude toward Argentina. The obstructionist tactics pursued by various Argentine governments during the 1930s enraged Hull and his associates to such a degree that by 1938 they were convinced that Germany was directing Argentine foreign policy. Moreover, when the government of President Ramón Castillo proclaimed a state of siege in January 1942 and set about systematically to suppress domestic dissent, the internationalists concluded that the people of Argentina were consumed by a desire to aid the Allies but were being prevented from doing so by an unscrupulous group of individuals who were temporarily in control of the government.[20]

Thus, by the time the Governing Board of the Pan-American Union responded to Secretary Hull's request for a meeting of foreign ministers, these two cliques—each with its own goals, priorities, and assumptions—had arrived at totally different conclusions as to the direction that United States hemispheric policy should take. The Latin American establishment had resolved to protect the Inter-American System and to preserve hemispheric unity, whatever the cost. The internationalists were equally determined to eradicate all traces of Axis influence in the Western Hemisphere and to get each state to sever all relations with America's enemies. The split within the State Department might well have remained hidden had Argentina decided to adopt a vigorous anti-Axis stance, but such was not to be the case.

Argentina's decision to continue her policy of nonalignment even after Pearl Harbor and to resist pressure from the United States to make a total commitment to the Allied cause at the forthcoming conference of foreign ministers was a product not only of the nation's location, economy, tradition of neutrality,[21] and burgeoning nationalism, but of an intense political rivalry between Dr. Ramón Castillo and Gen. Augustín Justo. Each had his agents and supporters within the federal bureaucracy, Congress, the army, and the general electorate. Each saw in the problem of Argentine policy toward World War II an issue that would not only vitally affect the national interest but one that could make or break his political future.

Of the two men, Justo was by far the more experienced in national politics, and originally at least, he possessed a much broader power base. Elected president in 1932, this brilliant, ambitious officer concentrated on creating a national rather than just a military following during his term in office, and he quickly earned a reputation as an adept political maneuverer.[22] During his stay in the Casa Rosada he continued to cultivate the military by increasing overall troop strength and coercing Congress into voting for ever-higher military appropriations. In addition, a working alliance with the Radical party, which at that time controlled the Chamber of Deputies in the national legislature, provided him with an impressive stronghold in the civilian sector. By 1938 Justo had gained enough control of the political process and enough support to choose his successor and to rig the election without fear of military intervention or popular revolution.[23] As heir apparent, he selected Roberto Ortiz, leader of the Radical party;

Justo believed that Ortiz was the man most likely to continue his economic policies, protect the Justo reputation, and pave the way for his return to the presidency in the next election.[24] In order to balance the ticket and preserve the delicate political truce that he had engineered, the general-president reluctantly accepted Sen. Ramón Castillo, a National Democrat, as Ortiz's running mate.[25]

With the ticket duly if fraudulently elected, Justo's scheme seemed to be developing according to plan. However, the collapse of Ortiz's health in 1940 allowed the vice-president to assume the duties of chief magistrate and radically altered the situation. It quickly became apparent that Acting President Castillo was not disposed to serve as a mere link between Justo administrations.[26] The new chief executive ignored pressing economic and social problems and devoted his efforts instead to attracting political allies in the hope of being able to defy Justo, serve out a full term in office, and hand-pick his successor.[27]

Casting about for means with which to enlarge his anemic constituency, Castillo quickly concluded that the most fertile area for political cultivation would be the integral nationalist movement then flourishing in Argentina.[28] In an attempt to draw this group into his camp, he proclaimed throughout 1941 his intention to keep Argentina nonaligned and to fend off all threats to the national sovereignty.[29] The army, by far the most important element in the nationalist coalition, refused to join forces with the acting president, however, until he made certain specific pledges.[30] Realizing that he must have the support of the military in order to survive, Castillo met secretly in October 1941 with a group of leading army commanders from the Campo de Mayo and promised that he would proclaim a state of siege at the earliest possible date, close various pro-Allied newspapers, and, above all, maintain strict neutrality.[31] With this meeting, the alliance between Castillo and the integral nationalists was consummated.

Justo, momentarily taken aback by his rival's audacity, responded by assuming a pro-Allied posture and urging intervention at every opportunity. An outspokenly anti-Axis stand not only provided the general with an issue over which to attack Castillo, it also further endeared him to the generally pro-Allied Radicals and, somewhat ironically, made him the spokesman for all liberal nationalists within Argentina.[32]

By the end of 1941, then, the battle lines between Castillo and Justo had been drawn on the issue of Argentine policy toward World War II.

28

The Japanese navy's destruction of the United States' Pacific Fleet and Washington's subsequent calling of the Third Meeting of Foreign Ministers of the American Republics set the stage for a showdown between the two political adversaries.

In the weeks following America's abrupt entry into World War II, President Castillo gradually realized that the forthcoming Rio meeting offered a unique opportunity not only to cement his relationship with the integral nationalists but also to discredit Justo and thus to win the support of the bulk of Argentina's citizenry. He realized that most Argentineans, however much they might despise Hitler and his associates in aggression, hoped to remain aloof from World War II.[33] Even pro-American groups in Argentina, such as the navy and a sector of the Radical party, had come out in favor of strict nonalignment. Citing, among other things, the nation's exposed position; its large German, Italian, and Spanish populations; and the inability of the United States Caribbean Defense Command to defend southern South America, they urged Castillo to resist any attempts to have Buenos Aires sever relations with the Axis or use Argentine ships for convoy duty.[34] The ambitious chief executive was also well aware that not only the integral nationalists but all of his countrymen were sensitive to any hint of foreign pressure.[35] Given the history of United States intervention and Anglo-American economic imperialism south of the Rio Grande, many Argentineans believed that they had almost as much to fear from an Allied as from an Axis victory. Thus, when in the opening weeks of 1942 the State Department made it quite plain that it was going to press hard at Rio for a severance of all hemispheric ties with the Axis, Castillo perceived an opportunity to strengthen his political position by using the meeting to portray Washington as the interventionist threat of old, his administration as defender of the national sovereignty, and Justo as the toady of a foreign power.[36]

Despite the history of Argentine obstructionism in the 1930s, both groups of policy-makers within the State Department were confident that Buenos Aires would join wholeheartedly with the Allies when the Rio Conference convened. True, Argentina's response to Pearl Harbor had differed markedly from that of the rest of Latin America. By the end of December 1941, most of the beneficiaries of the Good Neighbor Policy had either severed relations with or declared war on the Axis, while the Castillo administration had simply decreed that all American states that were at war with Germany, Italy, and Japan were nonbelligerents and hence not subject to the limitations of Argentine neutrality.[37] Still, reports from the American embassy in Buenos Aires were quite encouraging about the posture that Argentina would ultimately assume toward World War II. The same day that Hull roused the Governing Board to action, Ambassador Norman Armour informed him that the Conservative regime gave little evidence that it would not live up to its inter-American obligations or that it could not be trusted with lend-lease. Displaying considerable ignorance of the true situation and a lamentable inclination to believe the best about the government to which he was accredited, he predicted that nationalist-neutralist groups would be able to exert a significant influence on government policies only through a coup. Expressions of support for the United States in other Latin nations, revulsion at Japan's surprise attack, and Argentine economic ties with the United States were all important factors impelling Argentina toward a pro-Allied policy.[38]

Armour's rather misleading reports were only partially responsible for the general optimism that prevailed in Washington, however. For their part the Latin Americanists were willing to trust in the dividends that past United States diplomatic restraint would pay, and they were certain that the United States could achieve a pro-Allied consensus within the context of the inter-American consultative system. The internationalists, reflecting Hull's faith in the ability of trade concessions to win friends and influence governments, were confident that economic aid provided to Argentina since the outbreak of war in Europe would, in conjunction with other factors, be enough to draw Buenos Aires into the anti-Axis camp. And, in fact, the economic concessions made by the Roosevelt administration had been quite significant. By March 1941 the Export-Import Bank had committed itself to $62.42 million in loans to Argentina, by far the largest amount proffered to any one Latin American country.[39] In late 1941 Argentine and American diplomats concluded a reciprocal trade agreement that was extremely favorable to Argentina. The pact, which was to run through November 1944, lowered duties on thirty-nine items composing 18 percent of United States exports to Argentina, while cutting rates on items constituting about 70 percent of previous Argentine exports to America.[40] As a result of these breakthroughs and of heavy United States purchases of Argentine strategic materials, Argentina's $28 million deficit with the United States ballooned to a $53 million surplus within a year.[41] If anything, attempts to placate

Argentina increased during the two months between Pearl Harbor and the convening of the Rio Conference. In response to hints from Buenos Aires that the best method for keeping fascism from the Western Hemisphere would be to continue to lower tariffs and make other economic concessions, the State Department inaugurated a second aid campaign which included the dispatch of a complete military instructional mission and the extension of further Export-Import and Treasury Department credits.[42]

Whether they put their faith in Pan-Americanism or in foreign aid, those in Washington who took an optimistic view of the Argentine situation were destined to be disappointed. Gradually, from a variety of sources, the State Department began to glean Argentina's true intentions. In early January, during a discussion with Welles at the State Department, Ambassador Felipe Espil provided a clue to what would be the Castillo administration's attitude toward a United States–dominated security system. With tongue in cheek, Espil observed that the act of nine American states' declaring war on the Axis without first consulting with their neighbors constituted a violation of existing inter-American agreements, especially the Declaration of Lima. In view of their "high-handed action," there was absolutely no need for the Rio meeting. "The Argentine Foreign Office," Espil informed his bemused colleague, "could not keep silent with regard to this impression since it is its intention to join in loyal application of the consultative system."[43]

The following week a Radical member of the Argentine Chamber of Deputies and a visiting professor from the University of La Plata called at the State Department and informed Berle that Castillo and his foreign minister, Enrique Ruiz Guiñazú, represented nobody, that one-third of the army was Nazi, and that the United States would be able to get nothing out of the Argentineans at Rio. The only solution to the problem of pro-Allied hemispheric solidarity, they declared, was a change in the Argentine government.[44]

In addition, by the last week of December, Armour's dispatches had become extremely pessimistic, tending to confirm Hull's suspicions that Argentina would once again pursue an obstructionist course. The ambassador and his staff were quite sympathetic to Justo, and the embassy received most of its information on the state of public opinion, the intentions of the Castillo administration, and other vital matters from the general's followers. Armour's once-optimistic reports now indicated that Castillo meant to block United States attempts at Rio to secure a comprehensive rupture of relations with the Axis. Moreover, according to the embassy, the state of siege was being employed specifically to deny Justo outlets with which to promote his campaign for the presidency and generally to suppress the overwhelmingly pro-Allied sympathies of the populace.[45]

Even more alarming to Washington than the Espil interview, the information given to Berle, or Armour's dispatches were reports from American representatives in the other hemispheric republics that Argentina was seeking to persuade a number of southern South American states to form a neutralist coalition that would be capable of resisting United States economic and diplomatic pressure to sever ties with the Axis. Despite Welles's efforts to block such proceedings, Argentine officials held a series of preconference meetings in Buenos Aires and Rio. They urged the foreign ministers of Chile, Paraguay, and Peru to join with Argentina in combating North American "intervention" and in defending each American nation's right to pursue an independent foreign policy.[46] While the ultranationalist Ruiz Guiñazú spoke grandly of "austral republics" and "harmonizing the economic interests of neighboring countries," other Argentine diplomats warned their South American colleagues that Washington's policies would create an entity that would be superior to the state, a kind of "supersovereignty" that might outlast the war and pave the way for perpetual United States domination of the Americas.[47]

By mid January, then, there could be no mistake as to what Argentina's policy would be at the forthcoming conference of foreign ministers. The Castillo government's determination to remain nonaligned during World War II and its campaign to persuade as many South American governments as possible to follow suit precipitated a clash between the internationalists and the Latin Americanists. Because both organizations realized that the key issue at Rio would be Argentine opposition to Washington's attempts to line up the entire hemisphere behind the Allied war effort, the struggle between the two coalitions of policy-makers for dominance within the State Department and the conflict between their philosophies of inter-American relations centered on their differing views as to how the American delegation should react if Argentina sought to block a resolution committing the entire hemisphere to severance.

It must be noted that in the federal bureaucracy the ultimate objective of an agency advising the president is to obtain White House approval for its policies. Therein lies the key to larger budgets and wider responsibilities for the organization and to advancement and power for the individual administrator. In designing policy alternatives the internationalists and the Latin Americanists were motivated as much by their estimation of what would meet Roosevelt's approval as by their view of inter-American affairs or by their personal prejudices. Quite simply, the undersecretary and his colleagues reasoned that FDR's commitment to the Good Neighbor principles would cause him to endorse the unity-above-all approach, while Hull anticipated that the president's preoccupation with the war would lead him to approve a hard-line attitude toward all those who refused to cooperate.

The internationalists were certain for two reasons that their approach would prevail. Aside from Secretary Hull's preeminent position in the diplomatic chain of command, statements and actions made by the Latin Americanists prior to and during the Rio Conference indicated that they had acquiesced in their rivals' views. The United States delegation, which was to be headed by Welles and dominated by the Latin Americanists, met with Hull prior to its departure and agreed that no effort should be spared to secure from the American republics a declaration that would actually end relations with the Axis. Subsequently, dispatches from the United States delegation in Rio promised that if Argentina resisted a binding resolution regarding severance, the remaining republics would eject her from the inter-American community and proceed with a total rupture.[48]

The internationalists' sense of security was totally unwarranted, however. The power structure within the United States foreign-policy establishment bore no resemblance to the table of organization. Instead of there being a direct line of command from the president to the secretary and his staff (internationalists) and to the Division of American Republic Affairs (Latin Americanists), there existed two coequal organizations, both of which had direct and separate access to the chief executive.[49] In short, the department was compartmentalized rather than being unified under a single authority. The Latin Americanists' entrée to the White House, in conjunction with select information that came into their possession in mid January and a tacit coalition with a powerful intragovernmental ally, enabled them to put a particular face on the Rio situation. As a result they were able to gain presidential approval for their projected policy and at the same time to exclude their rivals from the decision-making process.

Of inestimable value to the Latin Americanists was the fact that the recommendations of the United States military with regard to hemispheric policy coincided with their own. Reflecting its traditional preoccupation with the security of the hemisphere, particularly the Panama Canal, top officials in the Caribbean Defense Command urged the State Department, on the eve of the Rio Conference, to persuade the republics of southern South America not to declare war on the Axis or commit any other provocative act that could lead to a military assault by Germany and its Allies.[50] In the wake of the destruction of the Pacific Fleet and the continuing drain caused by convoy duty in the Atlantic, the United States Navy barely possessed the resources with which to protect the canal; it certainly could not guarantee the safety of the southernmost republics. The military planners who were concerned with hemispheric defense were particularly troubled about Argentina's situation. During Argentine-American staff talks held throughout the winter of 1941–42, American officers had become acutely aware of the Argentine navy's weakness and of the potential threat that its anemic condition posed to the Straits of Magellan.[51] Consequently, United States strategists believed that Buenos Aires, perhaps more than any other capital, should avoid a tough anti-Axis posture.[52] The military's support of Argentine nonalignment stemmed not only from sound strategic considerations but from traditionally close ties with the Argentine officers' corps. A perpetual concern for similar problems and an identity of organizational goals caused a considerable degree of solidarity.

The information that Brazil would not sign a severance resolution unless the proposal met Argentina's approval was even more useful to the Latin Americanists than was the military's position. Although relations between Brazil and Argentina, who had sometimes been bitter rivals, were quite cordial during the late 1930s, ties began to weaken as the integral nationalists within Argentina clamored for a "Greater Argentina." Shortly before the opening of the Rio Conference, Brazil's President Getulio Vargas and his foreign secretary, Oswaldo Aranha, informed Welles and his associates that their government as well as the overwhelming majority of the Brazilian people were anxious to show complete support for the United States. Unfortunately, the general staff was apprehensive about the fate of southern Brazil if that nation became involved in World War II while Argentina remained neutral. As a result the officer corps would not allow the Foreign Office to place Brazil on a course that was diametrically opposed to that of her powerful neighbor to the south.[53]

Instead of going through channels with this vital intelligence, the Latin

Americanists held it until the last possible moment and then went straight to the White House. In a private interview with Roosevelt just prior to the delegation's departure, Welles confided that in his estimation, Brazil would be the key to the conference because that country and Argentina would not tread opposite paths. Warning that Hull's judgment was beclouded by an irrational antipathy toward Argentina and hence could not be trusted, he argued that whatever happened at Rio, inter-American unity should be preserved so as to prevent the Axis from fishing in troubled waters. In short, the undersecretary proposed, and Roosevelt agreed, that Latin America should be urged to take as tough a stand toward the Axis as the individual states could reasonably support, but that there should be unity when the meeting ended.[54]

The campaign to convince the internationalists that Welles and the United States delegation would brook nothing less than a binding severance resolution continued as the opening date for the conference approached.[55] When the undersecretary addressed the initial session of the Third Meeting of Foreign Ministers, his remarks were as tough and uncompromising as the internationalists could have wished:

> The shibboleth of classic neutrality in its narrow sense can . . . no longer be the ideal of any freedom-loving people of the Americas.
> There can no longer be any real neutrality as between the powers of evil and the forces that are struggling to preserve the rights and the independence of free peoples.[56]

The Latin Americanists' program of dissimulation worked to perfection, for as the American republics turned to the problem created by the coming of World War II to the Western Hemisphere, the internationalists were ignorant not only of the Latin Americanists' long-range objectives for Rio but of the Brazilian situation and the Welles-Roosevelt interview as well.[57] Only once, apparently, did Hull, Long, and their subordinates evidence any suspicion. On the opening day of the conference, Berle cabled Welles, outlining once again the course that negotiations should follow. "In the Department from the Secretary on down," wrote Berle, "the feeling is in accord with the belief that rather than a compromise formula, a break in unanimity would be preferable. . . . The Argentines must accept this view or go their own way."[58]

The Latin Americanists anticipated problems with Argentina and Brazil at Rio, but they were shocked by the degree to which hemispheric solidarity had been shattered. Almost as soon as they stepped off the plane on February 12, Welles and his colleagues learned that Argentina's power play to block a United States–sponsored obligatory severance resolution was approaching a successful climax. The inauspicious nature of America's entry into World War II and its alarming vulnerability during the first months of 1942 made ultimate Allied victory seem far from certain. It was obvious to representatives of many hemispheric republics that Latin America's extended coastline, the weakness of her navies, and the sharply reduced defensive capacity of the United States would make any nation that adopted a hostile posture toward the Axis extremly vulnerable to retaliation.[59] And, in fact, in late December and early January, Germany, Italy, and Japan had intimated to Chile and a number of other republics that if those countries were to break relations with the Axis, they would find themselves immediately at war.[60] These considerations, together with traditional fear of Yankee imperialism, had caused a number of states to entertain Argentina's suggestions. The American delegation realized that to run roughshod over Argentina, especially given Brazil's attitude, would polarize the hemisphere.

In talks with key figures of the Brazilian delegation, the undersecretary began to give ground immediately. He agreed with Foreign Minister Aranha that no greater encouragement could be given to the standard-bearers of fascism than a break in hemispheric unity, and he again expressed his belief that the conference could not take action except by a unanimous vote. Encouraged by the American's obvious willingness to compromise, Vargas and Aranha told Welles that the Argentineans were not as adamant as they appeared: Ruiz Guiñazú would almost certainly sign a severance resolution if he could fall back on some face-saving device.[61]

Before engaging the Argentineans in a test of wills, Welles and Jefferson Caffrey, the United States ambassador to Brazil, a man who thoroughly sympathized with Welles's point of view, began to sound out opinion in the other hemispheric delegations concerning mandatory severance of relations with the Axis. The Caribbean, Central American, and northern South American states presented little problem. After the United States promised the removal of all tariffs on war materials, negotiation of lucrative long-range contracts for raw goods, and aid for developing local industries with the objective of establishing more diversified economies, these states announced that Argentina's veto power should not be allowed to interfere with hemispheric defense. Turning to the South American republics, American officials used a variety of arguments in order to extract unenthusiastic endorsement of a rupture with the Axis from Bolivia, Paraguay, and Peru. These republics, no less than Argentina, were far from the protective arm of the Caribbean Defense Command and were very vulnerable not only to Axis attack but to Argentine pressure as well.[62]

Washington's success in lining up votes for an obligatory pledge initially had no effect on the Argentineans. Repeating his standard battery of arguments in support of nonalignment, Ruiz Guiñazú refused to even consider severing diplomatic ties with Germany, Japan, and Italy.[63] In Buenos Aires, Castillo promised Armour that his government would go along with all other political and economic measures, including the furnishing of essential raw materials and port facilities and the enactment of measures designed to prevent Axis propaganda and subversion; but Argentina would continue to maintain diplomatic ties with the Axis.[64]

Realizing that Argentina's position would likely determine the policies of Brazil as well as a number of lesser Latin American states, the Latin Americanists first sought to exert as much diplomatic pressure as possible on the Argentine delegation to sign an obligatory severance pact and then offered them a way out by suggesting a compromise formula. With Welles orchestrating their efforts, the foreign ministers of Mexico, Venezuela, and Colombia took turns urging the Argentineans to make a full commitment to the Allied cause. When their blandishments failed to move Ruiz Guiñazú and his colleagues, Welles's cohorts collectively introduced a severance resolution at the plenary session of the conference.[65] After Peru and Chile came out in favor of a rupture on February 19, Ruiz Guiñazú began to waver. United States military advisors subsequently informed their Argentine counterparts, who were intensely desirous of cashing in on the lend-lease bonanza, that financial and economic aid could be given only to those countries that cooperated in the defense of the hemisphere. The climax of the assault on Argentine neutralism came during three long conversations held between the nineteenth and the twenty-second. After haranguing Ruiz Guiñazú on the dangers of neutrality, the undersecretary, as the Brazilians had advised, proposed a middle course. Asserting that there could be no compromise on the severance issue, Welles promised: "I as well as the other chiefs of delegations will make every effort to find some phraseology acceptable to all, provided the necessary principles are maintained intact."[66] At this, the beleaguered foreign minister succumbed and agreed to cable his government, requesting permission to sign a severance resolution.[67]

The heads of the delegations moved quickly to write a compact that everyone could live with. The key paragraph awkwardly reflected the Argentine-American compromise:

> The American Republics consequently declare that in the exercise of their sovereignty and in conformity with their constitutional institutions and powers, provided the latter are in agreement, they cannot continue their diplomatic relations with Japan, Germany, and Italy, . . .[68]

Unfortunately, Ruiz Guiñazú apparently acted without authorization from Buenos Aires in agreeing to this resolution, and as a result, post-signing festivities were interrupted by the recall of the foreign minister. After being roundly berated by Castillo, the chastened diplomat returned to Rio and disavowed his signature. To charges of bad faith he replied only that his government was absolutely determined to avoid war.[69] Actually, the resolution, like all previous inter-American security pacts, committed Argentina to nothing specific. Castillo's willingness to scuttle the agreement for the sake of appearances was a product primarily of his plan to assume a highly visible anti-American, neutralist stance.

At this point an untimely outburst from Washington played into Castillo's hands by hardening the resolve of the Argentine citizenry to pursue an independent course. In response to Buenos Aires's disavowal, Tom Connally, the parochial and combative chairman of the Senate Foreign Relations Committee, declared to reporters that "we are trusting that Castillo will change his mind, or that the Argentine people will change their President."[70] Despite the State Department's hurried announcement that the views of the legislative branch did not represent those of the executive, many Argentineans were convinced that Connally was representative of the true spirit of the Good Neighbor Policy.

In order to retain an absolutely free hand, Welles had throughout the conference led the internationalists, who were then absorbed in strategic talks with British officials, to believe that not only he and the entire American delegation, but Brazil as well, were prepared to take a hard line against the Argentineans if they failed to cooperate. "President Vargas told me yesterday afternoon," the undersecretary reported to Washington on the twenty-third, "that the Argentines would come along and that he himself had made it clear to Ruiz Guiñazú that Brazil would support the United States 100%; that the final decision of Brazil in this regard had been reached and that he, Vargas, had the support of practically every citizen in Brazil."[71] Moreover, in the course of "reassuring" the State Department, the Latin Americanists either inadvertently or deliberately reinforced the internationalists' negative view of Argentina. In his dispatch to Hull informing him that Castillo had ordered Ruiz Guiñazú to disavow the first severance pact, the undersecretary remarked that "the very definite conclusion has been reached by all of the Foreign Ministers with whom I have spoken that some influence of an extra-continental character is responsible for the decision reached by Dr. Castillo."[72]

Meanwhile, the American delegation was retreating in order to establish a new position around which to rally the hemispheric republics and thus preserve unity.[73] After hours of tedious debate the conclave unanimously adopted a resolution representing the lowest common denominator. Of the pact's four major points, the third contained the crucial alteration. After reaffirming that an act of aggression against one of their number was an act against all and after vowing to cooperate for mutual protection until the current crisis had ended, the agreement proclaimed that "the American Republics consequently, following the procedure established by their own laws within the position and circumstances of each country in the actual continental conflict, recommend the rupture of their diplomatic relations with Japan, Germany, and Italy, . . ."[74]

Julius Pratt, in his biography of the secretary of state, has recorded Hull's reaction to the ratification of the Pact of Rio and the confrontation between him, Welles, and FDR that followed. On January 24 Hull was sitting calmly beside his radio, awaiting news of an ironclad hemispheric defense pact—with or without Argentina—when article three, which contained the innocuous severance provision, was announced. His first reaction was disbelief; his second was speechless fury at what seemed an American Munich. He immediately alerted FDR, and both men contacted Welles on a three-way telephone hookup. The secretary, his voice "quivering with rage," told his subordinate that article three was a basic change of policy which had been made without his knowledge. Terming the recommendatory resolution a virtual "surrender to Argentina," Hull ordered the undersecretary to repudiate it. Instead of submitting, Welles appealed directly to

FDR, who abruptly ended the debate: "I am sorry, Cordell, but in this case I am going to take the judgment of the man on the spot. . . . Sumner, I approve what you have done. I authorize you to follow the lines you have recommended."[75]

Adolf Berle's diary provides a similar but more personalized account. Berle and Laurence Duggan (chief of the Division of American Republic Affairs and one of the Latin Americanists) had been summoned to Hull's apartment shortly after the secretary learned of Welles's "betrayal" and were present throughout the entire telephone conversation. According to Berle, Hull became abusive of both Argentina and the undersecretary and repeatedly laid his authority on the line. FDR's subsequent approval of Welles's position was a crushing political and spiritual defeat for Hull. Duggan and Berle tried to calm him, arguing that the United States would still be able to hold the anti-Axis republics in line and thus salvage its "moral leadership" in Latin America, but to no avail. Declaring that "a lot of things were going to change" in the department, the secretary, despite Roosevelt's endorsement of the recommendatory resolution, even went so far as to draft a telegram (which was never sent) both repudiating the recommendatory resolution and recalling Welles. "Along past midnight," Berle wrote in his diary, "Duggan and I left to get a stiff drink, which represented my sole remaining idea of a tangible approach to the situation. For it is obvious that now there is a breach between the Secretary and Sumner that will never be healed—though the Secretary will keep it below hatches to some extent. . . . I felt that several careers were ending that night."[76]

In the days that followed, each group tried to vindicate its position. The Latin Americanists reiterated their view that preservation of hemispheric unity and the integrity of the consultative system not only would work to Washington's long-range interest in the Western Hemisphere but would serve America's strategic interests during World War II as well. If the delegates had been unable to agree to some type of severance resolution, however superficial, it appeared that Latin America would divide right down the middle between the pro-Allied and the nonaligned states. Those nations closer to the Canal Zone, and hence nearer to the protective arm of the United States, might follow Washington's lead even to the point of polarizing the Pan-American community. If, however, Argentina, Brazil, Chile, and their weaker neighbors were isolated, they would only fall into the arms of the hemisphere's enemies. Because of the intrinsic power of these republics and their distance from the defensive umbrella of the United States, they would become "untrammelled" centers of Axis activities in the Western Hemisphere. Moreover, contended Welles, Duggan, and Bonsal, if the United States had forced a break in ranks at Rio, it would have been attacked from one end of the hemisphere to the other for undermining the principles of democracy and unity upon which the Inter-American System was based. Undue pressure would have destroyed the trust that the Roosevelt administration had taken years to accumulate.[77]

To the internationalists, however, Latin America, not the United States, was on trial at Rio. During the 1930s Washington had shown meticulous respect for the sovereignty of her southern neighbors. Now that the very existence of the hemisphere was threatened, argued Hull and Long, Latin America must quickly fall into line behind the Allies, who, after all, were fighting and dying to preserve democratic institutions and to save the entire New World from Axis domination.[78] The internationalists believed that the global crisis warranted immediate action against all states that were not willing to cooperate fully with the Allies, and they were convinced that Roosevelt would eventually concur.

Apparently, to Roosevelt's mind the key to the situation was Brazil. During the anxiety-filled days after Pearl Harbor, American military leaders repeatedly advised the White House that because of the strategic position of Brazil, its wholehearted cooperation with the Allies was essential to the war effort.[79] During his preconference interview with Roosevelt and in several mid-conference phone calls to the White House, Welles convinced the president that if the United States continued to pursue a hard line, it would certainly alienate Brazil and drive that nation into the arms of the neutralists. Even if Vargas could be persuaded to sign a compulsory resolution, the undersecretary insisted, the military would eventually revolt, remove Vargas from office, and disavow the Rio agreements.[80]

Thus, the American position at the Rio Conference was shaped by Argentina's determination to remain neutral and by Brazil's refusal to isolate Argentina, but it was also a product of the goals and characteristics of a particular coterie within the foreign-policy establishment. By utilizing direct access to the White House, control over vital intelligence, intragovernmental allies, and its proximity to the actual negotiating process, the Welles-Duggan-Bonsal group eliminated their rivals from the decision-making process and secured approval of their policy recommendations. Like Germany in the aftermath of World War I, however, the internationalists, although humiliated, were left with the sinews of power. Their resolve to regain control of the Latin American policy of the United States and their bitterness toward both the Latin American establishment and Argentina would have profound implications for the wartime history of the Good Neighbor Policy.

3

SUMNER WELLES AND THE ART OF COERCION

In the weeks following the Rio Conference, the Hull-Welles controversy lay like a pall over the State Department. "This has been a bad week," Adolf Berle confided in his diary on February 1. "Welles has been away and the Secretary has been in bed. . . . Following the blow-up with Wells in Rio a week ago, he came to the office on Monday but was nervously and spiritually torn to pieces, to a point where his doctor kept him in bed. . . . He emerged Friday to go to the cabinet meeting, but this was about all." Peacemakers such as Berle and Acheson tried to mediate between the two warring factions, but with no success. The question boiled down to who would be secretary of state. At Rio, Welles and Roosevelt had made policy behind Hull's back. "Sumner is really preserving a direct line of power through the White House," Berle wrote. "The Secretary will be satisfied with nothing less than cutting that off."[1]

Although Roosevelt's approval of Welles's approach at Rio clearly shifted the balance of power within the department in favor of the Latin Americanists, time was on the side of the internationalists. In many ways 1942, which was punctuated by one military disaster after another, was the most trying year in the history of the republic. In late May the Germans launched a successful military drive designed to capture the Suez Canal; and by July, German troops were only seventy-five miles from Alexandria. In Russia a Nazi offensive pushed relentlessly toward the Volga and the Caucasus. German U-boat activity in the Atlantic became so effective that by summer the flow of United States goods to Allied Europe had slowed dramatically. The situation was no less discouraging in the Far East. As the last American forces surrendered in the Philippines in May, the Japanese were busy consolidating their positions in the Dutch East Indies and un-leashing their naval forces on New Britain and the Solomon Islands. With newspapers and newsreels recounting one military disaster after another, Americans became less and less willing to tolerate dissent at home and abroad.[2]

The reaction of the American press to the Castillo government's policy of nonalignment and to the Pact of Rio made it imperative, from a political point of view, that the Latin Americanists induce Buenos Aires to cooperate in the Allied war effort as fully and as quickly as possible. Ironically, those journalists who originally had been the strongest supporters of the New Deal and the Good Neighbor Policy were the first to link Argentine mili-tarism with National Socialism and to blast the Roosevelt administration for "appeasing" Buenos Aires at the Rio Conference. "If anyone thinks that a benevolently neutral Argentina is not an important asset to the Axis in America," said Freda Kirchwey in the *Nation*, "he has not followed Nazi methods of political warfare."[3] In an article in the same issue of that jour-nal, Hugo Fernandez Artucio labeled the Castillo government "the advance guard of an army of invasion against the shores of America."[4] Denouncing the Rio Conference as the most perfect example of appeasement since the Munich meeting of 1938, the *New Republic* charged that the State Depart-ment's past policy of seeking to persuade the Latin American dictatorships to merge their foreign policies with that of the United States through the open bribery of trade agreements, outright loans, and military supplies had simply strengthened the pro-Nazi and pro-Fascist groups that were now blackmailing the United States.[5] Virtually everyone within the "liberal estab-lishment"—that is, those Americans who by the early 1940s were denouncing, on the one hand, New Deal domestic policy for not going far enough in achieving economic and social justice and, on the other, New Deal foreign policy for not producing true Soviet-American solidarity—agreed that the "sellout" at Rio was basically an attempt to smooth over the damage caused by two years of trying to buy off the Castillo government.[6]

Some newspapers, primarily those that continued to support the admin-istration's domestic and foreign programs, were willing to give the Latin Americanists the benefit of the doubt as to whether or not the good faith displayed by the United States delegation at Rio would convince Argentina and Chile to throw in with the Allies. Nonetheless, they made it clear that their continued support of the administration's hemispheric policy was dependent on Buenos Aires's and Santiago's abandonment of neutrality. The *St. Louis Post-Dispatch* hailed the Rio accords as "the kind of compromise which remains after the concessions are made, a strong unmistakable definition of policy," but then warned that "Argentina and Chile must be won to the declaration which their diplomats have tentatively approved."[7] Other proadministration columnists simply chose to ignore the recommendatory nature of the January pledge and to view it as a binding agreement. One foreign-policy analyst declared that "the Pact of Rio unquestionably put Argentina and Chile under obligation to expel the Nazi Fifth-Column from their midst, and cooperate with the United States in defeating the Axis."[8]

Whether they were critical or tolerant of the administration's actions at Rio, the vast majority of commentators on foreign affairs took a negative view of the Castillo government and its policies. Even as early as the spring of 1942 many journalists began to join Cordell Hull, Breckinridge Long, and their associates in viewing the Castillo regime not only as a government that was refusing to join the free world in its struggle against the forces of evil but also as one that was destroying democratic institutions and suppressing the popular will within Argentina in order to do so. According to this segment of opinion, the Good Neighbor Policy had won the hearts and minds of the Argentine citizenry, who now trusted the United States and wanted Argentina to take its place beside the defenders of democracy. Only the small clique ensconced in the Casa Rosada prevented them from acting. "Dr. Ruiz-Guiñazú's obstructionist attitude went contrary to the expressed wishes of a large part of the Argentine population," observed the *Washington Post*, "and reflected only the views of the minority government which, by a fluke, happens to be in power in Buenos Aires."[9] The implication of such a view was clear: if the Castillo administration did not change its policies to reflect the pro-Allied sentiments of the people, then it was America's duty to help the Argentineans change their government.[10] Tom Connally may not have spoken for the chief executive, but his views apparently coincided with those of a sizable sector of the American public.

Franklin Roosevelt was as sensitive to public opinion as any president in the nation's history—a fact that was never far from the minds of those within the foreign-policy establishment. The Latin Americanists realized that if they were going to retain control of inter-American relations and implement their view of the Good Neighbor Policy, they would have to secure concrete proof that hemispheric solidarity and nonintervention had won Argentina and Chile to the anti-Axis banner. Shortly after the close of the Rio Conference, FDR dashed off a telegram in which he bemoaned unfavorable press comments on the Pact of Rio. Welles's reply indicated that he was well aware of the president's anxiety and of the tenuousness of the Latin Americanists' position. "I fully share the point of view you yourself expressed," he wrote to his former classmate at Groton, "and that is that immediate implementation in the sense of action is required in order to counteract the alleged mistaken press comments which have been reported."[11]

Nevertheless, the Latin Americanists believed as strongly as ever that overt coercion of Buenos Aires, whether verbal, economic, or military, would alienate the Argentine people and drive them to support the Castillo government and its neutralist policies. More importantly, a frontal assault would shatter hemispheric solidarity; convince the other Latin nations that Washington had returned to the era of the big stick; and during what many considered the greatest trial the United States had yet faced, undermine its influence south of the Rio Grande. In mid February 1942, in a speech to the Cuban Chamber of Commerce, Welles went to great lengths to reassure the American states that the entry of the United States into World War II did not sound the death knell of the Good Neighbor Policy. He blasted those in the United States who advocated the overthrow of those Latin governments that did not conform to Washington's expectations. The Roosevelt administration's hemispheric policy was still based on nonintervention in the political affairs of the other republics and on "recognition in fact, as well as in word, that every one of the twenty-one American Republics is the sovereign equal of the others." To condemn existing governments and to pit one political faction against another would "be to ape a policy which has been pursued during the past five years by Hitler."[12]

The problem, then, for Welles, Duggan, Bonsal, and their associates was to provoke the Castillo government to abandon neutrality and eradicate all traces of Axis influence in Argentina. At the same time they were determined to avoid blatantly coercive policies that would alienate friendly, pro-Allied elements in Argentina and would undermine Latin America's faith in the Good Neighbor Policy. From 1936 through January 1941 the Latin Americanists rejected unilateral coercion and attempted to use the consultative system in order to persuade Argentina to support, first, hemispheric defense measures and, then, the Allied cause. At Rio, however, the other republics had gone as far as they intended to go in pushing Argentina toward a break. Further attempts by Washington to invoke hemispheric opinion against Argentina would only lead to charges that the United States was trying to convert the Pan-American System into a blunt instrument with which to beat Argentina to its knees.[13] Denied this avenue of attack, faced with mounting criticism of their philosophy, and threatened by the feud with the internationalists, the Latin Americanists turned to propaganda and a policy of selective pressure to obtain a reorientation of Argentine foreign policy.

Welles and his cohorts were unwilling at this point to foment a revolution against the Castillo regime,[14] but they were certainly not averse to aiding those who advocated a pro-Allied change in Argentina's international posture. The Argentine press, one of the oldest and most articulate institutions in the Western Hemisphere, was a major factor in shaping not only Argentine opinion but the attitudes of *latinos* everywhere. The federally subsidized integral-nationalist sheets *El Pampero* and *El Cabildo* were vehement critics of the United States and were avid supporters of the administration's policy of neutrality, while the older, more widely read Buenos Aires dailies such as *La Nación, La Prensa,* and *Noticias Gráficas* generally favored a return to constitutional elections and sympathized with the Allied cause. Using powers granted to it under the state of siege to suppress dissenting opinion, the Castillo government sought through direct if rather inept censorship and restriction of newsprint (nearly all of which had to be imported) to control those papers that were most critical of its policies.[15] As a principal supplier of this critical material, the United States was in a perfect position to "aid its friends and punish its enemies." Amid cries from the Argentine Foreign Office that Washington was impinging on Argentina's national sovereignty, the United States began shipping paper only to those journals that urged alignment with the United States.

The Latin Americanists' program of selective supply got off the ground in early February when Armour notified his superiors of the newsprint shortage, and the State Department subsequently prevailed upon the Combined Shipping Board to create precious additional space for this commodity aboard Allied ships destined to call at Buenos Aires. Selective replenishment continued throughout the spring and summer, until finally the Casa Rosada retaliated. It first ordered the Flota Mercante, an Argentine shipping line under government supervision, to stop carrying American newsprint to Argentina, and then it announced a complete government takeover of distribution, thus effectively ending the State Department's power to influence domestic editorial opinion.[16]

By early 1943 the "democratic" press was suffocating for lack of paper. In a last-ditch effort to protect pro-Allied forums in Argentina, Washington attempted to use that nation's desire to export more fresh fruit as a lever to pry permission from the Foreign Office to resupply the anti-Axis press. Over lunch with Ambassador Espil, Philip Bonsal hinted that the United States would buy huge quantities of fruit in return for increased cargo space for newsprint aboard Argentine ships and, more importantly, for control over allocation. Replying that such an agreement would constitute a clear violation of Argentine sovereignty which would in turn provide the nationalists with a propaganda field day, Espil flatly rejected the scheme.[17] The Castillo administration was no longer inclined to permit Washington to supply its critics with the paper upon which to print their antigovernment broadsides.

Not content to rely solely on Argentine sources to sway public opinion in that country, the State Department turned to direct and inevitably more offensive methods of propaganda. In their search for more effective ways of influencing Argentine opinion, the Latin Americanists approached the Office of Coordinator of Inter-American Affairs (OCIAA). The agency had been established by President Roosevelt in 1941 to "formulate and execute programs in the commercial and economic fields and the fields of the arts and sciences, education and travel, the radio, the press and the cinema that would further national defense and strengthen the bonds between the nations of the Western Hemisphere."[18] Under Nelson Rockefeller, the OCIAA labored from 1941 through 1944 to mobilize *latinos* everywhere in behalf of the crusade against the Axis. Among other things, it served as a grievance board for cooperating governments, as an Allied propaganda bureau, and as an intelligence-gathering agency for other branches of the United States government. In April, at Welles's behest, the OCIAA set in motion plans to construct a long-range radio station in Uruguay that would be capable of beaming anti-Axis broadcasts to the Argentine provinces of Buenos Aires, Rosario, and Cordoba.[19] Program schedules were to be approved by the State Department. In August, Robert Wells, chairman of the coordinating committee for Argentina within the OCIAA, reported to Duggan that during the summer, OCIAA operatives had begun broadcasting three radio programs in Argentina which were designed to extol the virtues of the United States. Also they had hired Argentine nationals to complain to various papers that were running pro-Axis editorials, and they persuaded many American businessmen to cancel their advertising in unfriendly sheets.[20] Because, however, the source of this propaganda was so obvious and because Argentineans were so incensed at attempts to brainwash them, direct efforts to influence Argentine opinion were even less successful than were attempts to work through the indigenous press.

The Latin Americanists realized that it would be months, if ever, before their propaganda efforts bore fruit in terms of a firm Argentine commitment to the Allied cause. Given their tenuous hold on hemispheric policy within the foreign-affairs establishment, Welles and his colleagues found it imperative to apply pressure directly on the Castillo government in order to obtain immediate results. Several members of the group, most notably Norman Armour and Philip Bonsal, correctly perceived the source of Castillo's political power to be the Argentine military, so they began to urge adoption of policies that would exploit the officer corps' preoccupation with acquiring large quantities of munitions and the latest, most sophisticated military equipment. From Buenos Aires, Armour advised Welles and Bonsal that World War II had stimulated feelings of both insecurity and aggression within the military and that if Washington were to ignore Argentina's rather frantic requests for arms aid, while ostentatiously "building up" Brazil, Uruguay, Paraguay, and Chile, the officer corps would overnight become an advocate of Argentine-American cooperation in the struggle against the Axis.[21] Bonsal not only relayed Armour's recommendations to his superiors with his endorsement; in early February he also took it upon himself to suggest the establishment of a seaplane patrol base in southern Brazil—specifically at Rio Grande de Sul, only about four hundred miles round-trip from Buenos Aires. The stationing there of a dozen long-range bombers to be eventually turned over to the Brazilians, he observed, would have a useful effect on the Argentineans.[22] Both Welles and Roosevelt, who subsequently initialed an air-base agreement with Brazil, were enthusiastic about the balance-of-power approach, not only because it seemed to offer an opportunity to play on the military's fear that Argentina's neutralist policies were relegating her to the status of a third-rate power in South America, but also because it did not conspicuously violate the Good Neighbor Policy. To those who might accuse the United States of attempting to coerce Buenos Aires by denying it arms aid while building up its rivals, Washington could reply that it would be manifestly unjust to take from its allies in order to give to a neutralist power such as Argentina.

The State Department embarked on its campaign to maximize insecurity within Argentina's officer corps, and thus within the Castillo administration, almost immediately after the signing of the Pact of Rio. As the various delegations were preparing to depart, Ruiz Guiñazú informed Welles that his government expected to reach an agreement with American military representatives for the transfer of arms, ammunition, and ships under lend-lease provisions. Welles, whose capacity for chilling formality was notorious in diplomatic circles, replied stiffly that it would be the Roosevelt administration's policy to distribute materials of war only when such aid would contribute to the defense of the United States. Citing massive United States aid to Brazil and to numerous other nations that had not yet declared war on the Axis, Ruiz Guiñazú angrily charged the Roosevelt administration with pursuing a blatantly discriminatory policy. Welles retorted that so long as Argentina refused to contribute to the common defense of the hemisphere, it alone was responsible for its shortage of munitions.[23]

The foreign minister responded to the Latin Americanists' arms-aid diplomacy by trying to beat them at their own game. Throughout 1941 and into 1942 the United States held a series of meetings with high-ranking naval officers from the American republics to coordinate plans for the defense of the hemisphere. Members of the Argentine navy arrived in Washington in December 1941 and worked feverishly through the winter and early spring to coordinate Argentine-American naval operations in the Western Hemisphere before deteriorating diplomatic relations between their two countries wrecked the talks. Aware of the United States Navy's intense desire to gain effective control of the Straits of Magellan, Ruiz Guiñazú ordered Ambassador Felipe Espil to attend the sessions and to extract an unconditional pledge of military aid from the United States by playing off the navy's desire for a military accord against the State Department's desire to squeeze further diplomatic concessions from the Castillo government. In short, Espil was to sabotage the discussions unless American diplomats authorized a full measure of lend-lease aid to Argentina.[24]

The Latin Americanists were far less concerned about the military security of the South Atlantic than they were with securing a break in relations between the Castillo government, on the one hand, and Germany, Italy, and Japan on the other. Not only would a no-strings-attached aid agreement destroy any leverage the Latin Americanists might be able to exert on the Argentine army, but in addition, once the War Department had made a commitment to deliver lend-lease supplies, however small the amount, the Castillo regime would be able to hold up to the Argentine people these arms consignments as proof that Washington recognized Argentina's Rio policy to be consistent with hemispheric security. To forestall such an interpretation and to maintain the balance-of-power stratagem intact, the State Department instructed United States military representatives at the staff discussions to insert into the Argentine draft of an aid agreement a proviso making Argentina militarily responsible for Allied shipping in the South Atlantic.[25]

Despite repeated assaults on the obligatory patrolling section by a distraught Espil, the United States held firm. To the Argentinean's contention that the required convoy duty would lead quickly to a state of belligerency, Welles, knowing full well that American convoying in the winter of 1941 had led to a state of undeclared war between the United States and Germany, replied that the United States had managed to maintain its neutrality while guarding Allied ships in the Atlantic in late 1941. The undersecretary informed Espil that the State Department would like nothing better than to furnish its neighbor to the south with arms, but this was impossible without some positive action that would convince the rest of the Americas that Argentina was living up to its hemispheric commitments. To no one's surprise, Ruiz Guiñazú rejected the American proposal, and as a result, in late April, the negotiations between the Argentine mission and the War and Navy departments collapsed.[26]

The refusal of the State Department to make even token deliveries of arms to Argentina during 1942 and 1943, despite giving substantial aid to the neutralist governments of Chile and Spain, played into the hands of the nationalists. In the first place, Washington's attempts at lend-lease diplomacy proved of inestimable aid to the Castillo government in its continuing campaign to justify nonalignment. When the Argentine delegation returned home from Washington empty-handed, Ruiz Guiñazú told the nation that "the denial of military equipment to Argentina by the United States represented the most flagrant kind of discrimination as well as ill-concealed coercion."[27] In July he informed the Chamber of Deputies that the government's plans for an eventual break with the Axis could never be implemented as long as Washington denied Argentina the arms with which to defend herself against Axis aggression.[28] In the second place, because the State Department's policy of discriminatory lend-lease aid forced the Argentineans to search for alternative sources, it had the effect of driving Buenos Aires closer to Berlin.[29] Initially the balance-of-power technique did create insecurity within certain sectors of the officer corps and hence put pressure on the Castillo government to assume an actively pro-Allied role in the war. In early 1943 the United States military attaché in Buenos Aires uncovered a memorandum sent by the Argentine general staff to President Castillo, arguing that Argentina's position vis-à-vis her neighbors had become greatly weakened because of discriminatory lend-lease aid. The memo urged absolute conformity to the Rio declarations in order to end Argentina's isolation.[30] Castillo rejected the recommended solution, however, because he believed that the bulk of middle- and junior-grade officers and a majority of the citizenry favored a policy of strict neutrality and because he was himself an ardent nationalist. He sought instead to satisfy the military's demands by negotiating with the Third Reich for the munitions that would preserve Argentine ascendancy in southern South America.[31]

Topping the Latin Americanists' list of weapons in their war on Argentine neutrality and Axis activities within Argentina was a program of selective economic coercion. Various United States intelligence sources within Argentina advised the department throughout 1942 that there was little chance that the Castillo government would break relations with Germany, Japan, and Italy unless the Allies could inject an element of doubt into the booming Argentine economy. Because of the changes wrought in the international marketplace by World War II, the United States, in the wake of the Rio Conference, appeared to be in an excellent position to create anxiety and insecurity within the Argentine business community. With the fall of France and the advent of the Battle of Britain, the United States became virtually the sole supplier of steel machinery, railway replacement parts, tires, petroleum equipment, and other industrial items to Argentina.[32] Like discriminatory lend-lease aid, economic constriction could be justified on the basis of the war effort. Moreover, because the United States had by the end of 1941 concluded long-term contracts for a number of Argentina's strategic raw materials, including feldspar, manganese, antimony, silver, beryl, tungsten, tin, lead, and quebracho, the State Department believed that it could exert economic pressure without fear of endangering this vital source of goods. So immune did Washington feel from Argentine retaliation that in early 1942 Welles informed Espil that his government did not really favor successful consummation of pending raw-materials contracts. Since Argentina would have to sell in order to survive, and of course would not think of dealing with the Axis, the Allies could purchase all that they needed on the open market.[33]

The Latin Americanists realized that economic deprivation would exert pressure on Argentineans of virtually every political persuasion and every walk of life, from Conservative to Communist, from *estanciero* to *descamisado*, and they believed that if they could convince a majority of the citizenry that neutrality did not mean prosperity, then they would undermine a powerful argument in behalf of continued nonalignment. If, however, Washington engaged in gross and indiscriminate coercion, economic pressure would only unify the proud Argentineans behind the Castillo government's policy of neutrality and would revive latent anti-Americanism in Argentina and throughout the Americas. Thus, fearful of resurrecting charges of dollar diplomacy, Welles and his colleagues rejected traditional implements of economic compulsion such as an embargo or blockade and turned instead to a program of selective deprivation which was designed to reward pro-Allied groups while punishing those who advocated either neutralist or pro-Axis policies. In its desire to avoid a frontal attack, the State Department devised a formalized mechanism for systematic intervention into Argentine economic affairs that in the end antagonized Argentineans to perhaps a greater degree than the more direct methods that the Latin Americanists were striving to avoid.

Despite the desire of Welles, Duggan, and Bonsal to pursue a selective approach that would penalize only specific groups, early efforts at economic coercion were capricious and indiscriminate. In March 1942 the Board of Economic Warfare (BEW) began refusing export licenses to United States exporters wishing to sell electrical equipment, chemicals, and other items to Argentina. Later in the month the State Department notified the British Foreign Office that in order better to supply the needs of the Allies, the United States would henceforth restrict the exportation of a wide variety of goods to the Argentine. The British were requested in the name of the war effort not to make up these deficiencies.[34] By early April, Argentine importers of North American products were having so much difficulty obtaining export licenses for goods they had bought in the United States that the Castillo government ordered its official purchasing commission to come home. *Business Week* reported that, in the weeks after the Rio Conference, American traders had often been unable to obtain licenses for Argentina but had encountered no difficulty when it came to Mexico, Brazil and Chile.[35]

Such blanket tactics were only stopgap measures, however. In the last week of March the State Department presented BEW with a complex design that would pinpoint pro-Axis firms within Argentina for punishment. The plan sought to take advantage of an ardently pro-American clique within the Central Bank, the federally supervised but privately owned national bank of Argentina. In conformity with the State Department directive, the BEW announced that as of April 1, licenses for exports to Argentina, including goods in transit through the United States, would be granted only under certain procedures. Importers in Argentina who desired North American products would have to apply to the Central Bank in Buenos Aires for a Certificate of Necessity and would have to supply all information the bank might require. The bank, in collaboration with the United States embassy, would then issue certificates based on the needs of the Argentine national economy and on estimates of available supply and transportation facilities. Exporters in the United States would have to obtain an original copy of the certificate from the importer. After April 1, all applications for export licenses had to be accompanied by such documents. This licensing system put the State Department in a position to bring direct pressure to bear on the Castillo government by depriving the Argentine economy of vital raw materials and finished goods, thus creating a judicious amount of instability in the marketplace.[36] It would at the same time permit Washington to reinforce those firms that were cooperating with the Allies and to punish those dealing with Axis subsidiaries. From Buenos Aires, Armour advised that he, as well as "the bulk of the thinking Argentine people" heartily agreed with the department's recently implemented policy of freely sharing scarce commodities with America's allies while distributing Argentina's share in such a way that "the friendly majority of the Argentine people would be strengthened at the expense of the unfriendly but influential minority."[37]

Another, more traditional device utilized by the Latin Americanists to penalize the "influential minority" was the Proclaimed List. Established in 1941, it enumerated Latin American firms that were trading with the Axis and forbade United States concerns from having any contact whatsover with them. With an eye always to limiting commercial ties between Argentina and Germany and to enriching those businesses that supported the Allies, the State Department added more and more Argentine firms to the list during 1942. Buenos Aires, which viewed the Proclaimed List as nothing less than a crude weapon with which the United States was attempting to coerce a nonconforming nation, protested vigorously, pointing out that the United States and Argentina had joined together in 1916 to object to similar measures imposed on neutrals by the British. Sounding surprisingly like Hull, Welles replied that the fifth-column threat to the Western Hemisphere was immeasurably greater in 1942 than during World War I. The Roosevelt administration would continue to do everything within its power to "prevent the fires of Hitlerism in this hemisphere from being fed with our own resources."[38]

The undersecretary's rhetoric reflected his and his subordinates' growing sense of frustration. For despite the complex licensing system instituted in April, the Proclaimed List, and other subtle and not-so-subtle devices of economic compulsion, Buenos Aires remained as committed as ever to non-alignment. If anything, it became increasingly tolerant of German sympathizers and Axis activities in Argentina. Despite domestic discontent with the administration's exclusion of workers, peasants, and the petty bourgeoisie from the political process and despite its refusal to sponsor measures of social justice, Castillo's political position remained secure. His foreign policies more than satisfied the principle source of his support, the integral-nationalist middle- and junior-grade officers who wanted above all to maintain Argentina's freedom of action and to avoid any hint of truckling to United States demands.[39] In addition, the Proclaimed List and the licensing system served to heighten both nationalism and support for neutrality among groups otherwise quite critical of the Castillo government. Adding to the Casa Rosada's sense of security and the Latin Americanists' mood of frustration was a pervasive apathy among the populace that stemmed primarily from continuing prosperity. Although import-export cutbacks by the United States had some effect on the Argentine economy, the overall impact of the State Department's program was negligible. The Allied war machine continued to consume virtually all of Argentina's exportable surplus of raw materials. The British Ministry of Food—the sole purchaser of meat from Argentina, Brazil, Paraguay, and Uruguay for the United Nations—used lend-lease funds to purchase over 2.13 billion pesos in goods from Argentina during the period from 1941 through 1943. This transaction, coupled with

Argentina's skyrocketing trade with her South American neighbors, produced a net increase in foreign trade in 1942 of 11.5 percent over 1941. While imports declined, exports increased 21.79 percent, creating huge foreign-exchange credits abroad. The fact that imports of iron products from 1939 to 1943 dropped from 693,000 tons to 76,000 tons did not spell economic disaster, as so many in the United States had hoped. The decline only served to make Argentina more self-sufficient: between 1935 and 1943 Argentine manufacturing increased by 100 percent.[40] After 1942 Buenos Aires was able partially to fulfill the nation's requirements for certain machine parts and high-grade steel and iron by negotiating a series of very favorable trade agreements with Franco's Spain.[41] As 1942 drew to a close, *Business Week* painted a depressing picture for those who had hoped that economic instability would persuade Argentina to break with Germany, Italy, and Japan and to crack down on Axis sympathizers within its borders:

> Argentina has felt almost no disturbing business repercussions from the war. . . . There's tremendous volume of building in Buenos Aires; the streets are jammed with automobiles; hotels are full and nightclubs are doing a thriving business; the stock market is booming; export trade as a whole, despite the loss of continental European markets, is prospering because of huge meat sales to the United Nations and soaring export prices.[42]

In its efforts to resist North American economic pressures, the Castillo government was able to benefit immeasurably from a tacit coalition with Great Britain. Throughout 1942 and 1943 London displayed a marked unwillingness to join in the Latin Americanists' policy of selective coercion, while British businessmen and diplomats used the widening breach between Buenos Aires and Washington to increase England's economic and political influence in Argentina. Perhaps the most important factor behind British noncooperation was the important place that Argentina occupied in the Churchill government's plans to rebuild the empire in the postwar era. From 1940 through 1943 Britain was forced to liquidate a large part of her holdings throughout the world. In the United States, for instance, British assets melted from $4.5 billion to $1.5 billion. Latin America was the only area in which British investments held firm. Over one-third of the British capital in that area resided in Argentina, a nation that was traditionally favored by British businessmen because of high market potential, abundant raw materials, and a spotless record of debt repayment. As of May 1943, British nationals controlled over $1 billion in Argentine rails, $36 million in banking, $900 million in mining and manufacturing, and $177 million in government bonds. Whitehall's economic planners operated on the assumption that if the British Empire were to survive the war, then His Majesty's government would have to preserve investments and commercial ties with Argentina, the keystone in the economic arch connecting Britain and Latin America.[43]

That Whitehall believed that United States businessmen were seeking to take advantage of Britain's preoccupation with World War II in order to further their economic interests made the Churchill government even less willing to join in sanctions. As Europe's markets dried up during the dark days of 1940 and 1941 and as the United States' need for raw material increased, Argentine-American trade grew by leaps and bounds. The activities of aggressive American businessmen naturally prompted the well-entrenched and cohesive British colony to suspect that the Yanks were seeking to profit from Britain's distress. As the British Foreign Office put it, stepped-up United States business activity had "given rise to the impression, however false, that there may be some desire on the American side to supplant British traders in their established and traditional markets, not only for the war period but permanently thereafter."[44] This was certainly the view of Sir David Kelly, Britain's ambassador to Argentina:

> While the Americans were very resentful of the Argentine Government's refusal to line up with the other South American Governments by at least breaking off relations with the Axis, they were quite reasonably doing everything possible to build up the trade supremacy for which their geographical situation and the virtual cessation of British exports afforded a solid foundation.[45]

Indeed, the British business community in Argentina was so frightened of competition from United States traders that, from 1941 on, a number of them supported Ruiz Guiñazú and his neutralist policies. During an April 1943 visit to the State Department, José Augusti, publisher of *Noticias Gráficas*, told Sumner Welles that "whatever superficial appearances might be, the pressure of British interests in the Argentine Republic until the present moment has been for the retention of Ruiz Guiñazú in office and for the continuation of the foreign policy which he had pursued." According to Augusti, the British financial, railroad, public-utility, and commercial interests were persuaded that if the United States succeeded in diverting Argentina from its course of neutrality, North American influence would immediately become preponderant, as it had in all of the Latin republics that had either broken relations or declared war. These businessmen, he concluded, "were determined that British hegemony of the commercial and financial spheres should continue to be exercised in this remaining part of South America where for a hundred years they had been predominant."[46]

Despite the support for the neutralists that was shown by British nationals living in Argentina, Whitehall was for a brief period willing to take action to ensure that all the American republics line up solidly behind the Allied war effort. Shortly before the Rio Conference, Sir Ronald Campbell approached the State Department, suggesting that the United States and Great Britain collaborate in toppling those Latin governments that were proving less than enthusiastic about doing battle with Hitler and Mussolini. He mentioned Argentina and Brazil specifically. When Duggan and Berle demurred, Campbell asked permission to proceed unilaterally. The Americans, however, would have no part of it. Direct immediate intervention appealed to the British Foreign Office because it would be over with quickly and because there was a possibility that Britain's role might be concealed. British officials were not willing to participate in lesser sanctions, perceiving that half-way measures, while certain to provoke charges of British imperialism, stood little chance of success.[47]

In view of Washington's refusal to support direct clandestine activities leading to the overthrow of neutralist and pro-Axis governments and in view of a total lack of sympathy among British citizens toward the coercion of Argentina,[48] Great Britain launched an unofficial campaign in 1942 to soften the effect of United States sanctions and to use the widening breach between Washington and Buenos Aires to enhance Britain's prestige in Argentina. Argentine representatives, arguing that heavy United States lend-lease shipments to Brazil were threatening to upset the balance of power in southern South America, contacted Great Britain in June and requested assistance in building up their armament industry. Whitehall responded favorably, and Argentina subsequently began to export small arms to Britain in return for the raw materials needed to feed her munitions plants. In addition, Industrias Metalurgicas and Plastica Argentina contracted with Vickers and Armstrong, England's leading producers of arms, for technical experts in the manufacture of cannon, machine guns, and other weapons.[49] All the while, British officials were attempting to convince the Castillo regime that the United States was rendering aid and comfort to its political enemies. Throughout 1942 General Justo, with the tacit support of American officials in Buenos Aires, continued to rail at Castillo and to plot his own strategy for the presidential elections to be held in 1943.[50] As the United States embassy sought to conceal its support for Justo from the Castillo administration, British journalists and spokesmen exerted every effort to link the general with North American influence and interests.[51] Lastly, in conjunction with these stratagems, the British colony inaugurated an intense propaganda offensive to improve the United Kingdom's image in Latin America. As British traders sought to protect their economic sphere of influence through a vigorous promotional campaign, including shortwave broadcasts from London and coordinated marketing efforts by British businessmen in Buenos Aires, other "sources," both official and unofficial, circulated the rumor that Britain fully understood and approved of the reasons for Argentine neutrality; these sources compared their country's attitude of friendship and understanding with the seemingly implacable hostility of the United States.[52] In early 1942, for example, Evelyn Baring, a prominent British businessman who was Lord Halifax's brother-in-law, told Raul Damonte Taborda, a leading Radical politician, that London was not interested in Argentina's domestic political situation and did not find Argentine neutrality offensive. England was interested only in preserving its customers and markets in Argentina and in preventing the United States from absorbing them.[53]

All in all, British activities in Argentina did not facilitate implementation of the Latin Americanists' policy of propaganda and selective deprivation. State Department complaints served to produce changes only in Whitehall's rhetoric. When the Castillo government attempted to utilize the Anglo-American differences to rally support for its program of resistance to pressure from the United States, the State Department protested vigorously to London. Foreign Secretary Anthony Eden reluctantly agreed to instruct the Argentine ambassador that he should warn his government to avoid creating false impressions regarding British attitudes, and Eden consented to state publicly that His Majesty's government fully supported the position of the United States.[54] Nevertheless, Great Britain would continue to sell munitions and machinery to Argentine concerns, to expand its investments, to purchase all available Argentine food surpluses, and to profit generally from the Argentine-American rift. United States diplomats and businessmen learned quickly that Winston Churchill's oft-quoted observation—that he had not become His Majesty's first minister to preside over the dissolution of the empire—applied to England's economic satrapy in Latin America as well as to her more visible colonial holdings in the Middle East and Asia.

Despite British obstructionism, continued Argentine prosperity, and Castillo's talent for turning Washington's subtle attempts at coercion to his political advantage, the Latin Americanists were convinced that time would vindicate their policy of propaganda and selective pressure. As Argentina gradually realized that its national interest was inextricably intertwined with the Allied cause, hemispheric unity and the Good Neighbor Policy would remain intact. Unfortunately for Welles and his colleagues, their inability to modify the Castillo government's policy of neutrality and to eradicate pro-Axis activities in Argentina undermined the Latin Americanists' power and prestige within the Roosevelt administration and opened the way for other governmental agencies to issue a serious challenge to the State Department's authority in inter-American affairs. This challenge in turn played into the hands of the Hull internationalists and contributed ultimately to their triumph over Welles and his associates.

4

THE ROOSEVELT FOREIGN-POLICY ESTABLISHMENT AND THE FAILURE OF SELECTIVE INTERVENTION

As the Latin Americanists moved from stratagem to stratagem during 1942 in an unsuccessful attempt to modify Argentine policy, they were forced to deal with a challenge to their control of policy not only from the hard-liners within the State Department but from other groups as well. Franklin Roosevelt had in 1933 brought to Washington a small army of bright, innovative men who, the president hoped, would be capable of dealing with the problems created by the Depression. These men—Henry Wallace, Jesse Jones, Henry Morgenthau, Jr., Harold Ickes, Rexford Tugwell, and Adolf Berle, to name a few—were not only intelligent and inventive but self-willed and ambitious as well. The plethora of problems to be solved, coupled with Roosevelt's penchant for blurring lines of jurisdiction and inviting competition among his subordinates, meant that by the eve of World War II, the administration "team" consisted of a gaggle of accomplished bureaucratic empire builders who were bound together only by common ties of loyalty to Roosevelt.

To a large extent, foreign affairs had escaped the attention of the various department and agency heads during the 1930s, probably because the president himself had evinced little interest in diplomacy. State Department leaders had to contend only with each other for control of policy. With the outbreak of war in Europe in 1939 and with America's gradual shift from a policy of neutrality to one of undeclared war by the fall of 1941, powerful figures within the federal bureaucracy who had not heretofore been concerned with diplomacy turned their attention to foreign policy with a vengeance. As a result, fully a score of departments and agencies, some old and some spawned by the war itself, emerged to challenge the State Department

61

for control of policy-making—a development that profoundly affected Argentine-American relations and the course of the Good Neighbor Policy.

One of the most accomplished bureaucratic imperialists in the Roosevelt foreign-policy establishment was Secretary of the Treasury Henry Morgenthau, Jr. He perceived that the American public's growing disillusionment with the State Department's "soft line" toward Argentina offered a unique opportunity to add an important area in foreign affairs to his domain. As a result, he and his subordinates set about to convince FDR, who was acutely aware of the mounting anti-Argentine sentiment in the United States, that Argentina constituted a Nazi outpost in the New World, that financial coercion offered the best opportunity to force the Castillo government to abandon its "pro-Axis" policies, and that the Treasury Department's operatives and affiliated agencies were in the best position to apply pressure on Buenos Aires.

The Treasury Department's decision to advocate a get-tough policy toward Argentina was a product not only of its bureaucratic rivalry with the State Department but of the personal prejudices of the leadership within the department and of the parochial priorities and perceptions of the organization as a whole. Aware both of the strong anti-Semitic strain in Argentine nationalism and of the close relationship between the Argentine and German military organizations,[1] Morgenthau had come to the conclusion by 1942 that Argentina stood for the very principles against which America was fighting in Europe and the Far East. Much as Hull and Long, Morgenthau and his assistant for international affairs, Harry Dexter White,[2] were convinced that the totalitarian practices of the Castillo regime indicated affiliation with the members of the Tripartite Pact. The liberal White (who in 1948 was allegedly driven to his death by Elizabeth Bentley's charges that he was a Communist agent) found the totalitarian policies of the Conservative-backed Castillo particularly repugnant.[3]

Adding to the department's inclination to adopt the toughest possible stance toward Argentina was its tendency, as an organization, to judge foreign states solely on the basis of their international financial conduct. From the perspective of those who were responsible for measures of economic warfare, the Castillo government's financial policies were as damning as if Buenos Aires had permitted the armies of the Third Reich to use Argentine territory to launch an attack on New World members of the Grand Alliance. The Treasury Department's concern over Argentina's failure to sever financial ties with the Axis is well illustrated by a mid-1943 report from White to Morgenthau on the Argentine situation:

> In the weeks preceding the extension of our freezing order to the Axis (April 10, 1940) large sums were transferred to Argentina on behalf of the Axis countries in the form of bank transfers and currency shipments. In this way a large part of the funds which we had hoped to prevent from being used for Axis activities escaped our control. This accumulation of Axis funds in Argentina has resulted in the Axis' using Buenos Aires as the center point from which to transmit funds to Axis agents in all the other American republics.
>
> We have proof that Argentine holding companies and financial institutions are widely used by the Axis and its satellites to hold substantial amounts of dollar assets in the United States in evasion of our freezing control. With these funds they carry on transactions contrary to the purposes of our freezing order and inimicable to our war effort.[4]

Thus, uninhibited by concern for the well-being of the Good Neighbor Policy, the survival of the inter-American consultative system, or any of the other factors that restrained the Latin Americanists, Treasury Department officials urged measures of all-out economic warfare against Argentina throughout 1942 and attempted to run roughshod over the State Department when it objected.

In the struggle with the State Department, Morgenthau and his subordinates were able to take full advantage of Roosevelt's tendency to promote bureaucratic proliferation. The agency most useful to the Treasury in its drive to gain control of Argentine policy was the Office of Foreign Funds Control, established in 1940 under the control of the secretary of the Treasury. Among other things, this agency, which was headed by John W. Pehle,[5] was charged with preventing "all financial and commercial transactions between the United States and any other American Republic that directly or indirectly benefited the Axis" and with bringing a halt to "all financial and commercial activity on the part of persons or corporations in the United States whose influence or activity was deemed inimicable to the security of the Western Hemisphere."[6] Armed with this weapon, the Treasury Department was in a position to coerce the Castillo government by disrupting Argentine-American trade.[7] In addition to agencies under its direct control, such as Foreign Funds, the Treasury was able to count on the support of powerful allies within the foreign-policy establishment, most notably Vice-President Henry A. Wallace and the Board of Economic Warfare (BEW).

Established by an executive order on 17 December 1941, the BEW was placed at once under Wallace's control. He appointed as its executive director Milo Perkins, an old friend and a dedicated promoter of the vice-president's purposes. BEW was divided into three sections: the Office of Imports, which was charged with procuring strategic materials and with preclusive buying all over the world, but especially in Latin America; the Office of Exports, which was to use its licensing power to prevent goods from reaching Axis nations; and the Office of War Analysis, which selected targets of economic importance for strategic bombing. From its inception to its demise in mid 1943, BEW under Wallace and Perkins was involved in one dispute after another with the State Department. The conflict stemmed both from bureaucratic competition and from philosophical differences on the part of the leaders of the two organizations.[8]

Henry Wallace was, not surprisingly, bored and frustrated with the vice-presidency. A man of vision, ambition, and action, Wallace longed to play a major role in the struggle against international fascism and in the formulation and implementation of postwar programs. Establishment of BEW provided the vice-president with the bureaucratic vehicle he needed. Wallace and Perkins were determined to use their agency so as to control every aspect of overseas purchasing, from planning to financing. In reaching for these powers, BEW threatened to encroach on the jurisdiction not only of the State Department but of the Reconstruction Finance Corporation (RFC), under the powerful and conservative Texas financier Jesse Jones. Since the beginning of the war, the State Department had infuriated BEW officials by vetoing every BEW project that threatened to affect the international political situation, while Jones in RFC turned over the funds for BEW programs only after he was convinced that they would not damage private United States economic interests. To Wallace and Perkins, the State Department was a bureaucratic tar baby; Jones was a penny-pinching reactionary; and BEW was the only agency capable of bringing efficiency and speed to foreign procurement. In the same way that Donald Nelson and the War Production Board controlled every aspect of domestic purchasing,

BEW would dominate overseas procurement.[9] After weeks of intense lobbying at the White House by Wallace and BEW officials, FDR issued an executive order on 13 April 1942, authorizing BEW to represent the United States in its dealings with the economic-warfare agencies of other nations, to draw funds from RFC at will, and to dispatch its own agents to work directly in foreign capitals.[10]

The leadership within BEW viewed the April 13 order as nothing less than a carte blanche. As one interoffice memo put it, "The Presidential directive gives Wallace and Perkins the whip hand and they will not hesitate to use it."[11] On April 16 Perkins sent a terse directive to all government agencies in Washington that were concerned with procurement, including the RFC and the State Department. First, he called for a complete list of outstanding contracts between the procurement agencies and any foreign government or corporation; and second, he notified the agencies that thenceforth all purchasing and development work abroad was to be done solely under the direction of BEW. Perkins believed that he and his agency were embarked on a great crusade not only to win the war but to vindicate Wallace and punish those bureaucratic entities that he believed had been hindering BEW operations. "H. A. [Wallace] will stand or fall on the success of our efforts within the next six months," Perkins confided to a friend. "If we do the job we must do, then the faith of the President in us and in giving us our authority will be justified. . . . If we flop, we are going to catch hell, and with good reason."[12] As to BEW's rivals within the foreign-policy establishment: "I've been a pretty patient man because I'm more interested in winning the war and getting something done than I am in the matter of prestige and dignity. . . . But I hope Mr. Welles will realize that there is a limit to my graciousness and when that is reached somebody will have a fight on their hands."[13] Second-level officials in BEW could not contain their glee. A week before the presidential order, Sumner Welles had sent a stiff note to all government agencies, advising them that all foreign missions would be responsible to the State Department. "So far as BEW is concerned," wrote Jerry Greene to a fellow staff member, David Hulburd, "the presidential order . . . turns the Welles letter into a badly used pie plate. . . . Henceforth BEW can send whom it pleases where it pleases and the missions will be responsible to Wallace and Perkins, not to State."[14]

It quickly became obvious that in determining export and import priorities, Wallace and BEW officials would not hesitate to pursue political objectives. In mid 1942, for example, Welles had convinced FDR to continue United States oil shipments to Spain. The decision infuriated Wallace and Perkins, because they placed Franco in the same class with Hitler and Mussolini and because they were sure that some of the oil was being transhipped to Italy. In mid April, Wallace told Greene that no longer would BEW have to acquiesce in such accommodationist decisions. The agency, he said, was now in a position to take its case directly to the White House.[15]

State Department officials, whether disciples of Hull or followers of Welles, viewed the mere existence of BEW as an encroachment on the department's prerogatives, and they worked assiduously throughout 1942 and 1943 to decrease BEW's power. From February through April 1942, Welles complained strenuously to FDR that Perkins was trying to take control of all activities that were in any way related to foreign trade.[16] According to Dean Acheson, Hull regarded the April 13 executive order augmenting the authority of BEW as a "bitter and humiliating defeat," and the secretary moved quickly to have it rescinded. To the chagrin of Wallace and Perkins, Hull persuaded Roosevelt in early May to modify the order, causing BEW to have to go through the State Department in negotiations with other Allied agencies and subsuming BEW representatives abroad to the authority of the local American embassy.[17] The vice-president, an experienced infighter, had no intention of remaining quiet while his bailiwick was being attacked. When, in mid May, Wallace learned that Welles was working openly to place additional limitations on the jurisdiction of BEW, he declared that he and Perkins would "fight like hell."[18]

Further contributing to the row between BEW and the State Department was the latter's belief that Wallace was responsible for much of the left-wing criticism that was being leveled at its "expedient" policy toward Vichy France and, subsequently, toward Vichyite authorities in North Africa. Not only Hull but Berle, Welles, Acheson, and their subordinates were all extremely sensitive in this regard. Indeed, it is safe to say that by 1943 Hull, Long, and Berle in particular had begun to believe that a conspiracy to discredit them was being formed by ultraliberal publications such as the *New Republic* and the *Nation* and their hero, Henry Wallace. Thus, any augmentation of BEW's power was seen as a victory for the hated "left," for the "fellow traveller-type individual who has very little to recommend him except the rather slavish following of the Russian propaganda."[19]

The struggle between the State Department and BEW was accentuated by far-reaching differences between the leaderships of both agencies as to the role the United States should play in world affairs, especially in Latin America. Wallace, like Hull, was committed to free trade; but, unlike the secretary of state, Wallace envisioned a postwar world that would be characterized by international economic interdependence, complete with a world granary and other communal projects. Wallace was an outspoken champion of those submerged peoples who were struggling for political democracy and social justice. When pressed on the matter, however, he was not above sacrificing one for the other. When asked by Vice-President Sergio Osmeña of the Philippines to give his opinion on the function of dictatorships in Latin America, Wallace replied that as long as a great majority of the people in a country did not know how to read and write, a dictatorship that rapidly increased the percentage of literacy, improved nutrition, and increased industrialization might be justified as a preliminary to democracy. Moreover, Wallace believed that the United States should use its economic and political leverage to aid the exploited masses in their struggle for power and dignity —even to the point of intervening in the affairs of other states.[20] For example, he believed that Washington should require Latin American governments and/or businesses to guarantee certain wage levels and working conditions before it purchased products from them. Thus, for Wallace, the Good Neighbor Policy consisted of a hemispheric campaign to obliterate social injustice.[21] Hull viewed Wallace's quest for a social revolution as a threat to the war effort and to democratization in the postwar era.[22] Welles was convinced that the vice-president's approach to inter-American affairs was no better than Hull's. One wanted to export political democracy; the other, economic and social justice. To the undersecretary, Wallace's projected activities constituted unwarranted interference in the affairs of other nations, and in Latin America they would revive charges of United States imperialism. In turn, Wallace regarded State Department officials as a collection of reactionaries who openly supported the corrupt church-army-landowner alliance that dominated so many Latin American nations.[23]

Nonetheless, the Castillo government in Argentina was not originally that offensive to Wallace and Perkins. They found the regime's autocratic methods distasteful, but they were willing to walk the path of expediency. In mid April, Wallace advised BEW officials that the agency would not swing its economic club to bring Argentina and Chile into line with the rest of the Americas. Their neutrality was sufficiently unimportant to allow the State Department to handle the matter.[24] Only a month later, however, Wallace and Perkins were calling for all-out economic war against Argentina. The reason for this turnabout was twofold. The leadership in BEW quickly became convinced that the Castillo government was thoroughly and permanently pro-Fascist and that Argentina was serving as headquarters for all fifth-column activities in South America. By 1943 Wallace was announcing that Germany had decided that World War II was lost and that Germany was converting Argentina into a staging area for World War III.[25] Perhaps even more importantly, Wallace and Perkins sensed the State Department's vulnerability in regard to its Argentine policy and decided to exploit it. As a result, throughout the remainder of 1942 and 1943 the vice-president warned Roosevelt that the Castillo regime and its pro-Axis policies were very real threats to freedom and democracy in the hemisphere, and he attempted to use State Department "appeasement" of Argentina to discredit Hull, Welles, Berle, and Acheson within the foreign-policy establishment.[26]

From early 1942 through mid 1943 Wallace and BEW managed the licensing system in a way that would compel the Castillo government to prevent the use of its territory as a base for Axis subversive activities and prevent the use of its financial, trade, and communication facilities by the Axis.[27] The tendency of the BEW mission to operate independently of the American embassy[28] produced bitter complaints from Ambassador Armour, who railed against "duplication of effort" and charged that meddling by BEW and the Treasury Department was subverting Welles's policy of selective coercion.[29] Perkins was able to fend off all threats to the mission's control over licensing until November 1942, when the State Department persuaded the White House to create the position of Counselor of Embassy for Economic Affairs, which was to act in Argentina for the BEW as well as for other purchasing agencies. The counselor was to be directly responsible to the ambassador.[30] Despite, or perhaps because of, this loss of power, Wallace and the board continued to support the Treasury Department's arguments that Argentina was a Fascist pro-Axis nation and to advocate the strongest possible measures of economic coercion.

Given its rivalry with the State Department, the Treasury felt by 1942 that it could no longer count on the embassy or the American Republic Affairs Division for an adequate flow of information on the Argentine situation. Morgenthau and White, ever the resourceful bureaucrats, soon turned up alternative sources. The top echelon in Washington was kept abreast of domestic political developments and Axis espionage activities in Argentina not only by the Treasury Department's regular field agents but also by the FBI and by Military Intelligence. Indeed, J. Edgar Hoover fully supported Morgenthau's position and had offered the services of his agents to the secretary personally.[31]

From February through May 1942 the Treasury Department utilized its subsidiary agencies, its intragovernmental allies, and its intelligence sources to achieve one primary goal—namely, the freezing of Argentine assets in the United States. In the minds of Morgenthau and his associates, freezing would serve a twofold purpose: it would force the Castillo government to renounce neutralism and abandon its permissive policies toward financial transactions beneficial to the Axis, and it would allow the Treasury Department and BEW to control commercial and financial relations between the United States and Argentina.[32] On May 7 White proposed that BEW completely freeze $500 million in Argentine funds in the United States and that this be accompanied by a general licensing system to be administered by the board.[33] On May 12, at the first meeting of a special interdepartmental committee on Argentina, the vice-president and BEW representatives formally confronted the State Department delegation with a proposal relating to freezing. Admitting that certain actions had to be taken in order to curb financial transactions in Argentina that were favorable to the Axis, Assistant Secretary for Economic Affairs Dean Acheson and Duggan urged the Treasury Department not to "walk in with a club to kill a mosquito."[34] Freezing, which is generally regarded among diplomats as the most extreme action that one nation can take against another short of war, would be counterproductive in a number of ways. Besides alarming the entire hemisphere, it would strengthen the hand of the nationalists and "would reverse the present perceptible trend against the Castillo government in Argentina."[35] White was not persuaded. The time for negotiation and accommodation was past, he declared: "The broad and inescapable fact is that Argentina is not cooperating, has no intention of cooperating, and is a hotbed of intrigue against the United Nations."[36]

The first phase of what was to prove a continuing clash between the State and Treasury departments over freezing reached an angry climax on the thirteenth and fourteenth of May. Ignoring the State Department's long-observed prerogative of vetoing action by other executive departments in the field of foreign affairs, Morgenthau decided to by-pass Hull and go directly to the president. On the day after the interdepartmental committee meeting, he called at the White House and asked FDR for an executive order freezing Argentine assets. The secretary not only went to great lengths during the interview to prove that Argentina was being used as a cloak by the Axis for "important economic and financial operations" but also implied that the State Department was doing a very poor job in preventing such activities. Not only would a freeze forestall specific financial abuses; it would also drive the Castillo regime into close collaboration with the United States and show the rest of the Americas that Washington would not hesitate to use its vast economic power to obtain solid hemispheric support for the war effort.[37]

Morgenthau's initiative, which the Treasury Department did not attempt to conceal, infuriated both the Hull group and the Latin Americanists and drove them into a momentary alliance. Hull detested Morgenthau for his bureaucratic aggressiveness and his intimate relationship with FDR.[38] The freezing proposal angered the Latin Americanists for the same reasons that Acheson and Duggan had outlined in their meeting with White and BEW officials—freezing would convince many Latin Americans that the United States had reverted to using the big stick, and it would destroy any chance that Washington had of achieving a peaceful reorientation of Argentine foreign policy. On May 14, Hull, Long, Welles, Bonsal, and other top officials in the State Department gathered in the secretary's office, drafted a comprehensive refutation of the Treasury Department's proposal, and sent it to the White House. This note first tried to counter the absolutely negative image that Morgenthau and White had painted of Argentina. Was not Buenos Aires selling strategic materials to the Allies, allowing Allied ships to utilize Argentine ports, and refusing to sell gas to Axis-controlled airlines? Moreover, a freeze would be particularly unfortunate at that time because the policies pursued by the State Department since Rio were starting to bear fruit. Not only public opinion, "carefully influenced by us," but "the powerful military and naval elements in Argentina, which really maintain the present Government in power, are beginning to question the desirability of Argentina's present policy." Most importantly, a freezing order would destroy the good will established throughout Latin America by a decade of restraint. Freezing would confirm "the thesis which the Axis is subtly promoting, namely, that the United States, under the guise of hemispheric solidarity is actually embarked upon a policy of ruthless economic imperialism."[39]

This broadside, the product of a momentarily unified State Department, was sufficient to overwhelm the Treasury Department's arguments. Roosevelt effectively shelved the freezing proposal with a one-sentence scrawl on Hull's memorandum: "C.H. Not in accord with Good Neighbor Policy. F.D.R."[40]

The president's decision to reject a general freeze, however, produced only a momentary respite from Morgenthau and his men. In conjunction with BEW, the Treasury Department had been conducting an independent study of the complicity of the Argentine government in German espionage, propaganda, and financial activities. At Hull's behest, FDR had told Morgenthau to halt the project and "keep out of there."[41] During the course of a cabinet meeting on May 15, however, Morgenthau passed Wallace a note saying that he had persuaded the president to allow the Treasury Department and BEW to continue their study. A week later, White notified Breckinridge Long that the Treasury Department was preparing a special mission to go to Argentina in order to conduct a complete investigation of Axis activities there.[42] Long replied that such an expedition would prove a hindrance rather than a help in gathering intelligence in Argentina and that the embassy would refuse to cooperate with any Treasury men who were sent. "We are supposed to be equipped to get what you want," the assistant secretary informed Morgenthau, "and if we are not equipped, we will get equipped."[43]

Evidently afraid that White and Morgenthau might use the State Department's intransigence to elicit an executive order creating some new bureaucratic apparatus, Hull on May 30 notified the Treasury that Merle Cochran, a State Department economic officer who had wide experience in Latin America, was being ordered to Argentina to gather complete information on "transactions which appear to involve directly or indirectly Axis interests."[44] Moreover, Cochran was to carry with him explicit instructions to Armour to make "strong representations" to the Argentine government "regarding its failure to implement Resolution V passed by the Rio Conference by severing commercial and financial intercourse between Argentina and the Tripartite Pact and its failure to take measures to eliminate financial and commercial activities which are prejudicial to the welfare and security of the American republics."[45]

The Cochran mission hardly mollified Morgenthau and his cohorts. Convinced that the United States could never hope for real cooperation from Argentina in any matter and sure that the Treasury Department possessed a presidential mandate to uncover and uproot pro-Axis activity in that nation, Treasury officials complained bitterly throughout 1943 that the State Department was hoarding vital information. Moreover, the Treasury Department continued to criticize the State Department's handling of financial control measures. White pronounced Cochran's mid-September report totally insufficient.[46] "Many matters which the Treasury is interested in are not even discussed in the report and those matters which were discussed only cover the situation on a superficial basis."[47] Not only was the report useless, but the solutions suggested to deal with the few problems that were uncovered were insufficient as well. "The primary purpose of the State Department's letter," concluded White, "was an effort to 'make a record' in this matter."[48]

State Department officials bitterly resented the Treasury Department's constant criticism and demands. Complained a young officer to Bonsal, "Treasury thinks we have done a lousy job on Argentine freezing and tells us so half a dozen times a day. . . . Don Hiss told me he is getting plenty fed up. . . . I have been fed up a long time."[49] Nevertheless, the State Department's resistance to the Treasury's demands for a larger voice in policy decisions and to its calls for an overall tougher line toward Argentina gradually began to weaken. When White cut off Export-Import Bank loans to all Argentine banks, the State Department could manage only a mild protest. Subsequently the State Department approved for ad hoc freezing forty-four of the sixty-four Argentine firms suspected of trading with the Axis (from a list submitted to it by White in November) and agreed to cut off credit facilities in the United States to Argentina's two largest financial institutions, Banco de la Nación and Banco de la Provincia. The two banks, one partly owned by the Argentine central government and the other by the provincial administrations, had incurred the Treasury Department's wrath by not cooperating with the United States in eliminating all transactions that would be of possible benefit to the Axis powers or their citizens.[50]

Hull's vigorous support of Welles's policy of selective pressure, which was expressed in the State Department's note of May 15 to Roosevelt, was a product of the bureaucratic stiuation. He and his colleagues viewed Argentina basically as a Fascist threat to the security of the hemisphere and viewed the Latin Americanists as a group of insubordinate usurpers, and these perspectives had changed not a bit. Indeed, in late June, Berle noted in his diary that Hull and Welles were farther apart than ever. Welles had committed the sin of speaking and acting as if he were the secretary "when there is an alive and very active Secretary of State in the immediate vicinity." According to Berle, Hull had been working to "clear the decks." Welles in turn retaliated by seeking to gain control of as much of the departmental machinery as possible.[51]

Throughout the fall and winter of 1942-43 the internationalists used the pressure being applied by the Treasury Department and BEW to force the Latin Americanists to acquiesce in a tougher policy toward Argentina. Hull and Long argued not only that the evidence dredged up by White and his associates constituted further proof of Argentine perfidy but that if the State Department did not seize control and launch an all-out campaign to obliterate Axis activity in Argentina and turn the Castillo government away from nonalignment, then the Treasury Department would. Thus, although the threat to the State Department's control over policy regarding Argentina that emanated from the Treasury Department and BEW during 1943 had the immediate effect of uniting the internationalists and the Latin Americanists behind a policy of selective coercion, in the long run the rivalry between the two departments played into the hands of Long and Hull and paved the way for the adoption of a hard line toward Argentina.

Meanwhile, domestic developments in Argentina during the latter half of 1942 were contributing to the Latin Americanists' continuing loss of power and prestige within the foreign-policy establishment. Intelligence reports in August and September provided virtually irrefutable proof that Argentina had become the center for Axis espionage and subversive activities in the Western Hemisphere, and those reports intimated that members of the Castillo government were planning right-wing *Putschen* in neighboring nations.

At the beginning of World War II the staff of the German embassy in Buenos Aires was overly large, numbering some one hundred and fifty compared to a mere thirty for the British.[52] This establishment became the headquarters for efforts to propagandize Latin America into a pro-Axis stance and to acquire all information that might profit Germany in the struggle against the Allies. Funds to support espionage operations poured into the embassy from trade balances in Argentina (which, because of the war, could not be liquidated through regular trade channels) and from various German bank accounts in Buenos Aires. Newspapers and pamphlets spread Goebbels's blandishments throughout the interior of South America. Espionage cells, reporting directly to the embassy, attempted to infiltrate and influence various Latin American governments, pinpointed Allied ship movements, and labored in numerous other ways to facilitate the Axis war effort.[53] Armour rather provocatively described the Nazi intelligence network as "a state within a state."[54] President Castillo reacted to this threat, not by ordering a roundup of all suspected German agents, but by issuing a decree ordering that fifty-nine alleged Communists be interned or expelled from the country.[55] Shortly thereafter, the Casa Rosada declared that as part of its continuing effort to protect the internal security of the republic, it was imposing a complete ban on press reports of foreign-policy debates within the Chamber of Deputies.[56] To Armour's complaints that the government's permissive policies were allowing "the criminal attacks of the Axis aggressors" to come ever closer to the Americas, Foreign Minister Ruiz Guiñazú replied that there had been energetic official intervention by the very efficient agency within the Ministry of the Interior that existed in order to stamp out all anti-Argentine activity.[57] When the United States embassy and the FBI investigated the efficiency and objectives of the Interior Ministry's spy-prevention machinery, however, its appraisal differed sharply from that of the Argentine Foreign Office. Reports on the Castillo regime's efforts to suppress Axis activity, which were submitted in September, indicated that such an agency did exist but that it had received practically no funds. Moreover, the police had devoted their efforts under the existing state of siege to stamping out "Communist activities" and to restricting the operations of "pro-democratic organizations."[58] Axis agents continued to enter Argentina both from other Latin American states and by way of Spanish vessels bound from Europe. The study concluded that Argentine measures for implementing the Rio resolutions were negligible and observed that the attitude of the Argentine government was still one of "intransigent isolationism."[59]

As long as the Castillo regime appeared to be guilty only of neutralism and a tolerant attitude toward pro-Axis activities within Argentina, the Latin Americanists could argue with some effect that a blatantly coercive policy was inappropriate. If, on the other hand, advocates of a get-tough policy could prove that Argentina was deliberately following a pro-Axis policy and was itself a threat to the security of South America, then their opponents' position would become untenable. In August 1942 the State

Department received from an unusual source a series of reports that seemed to substantiate the internationalists' view of Argentina and that facilitated their drive to snatch control of hemispheric policy from Welles, Duggan, and Bonsal. Very early in the war, intelligence agents of the Polish government-in-exile penetrated Argentina's ruling circle. From time to time throughout 1942 and 1943 Anthony Biddle, Washington's ambassador to the London-based Poles, received detailed reports on policy-planning within both the Argentine government and the military establishment. In mid August, Polish secret agents in Buenos Aires infiltrated a secret meeting of the nation's highest-ranking military officers, who had come together to discuss Argentina's relationship to World War II. Those in attendance, all of whom were integral nationalists, decided that in view of recent German successes, Argentina should indicate as much sympathy for the Axis as possible. The collapse of the United Nations was to be followed by a campaign in Argentina against Communists and Jews and by the establishment of a thoroughly totalitarian system. At the end of the meeting, the generals and colonels approved detailed plans for facilitating right-wing coups in neighboring states. The resulting governments would presumably favor creation of an anti–United States bloc in South America.[60]

Meanwhile, dispatches from the United States embassy in Buenos Aires and public utterances by officials of the Castillo government seemed to indicate that Washington's policy of aiding its friends and punishing its enemies was having no impact whatsoever. Chargé d'Affaires Edward Reed reported in late September that Castillo's determination to pursue a policy of nonalignment was as firm as ever. Although aware that a majority of Argentineans were pro-Allied, Castillo claimed that nearly everyone wanted to avoid war. Thus, according to Reed, the president perceived that neutrality would please both the public in general and the integral nationalists in particular.[61]

In a major policy speech given during Argentina's ninetieth anniversary celebration, Ruiz Guiñazú outlined the administration's foreign-policy objectives for the rest of the war. Argentina would adhere to a strict neutrality as being the course most beneficial to the national interest. Aside from shielding the country from a war in which it had no real stake, nonalignment was producing an autonomous economy, one dependent on no single nation or bloc of countries. Proclaiming that every war had produced a victor who was determined to establish economic hegemony over its part of the world, the foreign minister declared that it would be Argentina's aim to establish closer relations with neighboring states in order to resist economic and even political absorption in the postwar period.[62]

Then, in September, a ground swell of antigovernment sentiment swept Argentina, and it seemed that the Latin Americanists' long-held faith in the Argentine people was about to be rewarded. On September 5 the Chamber of Deputies summoned the minister of the interior so that he could explain why his department had not taken measures to suppress the Nazi party in Argentina. Meanwhile, former President Justo, who was still championing Allied-Argentine solidarity, stepped up his campaign against the government and its "pro-Axis" policies. When Brazil entered the war in late August, three hundred thousand Argentineans gathered under Justo's leadership to express their support. The climax of the pro-Allied movement came on September 28, when the Radical-controlled Chamber of Deputies passed a resolution by a vote of 67 to 64, urging the administration to sever all ties with the Axis nations. Castillo moved quickly to stem the pro-Allied tide. Declaring that the conduct of foreign relations was a function of the executive branch, he simply ignored Congress's severance resolution.[63] At his direction the Conservative-dominated Senate refused to endorse the Chamber's rupture resolution. Turning to Justo himself, the president launched a propaganda campaign to offset interventionist agitation, and he neutralized the general's key supporters in both the army and the government. Of particular importance was the forced resignation of Gen. Juan Tonazzi as minister of war. Castillo selected as his successor Gen. Pedro Ramírez, a prominent integral nationalist who quickly set about replacing Justista army officers with men of his own philosophical bent.[64] In November the Conservatives, who were supporters of Castillo's "prudent neutrality," swept the legislative elections, improving their advantage in the Senate and coming within just a few seats of controlling the Chamber of Deputies.[65]

Thus, it appeared by the fall of 1942 that all the carefully laid plans of the Latin Americanists were going awry. As Castillo became more entrenched and as evidence of close ties between the government and Axis interests in Argentina mounted, Welles realized not only that his policy of selective pressure had failed but that he was not going to have another chance. The Hull internationalists, aided by mounting public anger at Argentine nonalignment, a politically sensitive president, and two aggressive bureaucracies, were waiting in the wings, ready to mount a massive frontal assault on Argentine neutrality. Frustration breeds aggression, and Welles was no exception. Whether out of blind rage or a calculated attempt to retain control of Latin American policy, the undersecretary, in a speech to the National Foreign Trade Convention on October 8, delivered the most blistering attack yet made by an official of the Roosevelt administration on Argentina and her fellow neutral, Chile:

> I cannot believe that these two republics will continue long to permit their brothers and neighbors of the Americas, engaged as they are in a life and death struggle to preserve the liberties and the integrity of the New World, to be stabbed in the back by Axis emissaries.[66]

Repeatedly alluding to unspecified evidence gathered by the FBI, he charged Argentina with permitting activities that had led directly to the sinking of Brazilian, Colombian, Mexican, Dominican, Argentine, Paraguayan, Uruguayan, and United States ships.

Opinion on both sides of the Rio Grande correctly viewed the Trade Convention speech as marking the dawn of a new, get-tough era in Argentine-American relations. Foreign-affairs observers in the United States greeted Welles's broadside with thunderous approval. After enduring a year of global war, the American public was even less willing to tolerate independent action within the hemispheric community than it had been in the aftermath of Pearl Harbor. The *Washington Post* spoke for the vast majority of Americans when it lauded Welles for his forthright stand:

> The fact is that at a time when we are fighting for our very lives and for the freedom of all nations . . . the time has come for every nation to stand up and be counted. They must choose whether they are prepared directly or indirectly to aid the enemies of world freedom or sever their relations with the forces of evil.[67]

Predictably, the undersecretary's attack brought a storm of protest from the Argentine Foreign Office. In an indignant note to the State Department, Argentine officials maintained that the speech was nothing less than an insult to their nation's honor. The information in the address was imprecise, and the charges were vague. The Foreign Office informed Washington that not only was Mr. Welles's "crude" address slanderous; it had come at an inopportune time for Argentine-American relations. According to Ruiz Guiñazú, Buenos Aires had been planning to conclude with the United States a definitive agreement on Argentina's role in the war; but given the public's anger over the Trade Convention speech, this would be impossible.[68] This "definitive agreement" was a figment of the foreign minister's imagination. Welles's speech, however, allowed the Castillo government to act the injured party and to take the propaganda offensive.

The Trade Convention address marked a turning point both in the history of Argentine-American wartime relations and in the bureaucratic struggle for control of policy formulation. Despite Welles's momentary popularity in the United States, his public indictment of Argentina and Chile marked the beginning of the end for the Latin Americanists' influence within the foreign-policy establishment. By revealing to the world that the Western Hemisphere was divided by two competing power centers with widely divergent attitudes toward World War II, Welles destroyed the façade of unity which he long had argued was necessary in order to prevent Axis penetration of the New World and to preserve the Good Neighbor Policy. Because the address invoked one American state against another, it undercut the principles upon which the Inter-American System was based, principles which the Latin Americanists had said should form the basis not only of the United States' relations with Latin America but of its relations with the rest of the world as well. In short, the Trade Convention speech constituted an admission by Welles that the United States could not produce a basic reorientation of Argentine foreign policy within the context of the Good Neighbor Policy. As the undersecretary's credibility evaporated, so did his power. In the wake of the Trade Convention address, those who continued to argue for a policy of restraint were left leaderless and were increasingly unable to prevent themselves from being excluded from the decision-making process.

5

THE TRIUMPH OF THE INTERNATIONALISTS

As the first year of America's participation in World War II came to a close and the second began, those within the Roosevelt foreign-policy establishment concerned with hemispheric affairs were as determined as ever to secure a severance of all relations between Argentina and the Axis powers. The discrediting of the Latin Americanists' policy of selective pressure and the resulting loss of power permitted the internationalists to assume control of policy and to initiate a totally new approach to Argentine-American relations. With Sumner Welles taking a me-too position until his departure in September 1943, and with Morgenthau and Wallace continually maneuvering to seize control of Argentine policy, Hull, Long, and their subordinates acted to weld the American republics into a solid anti-Argentine front, tried to force a severance of telecommunications between Buenos Aires and the Axis capitals, and then launched an intensive propaganda campaign designed to link Argentina with international fascism.

The State Department's decision to employ the techniques of overt coercion was the product of a number of factors, not the least of which was pressure from both within and without the formal foreign-policy establishment. Charges of appeasement, which were leveled at the State Department by a number of newspapers and prominent figures in the United States because of its dealings with the Pétain and Badoglio governments, made Hull and his associates particularly sensitive to Argentina's continuing ties with Germany, Italy, and Japan and to the autocratic nature of Argentina's wartime governments. Moreover, despite the fact that 1943 witnessed a turning of the tide in favor of the Allies in virtually every theater of war, the American public was even less willing than it had been in 1942 to tolerate nonalignment by any American state. Adding to pressure on the State Department to adopt a get-tough policy was its bureaucratic rivalry with the Treasury Department and BEW. Morgenthau, White, Wallace, and Perkins continued to hammer away at the freezing issue and to go over Hull's head to the White House at every opportunity. No less important was the internationalists' determination to vindicate the position they had taken in the wake of the Rio Conference. They were determined to prove that isolation and coercion were the only ways to deal with nations who dared to "dally with evil."

Finally, the State Department's hard line stemmed from disappointed hopes associated with the revolution of June 1943. When a coalition of army officers overthrew the Castillo government, both the American people and administration officials mistakenly assumed that the cause of the revolt was a desire to align Argentina with the Allies. When the new regime failed to sever ties with the Axis, disillusionment in the United States caused a backlash that strained Argentine-American relations to the breaking point.

Prior to Welles's fateful Trade Convention speech, the State Department, under the direction of the Latin Americanists, had attempted to achieve a realignment of Argentine foreign policy within the context of hemispheric solidarity. After the undersecretary's blast, however, Washington abandoned the principle of inter-American unity and labored to forge the other American republics into an anti-Argentine phalanx that would, by creating within Argentina a sense of isolation and guilt, force the Castillo government to adopt an active pro-Allied stance. Hull and the internationalists operated on the assumption that if they could Pan-Americanize censorship of Argentina, they could immeasurably increase pressure on Buenos Aires for a rupture and at the same time neutralize charges of North American imperialism. Welles, who by this time had completely abandoned his Rio philosophy, joined in the drive to pit one American republic against another.

Hoping to camouflage Washington's attempts to discredit the Castillo government, the State Department sought to work through the various inter-American bodies created at Rio to coordinate the defense establishments and mobilize the resources of the hemisphere. Of these bodies, the most useful proved to be the Emergency Advisory Committee for Political Defense of the Hemisphere (the Montevideo Committee). Established at the Rio Conference in January 1942 to prevent clandestine Axis operations in the Western Hemisphere, the committee was first to set forth general anti-espionage guidelines for the entire hemisphere and was then to evaluate the threat of Axis subversion in each republic, study the countermeasures being taken, and make specific recommendations to the government in question. Representatives of the seven member nations—the United States, Mexico, Argentina, Chile, Brazil, Venezuela, and Uruguay—were not to act as agents of their home governments but were to work for the best interests of the hemisphere as a whole.[1]

From the outset, the Argentineans and the Americans rejected the Burkean concept underlying the committee. Privately denouncing the body as a tool of United States imperialism, the Argentine member notified the other representatives that any resolution passed would be binding only when ratified by the home government of each republic.[2] Meanwhile, the American representative, Carl B. Spaeth, attempted to use the committee to stimulate anti-Argentineanism throughout the hemisphere, primarily by persuading it to brand Argentina as a haven for Nazis and as a threat to the peace and safety of the hemisphere.[3]

Spaeth's approach to inter-American affairs actually went beyond Hull's and represented an amalgam of the views of the secretary of state and Henry Wallace. That Spaeth should take this approach was hardly surprising, since he had been head of the Western Hemisphere Division of BEW before coming to the State Department. The United States, he believed, should act vigorously to foster political democracy and social justice south of the Rio Grande. During a conversation with Berle in August 1943, Spaeth confessed that the tendency on the part of some in the Roosevelt administration, who were ostensibly "New Dealers," to cooperate with "old dealers" in various Latin American countries was quite distressing to him. It was apparent, he said, that the leadership in the State Department was doing everything possible through loans and other forms of aid to maintain in power those who were in positions of special privilege. Whatever his misgivings about the conservatism of the Roosevelt foreign-policy establishment, however, Spaeth sympathized thoroughly with the anti-Argentine views of the Hull internationalists. Determined to eradicate every vestige of Axis influence in the Western Hemisphere, he perceived Buenos Aires to be nothing less than an active ally of the Third Reich.[4] To charges by some of the Latin Americans that his vigorous efforts to compel the Latin countries to adopt uniform legislation against Axis activities threatened their national sovereignties, he replied, "Eyewash."[5]

In late 1942 Spaeth began pressing his colleagues on the committee to accept the results of a study of German, Japanese, and Italian spying efforts in South America, which had been conducted by the United States, and to publish it as their own. It was, not surprisingly, a scathing indictment of the Castillo government and its policies. The document that Spaeth attempted to foist upon the Montevideo Committee proved, among other things, that the German high command had transformed Argentina into headquarters for its South American spy network. At least four groups of espionage agents, many of whom were aides to the military attachés of the German embassy in Buenos Aires, were gathering information and transmitting it to Berlin. Included in these communiques were reports on arrivals and departures of Allied merchantmen and the movements of British and United States fleets, data on the location and production levels of Allied armament and munition industries in South America, and details of hemispheric arrangements for defense of the Panama Canal and the Brazilian coastline. Attached to Spaeth's incriminating report were appendices naming members of the four Axis cells and actual copies of messages sent by these cells to Germany by way of illegal radio transmitters.[6] As soon as the bill of particulars was completed, Spaeth began to lay the groundwork for publication by making the espionage memo available to the more "dependable" members of the committee.[7] Arguing that hemispheric defense required that all American states be made aware of German espionage and subversion, the American delegate managed to convince the chairman of the body, Uruguay's foreign minister Alberto Guani, that he should support eventual publication. Guani strongly suggested, however, that the committee first notify Buenos Aires and then allow the Castillo regime ample time to rectify the situation. Hull protested that making the report available to Argentina would cause Axis agents to take cover and would give the Castillo government an excuse for inactivity. Nonetheless, he subsequently agreed in the name of "hemispheric cooperation" first to show the memorandum to Buenos Aires and to warn that publication was being considered.[8] At the same hour that Armour called on the Argentine Foreign Office to deliver the text of the espionage report, Welles in Washington summoned Espil to the State Department. After handing the ambassador a copy of the memorandum, the undersecretary launched into a diatribe against Argentine neutrality during which he accused the Castillo government of only paying lip service to the ideal of inter-American solidarity and, by permitting German spy rings to flourish in Argentina, of endangering the security of the entire hemisphere. Espil implored him not to publish the document lest it provoke widespread anti-Argentine feeling in the United States and throughout Latin America and thus end all chance for reconciliation and reunification. Welles replied somewhat self-righteously that Argentina had only herself to blame and that the United States reserved the right to take whatever action it deemed necessary if the Castillo government's counterespionage efforts proved to be insufficient.[9]

Ironically, the chief advocate of immediate publication during succeeding weeks was Sumner Welles. As part of a continuing effort to retain some degree of influence in the making of hemispheric policy, the undersecretary had adopted an ultra-hard-line posture toward Argentina and now urged that the report be released either by the Montevideo Committee or, if it refused, unilaterally by the State Department. Publication, he proclaimed, could only strengthen the hand of "friendly" elements in Argentina.[10] To Welles's chagrin, his former supporters joined with his traditional enemies within the State Department in quashing his motion for immediate release. From Buenos Aires, Ambassador Armour pleaded for enough of a delay to allow the increasingly cooperative Argentine authorities to move against the network of German spies. The bureaucratic threat from the Treasury Department had driven Hull into a momentary alliance with the Latin Americanists in mid 1942; now he joined with them once again, this time to block Welles's bid to regain control of Argentine policy. Agreeing with Armour that Washington appeared to have found a vulnerable spot and should exploit it to the fullest, Hull flatly rejected the undersecretary's suggestion.[11]

By December 1942 the threat of publication appeared to be bearing fruit. Early in the month the Castillo government formally charged as spies six alleged Nazi agents, one of whom was the German naval attaché, Captain Dietrich Niebhur. Niebhur was named as chief of the entire Axis espionage system in Argentina. In addition, the minister of the interior in January 1943 ordered the governors of the fourteen Argentine provinces to preempt any activity that might be detrimental to the individual or collective security of the American republics.[12]

The goal of American policy-makers in late 1942 and early 1943, however, was a rupture of all relations between Argentina and the Axis, not the perfection of Argentine neutrality. Thus, the Castillo government's counter-espionage and antisubversion activities, no matter how effective, proved incapable of halting publication of the report. With Buenos Aires as committed as ever to nonalignment, the State Department gave Spaeth the go-ahead on 21 January 1943 to present the espionage memorandum to the Montevideo Committee with a recommendation for its immediate publication. The Argentine representative protested vigorously, arguing in vain that the memo involved United States–Argentine relations only, that Buenos Aires was taking vigorous action to prevent Axis abuse of Argentine neutrality, and that the present investigation would be compromised by release of the document. His objections were all to no avail, however, for the remaining five members voted to adopt Brazil's resolution in favor of immediate promulgation.[13] As a result, during the first week in February, the committee's "findings" were broadcast throughout the Americas by means of United States shortwave radio stations. During the days that followed, American radio stations in Uruguay beamed anti-Argentine comments, which had been extracted from various Latin newspapers by the OCIAA, throughout Argentina.[14]

Though it had been deprived of its leadership and its privileged access to the White House, the Latin American establishment continued to function within the State Department and to oppose the hard-line policies initiated by the internationalists. Duggan, Bonsal, and lower-level officials in the American Republic Affairs Division argued throughout late 1942 and 1943 that Argentine neutrality posed no real threat to the Allied war effort and that continued hemispheric unity was the most effective weapon that could be employed against Axis penetration of the New World. Warning that overt coercion and public attacks on the Castillo regime would simply arouse nationalism and latent anti-Americanism in Argentina and throughout Latin America, they held that the only positive leverage the United States could exert on Buenos Aires was by withholding arms aid and by winning the war in Europe.[15] Bonsal had argued long and hard against publication of the espionage memorandum, and both he and Duggan had objected to Spaeth's repeated suggestions that Argentina be ejected from the Montevideo Committee.[16] Nothing better illustrates the Latin Americanists' ongoing opposition to the get-tough policies and their inability to control policy in general, however, than an intradepartmental dispute involving

Washington's attempts to sever cable communications between Buenos Aires and the Axis capitals during late 1942 and early 1943.

In the fall of 1942 Hull and Long decided that continued telecommunications between Argentina and the Axis nations represented both a flagrant breach of the Rio resolutions and a major threat to the Allied war effort and that, as such, they had to cease. Transatlantic wireless service from Argentina to Europe was provided by Transradio International Argentina, a firm jointly owned by British, American, and Argentinean companies. The dominant partner was Great Britain. Cable and Wireless Ltd., the British holding company involved, controlled 65 percent of the stock. While Argentineans owned 65 percent of the bonds issued by the consortium, they controlled only 16 percent of the stock. The remainder of the stock was held by the Radio Corporation of America. Although Transradio operated by virtue of a direct grant of authority from the Argentine national government, Washington went to the British, not to the Argentine Foreign Office, in its campaign to interdict communications between Buenos Aires and occupied Europe.[17] Late in the summer of 1942 Breckinridge Long began pressuring Whitehall to have Transradio cut its circuits to the Axis capitals and fire its "pro-Axis" employees. Fearful of alienating both Cable and Wireless Ltd. and the Castillo government, the British Foreign Office resisted Long's blandishments, arguing that if Transradio were closed down, purely Axis-controlled communications companies would step into the void.[18] Nevertheless, Washington continued to harangue the British on the dangers of permitting radio communications between Buenos Aires and Europe. After the RCA representative on Transradio's board of directors voted for severance in October, the British Foreign Office capitulated and ordered Cable and Wireless Ltd. to vote similarly. Whitehall insisted, however, that the Castillo government be advised of the company's decision well before service was interrupted, since Transradio was operating under a federal charter and providing an essential service to the country.[19]

At this point the Latin Americanists, led by Bonsal, entered the fray and vigorously supported Whitehall's demand for prior notification. Ordering the consortium to close its European circuits and to fire certain employees labeled by the United States as undesirables without first consulting the Casa Rosada would be worse than pointless. Unilateral action by Transradio would most likely produce nationalization, and it would drive the Castillo government and the Argentine people into an anti–United States coalition.

"The Argentine Government together with a great many Argentineans, many of them good friends of ours will be highly indignant that a foreign company operating in Argentina should presume to dictate to the Argentine Government about what it should do in carrying out its international commitment,"[20] argued the chief of the Latin American desk in a memo to the secretary. Hull and Long disagreed. The internationalists asserted that because the Castillo government would not voluntarily sever telecommunications with the Axis, as provided in the Rio resolutions, the Allies would have to present Buenos Aires with a *fait accompli*. In short, if the Argentine government refused to act in its own best interest and that of the hemisphere, the United States would have to act for it. Accordingly, Hull overruled the British and the American Republic Affairs Division of the State Department (ARA), and Long ordered the board of Transradio to shut down its European operations immediately.[21]

Before the British-dominated consortium could decide whether to comply with the secretary's demand or to put forth additional arguments, the Argentineans moved to nip the threat to their transatlantic lines of communication in the bud. On October 9, a spokesman for the Casa Rosada announced that government interveners were being placed in all telecommunications companies operating in Argentina so as to prevent transmission of information prejudicial to the Argentine national interest and detrimental to those American republics involved in the war. When the Castillo regime announced a month later that it would in the immediate future issue an edict prohibiting either diplomatic missions or private firms from sending coded messages to points outside the Western Hemisphere, it appeared that Washington's threats had paid off.[22]

After prominent Argentine nationalists denounced the proposed decree as prejudicial to Argentine neutrality and derided Castillo for truckling to Allied demands, the Casa Rosada began to reconsider its position. To the enragement of the internationalists, the long-awaited proclamation regarding telecommunications, published on December 4, suspended international exchange of radiograms in code but exempted one hundred words per day for each embassy and consulate. The Argentine undersecretary for foreign affairs explained that to forbid all privileged communication would be a violation of international law and would almost surely lead to a break in relations with Germany, Italy, and Japan.[23]

Although they had given up hope of cutting all radio communications between Argentina and occupied Europe, the internationalists still believed that they could act through Transradio to deny code facilities to the Axis. Over the repeated and strenuous objections of the Latin Americanists, the State Department compelled Transradio to notify the Argentine Foreign Office on 19 January 1943 that it intended to deny code facilities to the Axis with or without the government's permission.[24] Issuing a press release that proclaimed that Transradio International was an Argentine company providing a vital service to the Argentine people and hence could not accept orders from any foreign government, the Castillo regime once again intervened in the cable matter. At this juncture, intervention was designed to ensure that the German and Italian missions had access to Transradio's facilities rather than to prevent transmissions detrimental to the Allied war effort. As the Latin Americanists had predicted, Washington's tactics not only failed to interdict Argentine-Axis telecommunications but enabled the Casa Rosada to denounce the United States for its interventionist tactics.

One of the most prominent organizational characteristics exhibited by the internationalists was a tendency to view all developments in Argentina through the prism of World War II. Every shift in the political arena, every public disturbance, and each new edict handed down by the Castillo government were interpreted as additional manifestations of the internal struggle that was supposedly raging between Argentine interventionists and neutralists. Consequently, when the Castillo regime was overthrown by a military junta in 1943, the internationalists and most members of the American press, who shared the Hull group's preoccupation with World War II, assumed that the new regime intended to sever all ties with the Axis nations, to join wholeheartedly with the Allies, and to inaugurate a new era of democracy. Norman Armour, who hoped for a number of reasons that the new regime would be all that the Castillo government was not, and Sumner Welles, who convinced himself that the coup would pave the way for a restoration of hemispheric solidarity and of his control over Latin American policy, also labored under this misapprehension. When it became apparent that the new government in Buenos Aires was the product of a number of forces and events, most of them unrelated to Argentina's posture toward the war, that it intended to preserve Argentine neutrality, and that the junta was determined to govern without benefit of Congress or constitution, the disappointed and disgusted internationalists, joined by the bulk of the American people, became more determined than ever to force Argentina into a pro-Allied stance. Moreover, as a result of their unfulfilled expectations in connection with the June revolution, many Americans both inside and outside the State Department became convinced that Argentina would assume the proper attitude in foreign-policy matters only after a "fundamental upheaval" in domestic politics and a return to democratic procedures. Consequently, following a brief period of grace immediately after the revolution, the State Department resumed its get-tough policy with the explicit objective of forcing Argentina to abandon neutrality and with the implicit goal of returning that nation to free elections and constitutional government. In the process of implementing this new, stridently hard-line approach, American policy-makers developed a disturbingly familiar justification for coercion and, in so doing, threw into sharp relief their assumptions about the relationship between foreign policy and domestic affairs.

By the spring of 1943 Ramón Castillo had managed, despite his success in keeping Argentina out of World War II, to alienate the one faction that was absolutely necessary to his continued presence in office—the military. In April 1943 Castillo made it clear that while he did not intend to stand for reelection in 1944, he would hand-pick his successor and do whatever was necessary to ensure his election. The heir apparent was Senator Robustiano Patrón Costas, who was a sugar magnate, a prominent figure in the National Democratic party, and provisional president of the Senate.[25] Since Patrón Costas had no national following to speak of, it was obvious to most Argentineans that he, like virtually every other political candidate in Argentina after 1930, would succeed to office through fraud.

The army was determined for a variety of reasons to prevent another illegal election, even if it had to assume direct control of the central government. Many were simply growing weary of what they believed to be the manipulation of the armed forces by corrupt politicians. Integral nationalists within the officer corps were convinced that the two dominant political parties were thoroughly corrupt, that representative democracy was a failure, and that it was the army's duty to seize control of Argentina and to restore order and discipline to national life. These individuals also hoped that by establishing a military government, they could purge Argentina of all foreign (British and American) influences. A pro-Allied liberal-nationalist faction, which drew its strength primarily from the navy, favored the ouster of Castillo because of his refusal to align Argentina with Great Britain and because of his toleration of Axis espionage activities within the republic.[26] A third, apolitical group agreed to participate in a coup purely for the good of the military. Before 1941 the Argentine military was probably the best equipped and most formidable force in South America, but with massive lend-lease aid to Brazil, the balance of military power in South America had shifted in favor of Argentina's northern neighbor. Thus, a large number of officers were clamoring for Castillo's removal because he had not secured the hardware necessary to maintain Argentine military superiority on the continent. By far the strongest of the components in the anti-Castillo coalition were the integral nationalists, who were led by a group of political opportunists including Generals Pedro Ramírez and Edelmiro Farrell and Colonels Enrique González and Juan Perón. These fascistoid (to borrow a term from historian Marvin Goldwert) officers hoped to use the widespread discontent within the military and Castillo's political vulnerability in order to further their own ambitions.[27]

During the first months of 1943, dissatisfaction with Castillo's policies and the desire among integral nationalists to "revitalize" Argentina spawned a mysterious military organization called the GOU (variously interpreted as Grupo Obra de Unificación; Gobierno, Orden, Union; and Grupo de Officiáles Unidos). This secret clique within the officer corps was united only in its determination to overthrow the existing regime and then install a military junta.[28] Shortly after its founding, the charter members of the GOU, led by González and Perón, initiated a drive to broaden the base of the anti-Castillo movement both by adding new converts from within the military and by establishing an alliance with the Radical party. Warning of the need to guard against a Communist conspiracy, playing upon fear of involvement in the war, appealing to the desire to resist external pressure, and utilizing a variety of other themes, the GOU attracted disciples in barracks throughout Argentina. Meanwhile, in the civilian sphere, the anti-Castillo officers openly courted the Radical party, which readily agreed that Castillo was impossible, pronounced Patrón Costas totally unacceptable, and hinted broadly that they would support Gen. Pedro Ramírez for the presidency.[29]

The confusion surrounding the coup of June 5–7, particularly in regard to who was to head the new government, reflected the lack of consensus on policy within the GOU. General Ramírez, the Radicals' choice, was minister of war at the time of the coup and thus, in terms of political experience and continuity, was the logical figure to succeed Castillo in the Casa Rosada. Moreover, his leadership traits and professional conduct had won him respect throughout the army. Pro-Allied liberals within the GOU distrusted Ramírez, however, because they thought that he was too closely identified with the ultranationalists. This group's first choice to head the new government was Gen. Arturo Rawson, commander of the huge Campo de Mayo military base and the man who was slated to lead the "revolutionary" troops into the capital on the appointed day. Because of the GOU's internal divisions and the overriding need to preserve unity within the anti-Castillo coalition, the officers who were planning the coup had made no definitive decision as to who was to head the new government even as the troops at the Campo de Mayo boarded their trucks for the assault on the seat of government.

As a result of this confusion the coup perpetrated on the morning of June 4 produced two governments in three days. As Rawson's column approached, President Castillo fled the Casa Rosada for the safety of a minesweeper situated in the Rio de la Plata. Impressed with the apparent unity of the military and the almost complete public apathy at his ouster, Castillo resigned without a murmur on the fifth. Meanwhile the ambitious Rawson had taken advantage of his position as commander of the revolutionary forces and had proclaimed himself president. His subsequent announcement that he intended to sever all ties between Argentina and the Axis nations ensured that his administration would be brief. On June 7 the GOU, the majority of whose members were either pro-Axis or neutralist, forced Rawson to step down in favor of former Minister of War Ramírez.[30] He in turn was succeeded as head of the War Ministry by Edelmiro Farrell; and Juan Perón, destined to become Argentina's next man on horseback, became undersecretary.[31] During the nine months that followed, Ramírez attempted to retain control of a military-political coalition whose only common denominator was opposition to Castillo. All the while the ambitious officers around him, most notably the young undersecretary of war, maneuvered to establish a power base that would perhaps permit one of them to seize control of the government if Ramírez should falter.[32]

Reports from the American embassy in Buenos Aires on both phases of the revolution correctly identified the Argentine military as the driving force behind the coup but mistakenly assumed that the sole motive of the officers involved was to align Argentina with the Allies and thereby to acquire the massive lend-lease aid necessary for Argentina to reestablish its military preponderance in southern South America.[33] On June 1 Armour reported that rumors were rampant in Buenos Aires that a group of activist officers headed by General Ramírez was plotting revolution because of their concern over Argentina's inability to obtain enough armaments. Conscious of the shifting balance of power in South America, this group, according to the ambassador, had continually urged solidarity with Britain and the United States in order that Argentina might become eligible for lend-lease.[34] In the wake of the general's pronouncement that henceforth Argentina would live up to all of her international obligations, Armour predicted that the revolution, though carried out by the army, not only would bring about a basic realignment in foreign policy but would usher in a new era of democracy in the domestic political arena as well.[35] That the GOU replaced Rawson with Ramírez on the ninth in no way altered the embassy's estimation of the rationale or objectives behind the coup. Pronouncing Ramírez a political opportunist whose views differed only slightly from those of Rawson, Jack Camp, one of Armour's lieutenants, summed up both revolutions as "the work primarily of a group of 18 colonels who call their organization 'GOU' and who were dissatisfied with the corruption and fraud in the Argentine Government and wished Argentina to take its place in the American community of nations by breaking relations."[36]

Despite these optimistic predictions, Hull made a half-hearted attempt to use the threat of nonrecognition in order to obtain specific assurances from Buenos Aires. Both after the coup of June 5 and the Ramírez succession on June 7, the ambassadors of the various American republics entered into consultations looking toward recognition of the new governments. The overwhelming sentiment among the Latin American envoys was for immediate de facto recognition.[37] When Armour, acting at Hull's behest, pressed for a delay in order to give first Rawson and then Ramírez a chance to outline the specific steps they planned to take in order to align Argentina with the Allies, the Latin diplomatic corps accused Washington of attempting to use recognition to bargain for a rupture, and they refused to wait more than twenty-four hours before establishing relations with the new regime.[38] To the State Department, the foreign-policy statements of both of the soldier-presidents were disturbingly vague. Rawson proclaimed that he did not intend to continue Castillo's "incomprehensible" policy of isolation, but he warned the United States not to expect extreme measures right away. On the ninth, Ramírez informed the head of the United States Air Mission in Argentina that his government might break with the Axis if there were a specific provocative act and if there were no hint of pressure from Washington.[39] Chile, Bolivia, Brazil, Uruguay, and Paraguay were more than satisfied with these pledges, however, and indicated that they would extend recognition, with or without the United States. In view of the intention of certain American republics to proceed with recognition and in view of the embassy's continuing reassurances, Hull authorized the establishment of diplomatic relations with the Rawson government on the sixth and with the Ramírez regime on the ninth.

In spite of the fact that Ramírez clung steadfastly to neutrality, refused to convene Congress, and suppressed domestic dissent, Armour continued throughout June and July to send glowing reports to Washington about the new administration and to plead for a conciliatory policy.[40] As late as July 13, Armour, no doubt reflecting the views of his contacts in the Radical party, cabled Hull that "Ramírez' popular strength is growing and it is not illogical that he wants to become the legally elected President. . . . With proper use of the press, the President can break relations and return Argentina to democracy without precipitating internal conflict." Moreover, compared to Castillo, Ramírez was a rabid reformer: "The present movement did dislodge the Conservatives from their entrenched position . . . and are [*sic*] taking measures to clear up all the graft and corruption of the old regime." He urged Washington to provide Buenos Aires with positive incentives in the form of aircraft parts and increased allocation of petroleum.[41] With proper support from the United States, Ramírez would unite with the Radicals behind a program of national union, and a "new Argentina" would emerge, one that would be ready to live up to its defensive commitments and to play a constructive role in postwar planning.[42]

The American embassy's optimism and its erroneous evaluations stemmed from faulty intelligence, a natural tendency to identify with the host country,[43] continuing ties with the Radicals, and pressure from two other American organizations operating in Buenos Aires. Although the State Department had moved in November 1942 to subordinate to the ambassador the representatives of the Board of Economic Warfare, the Treasury

Department, and other agencies concerned with measures of economic warfare, its efforts had been only partially successful. Throughout the remainder of 1942 and 1943 Armour repeatedly warned Washington that BEW operatives in particular were making policy on their own, not only in the economic sphere but in the political arena as well. BEW's absorption by the newly created Foreign Economic Administration (FEA) in July 1943 augmented rather than lessened the pressures on Armour and his staff.

By mid 1943 the struggle for control of foreign economic policy within the federal government was becoming openly rancorous and, as a result, increasingly embarrassing to the administration. While Wallace's and BEW's relationships with the State Department grew more and more strained during the year following Roosevelt's executive order of April 1942, their feud was relatively mild compared to the one that developed between BEW and RFC. Wallace and Perkins viewed Jesse Jones as Wall Street's preeminent representative within the administration. His economic nationalism and financial elitism were, they believed, not only hindering the war effort but laying the groundwork for a third world conflict. Jones, in turn, dismissed Wallace as a wild-eyed radical who, if left to his own devices, would destroy capitalism in the United States and facilitate Communist expansion abroad. In the spring of 1943, BEW, in an attempt to seize control of the financial apparatus through which RFC funded overseas procurement, began to press the White House to transfer supervision of the United States Commercial Corporation from Jones to Wallace. Jones retaliated by attacking Wallace through the press and through his conservative allies in the Senate. When the vice-president issued a public statement intimating that Jones cared more about the fiscal integrity of RFC than about winning the war, Roosevelt decided to call a halt to the confrontation.[44]

Not surprisingly, the president solved the problem by creating a new agency, the Foreign Economic Administration, to which he allocated many of the duties pertaining to economic warfare that had previously been performed by the State Department, BEW, and RFC.[45] To head this new bureaucracy, Roosevelt and Harry Hopkins, whose advice on personnel matters was crucial, chose Leo Crowley, a Wisconsin Democrat who had come to Washington in 1934 as chairman of the Federal Deposit Insurance Corporation.[46] In Roosevelt's and Hopkins's eyes, Crowley was particularly well suited for his new post. Identified with none of the major factions then contending for control of foreign policy, Crowley was also a prominent

Catholic layman who could and did serve as liaison man with the Irish Catholics during the 1944 campaign.[47] Other members of the foreign-policy establishment were not as enthusiastic. Both Wallace, who was of course prejudiced against Crowley because of the demise of BEW, and the Latin Americanists were distressed by Crowley's appointment of the president and executive vice-president of the United Fruit Company as chief consultants to FEA. Moreover, virtually everyone agreed that Crowley was a bureaucratic entrepreneur whose sole guide in the formulation of policy was the principle of organizational aggrandizement.[48]

Shortly after his confirmation, Crowley warned Dean Acheson in connection with the Argentine situation that his agency had "clear authority from the Congress to act in all matters relating to economic warfare."[49] It became increasingly obvious during 1943 that first BEW and then FEA believed that the political situation in Argentina was having a decisive impact on their efforts to deny the Axis financial facilities, markets, and other economic assets in the New World and that the two agencies were determined to wrest control of United States economic policy from the American embassy in Buenos Aires.[50] Although BEW had advocated a hard line toward the Castillo government throughout 1942 and had used the certificates of necessity in order to force a basic reorientation in Argentine foreign policy, it, like the regular staff of the American embassy, interpreted Ramírez's accession to office as a prelude to the assumption by Argentina of an actively pro-Allied policy. Immediately after the coup, BEW officials began arranging for delivery of power and utility equipment and other vital industrial goods.[51] On June 10, Hector Lazo, a top field agent for BEW and subsequently for FEA, arrived in Buenos Aires and began to administer the new policy with a degree of vigor and independence that was alarming to the American embassy. Armour reacted to what he considered an open challenge to his authority first by having the State Department demand that BEW-FEA submit to him[52] and then by engineering an Argentine-American rapprochement in hopes of stealing the rival agency's thunder.

The high expectations and optimistic predictions contained in the ambassador's cables were echoed by newspaper editors across the country during the days immediately following the coup.[53] As previously noted, many moderate-to-liberal journals had assumed throughout the period after the Rio Conference that the great mass of Argentineans were friendly toward the United States and would support Argentine alignment with the

Allies but that their desires were being suppressed by an autocratic, pro-Axis dictatorship. Just as had Armour and his colleagues, foreign-policy observers in the United States interpreted the June revolution as a manifestation of the people's will and as a prelude to democracy at home and solidarity with the Allies abroad. The *New York Times* was cautious but hopeful: "We feel sure, as we have always done, that the masses of the Argentines are friendly to this country and to the cause of the United Nations. This friendship may now have greater opportunity to express itself."[54] Typifying the false logic that entrapped so many other Americans, the *St. Louis Post-Dispatch* proclaimed that since Castillo had been autocratic and pro-Axis, the men who had overthrown this malefactor must be devoted to democracy and committed to the Allied cause. Arguing that "a good 90% of the country's population was . . . opposed to his [Castillo's] policy of prudence —a policy which meant theoretical neutrality as far as the war was concerned, a cold shoulder to the Pan-American solidarity agreement of Rio de Janeiro, and a foothold for the Axis propaganda and espionage network,"[55] the *Post-Dispatch* assured its readers that the recent changing of the guard at the Casa Rosada meant compliance with the Rio resolutions and a break with the Axis.

Despite a steady flow of favorable reports from the embassy, the events that transpired in the fortnight immediately following Castillo's ouster dispelled the aura of optimism and convinced the State Department and much of American press opinion that the new regime in Buenos Aires was as totalitarian and pro-Nazi as its predecessor had been. Postcoup promises to convene Congress, to set a date for national elections, and to sever relations with the Axis remained unfulfilled.[56] In addition, reports from the FBI to the White House painted an alarming picture of the new regime. Hoover had never been optimistic about the Argentine situation. On June 8 he transmitted to Hopkins a 500-page volume entitled *Argentina Today*. Significantly, pages 92 through 369 were devoted to "The Axis in Argentina." On June 12 Hoover provided Hopkins and Roosevelt with a brief sketch of Ramírez and his cabinet members. The profile emphasized that Ramírez had served a total of four years in Germany and Italy and characterized him as a neutralist, as a devout Hispanist, and as pro-Nazi; Vice-President Saba Sueyro "is a Nationalist and entertains pro-Axis sympathies." With two exceptions, other cabinet members were labeled either neutralist or pro-Axis.[57]

On 14 June 1943 the Casa Rosada suspended Acción Argentina, an organization of some four hundred thousand members that had supported the United Nations financially and morally throughout the war and had consistently advocated a return to constitutional government in Argentina.[58] More than anything else the suspension of this association precipitated American opposition to the new regime.[59] On June 16 the *New York Times* observed with obvious dejection that there had evidently been two contending revolutions within Argentina, one spearheaded by the prodemocratic Radicals and one fomented by the military. It was clear that the latter had triumphed and that there now existed a purely military dictatorship in Buenos Aires.[60] Claiming to have recognized the true nature of the Ramírez regime from the outset, liberal newspapers urged the State Department to once again wield the big stick in the name of freedom and democracy.[61] The *Nation* berated Washington for not having insisted from the very beginning upon a constitutional government that would surely have adopted an anti-Axis attitude:

> Washington's misguided haste in giving diplomatic sanction to the new regime must have greatly enhanced its prestige. . . .
> It took us sixteen years to decide to recognize the Soviet government, which had been established by a people's revolution; we might profitably have waited sixteen days to recognize the reactionary government of Argentina, set up by a military coup.[62]

Deeply troubled by the closing of Acción Argentina as well as by the revulsion evidenced by the domestic press, the secretary of state cabled Armour on June 16 that he and the rest of the department were becoming increasingly concerned about the Argentine situation, and he chided the ambassador for painting a falsely optimistic picture.[63]

Ramírez's refusal to break with Rome, Berlin, and Tokyo, to restore constitutional government in Argentina, and particularly to permit Acción Argentina to continue operating linked him with Ramón Castillo in the minds of both the internationalists and the American people. Moreover, to Hull, Long, Spaeth, and their associates, Ramírez's suppression of an organization that advocated democracy at home and a pro-Allied posture in foreign affairs validated their belief that autocracy and neutralism were inextricably intertwined. Gradually, Hull and his colleagues were coming to the conclusion that democratization of the Argentine political system was an essential precondition to Argentina's assuming a truly pro-Allied posture.

Although they were unable either to emulate Roosevelt, Wilson, and Taft or to use military force in order to institute political reforms in Latin America, the internationalists in the summer of 1943 did launch a frontal assault on the Ramírez government, using the presumed division between government and people in Argentina as justification.

Ironically, it was Sumner Welles who articulated the citizen-versus-government rationale and who announced the department's decision to initiate a new era of confrontation. The undersecretary had originally shared Armour's optimism and had joined with the ambassador in urging that Washington adopt a conciliatory posture, but after the closing of Acción Argentina, he quickly tacked before the prevailing wind. In response to a request by the secretary that he "straighten Armour out,"[64] Welles wrote his colleague in Buenos Aires on June 24 that the recent change of government provided a golden opportunity for reviewing the goals and assumptions underlying United States policy toward Argentina.

Welles observed that the Good Neighbor Policy, initiated over a decade before, had succeeded in convincing the Americas of the sincerity of United States pronouncements about nonintervention and hemispheric defense; and as indicated by the tremendous reception accorded to FDR in Buenos Aires in 1936, the Argentine people were among the most enthusiastic in Latin America about New Deal diplomacy. Although the Argentine delegates at Rio indicated that they thought that it was in the best interests of their country to go it alone, this attitude was not shared by many millions of Argentineans. Unfortunately, due to the autocratic methods pursued by both the Castillo and the Ramírez governments, they were not able to express their opinion or to effect a change in official policy. The high hopes generated by the June revolution were illusory, and the autocratic-neutralist policies followed by the military junta proved that the United States could not rely on subtle pressure techniques and public opinion—both inside and outside of Argentina—to bring about a change in Argentine foreign policy. The only alternative, he suggested, was a direct get-tough confrontation with the strong men in power.[65] Implicit in Welles's communique was the assumption that the Argentine people would accept virtually any pressure tactic designed to force Ramírez to sever relations with the Axis, because a continuance of relations with the Axis powers was contrary to the will of the majority. From this point until the end of 1944 the State Department operated on the supposition that it possessed a mandate from the Argentine citizenry to force the Casa Rosada (1) to break relations with Germany, Italy, and Japan and (2) to lend all possible aid to the Allies. For Welles, adoption of the citizen-versus-government rationale was both a result and a reflection of his impotency in the area of hemispheric policy-making. For Hull, Long, Spaeth, and their colleagues, it was the natural outgrowth of their Wilsonian view of international relations.

Convinced that they had the full support of both the Argentine and the American people, the hard-liners within the State Department once again set about the business of forcing Buenos Aires to sever all ties with "international fascism." Throughout June and July, Washington lectured the Ramírez government on the steps it must take to align Argentina with the Allies. Among the most important were (1) an immediate break in diplomatic relations, (2) complete interruption of telecommunications, (3) censure of all press and radio opinion that was in any way favorable to the Axis, (4) complete cooperation in implementing the Proclaimed List, and (5) conclusion of a comprehensive petroleum agreement that could make Argentine oil and tankers available to those hemispheric republics that were at war with the Axis. Moreover, Washington now required Buenos Aires to employ a particular justification for the break when it came. Hull rejected Foreign Minister Segundo Storni's contention that Argentina must wait for some specific provocative act before withdrawing her ambassadors from the Axis capitals. The secretary demanded not only that Buenos Aires break immediately but also that severance be based explicitly on the Rio resolutions.[66] As both parties knew, a rupture founded on principle rather than on a particular offense would constitute a tacit admission by the Argentineans that neutrality was incompatible with hemispheric solidarity and that its foreign policies had been in violation of the inter-American agreements initiated at Rio. It would, in short, be an implicit admission of guilt by Buenos Aires and a complete vindication of the internationalists, wiping out, for them, the humiliation of their defeat at the hands of the Latin Americanists.

But the Ramírez regime refused to sever ties with the signatories of the Tripartite Pact. It decided in late July to plead its case before the bar of hemispheric opinion in hopes that it could generate a ground swell of sympathy within Latin America, which would in turn compel Washington both to stop pressuring Buenos Aires and to meet Argentina's demands for lend-lease aid. Contrary to the Casa Rosada's expectations, this ill-conceived stratagem played right into the hands of the hard-liners, who used the incident to portray Argentina as a nation that was both insensitive to the needs of those engaged in the monumental struggle against the Nazi-Fascists and as a threat to the peace and safety of South America as well.

Quite aside from the fact that neutrality served the organizational goals of the military, conformed to traditional principles of Argentine diplomacy, and reflected widespread public apathy toward the war, those in charge of the Argentine Foreign Office in the summer of 1943 believed that nonalignment was in perfect harmony with the principles of hemispheric solidarity and that it was in no way harmful to the inter-American community. Moreover, they believed that Washington's withholding of lend-lease aid, imposing of economic sanctions, and launching of a propaganda war against Argentina constituted gross coercion, designed to force Buenos Aires to take a position not in the national interest. They believed, in addition, that Washington's policies would so appear to the rest of the hemisphere if only the facts were made known. Thus, when Washington decided to recall Ambassador Armour, the Argentine Foreign Office proceeded with plans to publish both a public indictment of United States policy and a comprehensive defense of Argentina's position.

When it became evident that the new government in Buenos Aires had no intention whatsoever of ejecting Axis diplomats and interests from Argentina, the Roosevelt administration began to search for some method of showing its displeasure and for a specific event to serve as a "last straw." When in late July the Ramírez regime placed government interveners in eight important United States plants in Argentina—including Ford, International Harvester, General Motors, Goodyear, and Firestone—Hull cabled Armour that the president had decided on a full-scale review of United States policy toward Argentina, and Hull ordered the ambassador home for consultation.[67] Before Armour left, the Foreign Office presented him with an *aide-mémoire* covering the entire scope of American-Argentine wartime relations.

Although the Argentine Foreign Office first presented its case privately to the State Department via Armour, the text of the note seems to indicate that it had been designed from the beginning to appeal to a hemispheric audience.[68] Complaining that name-calling in the United States press was endangering relations between the two countries, Foreign Minister Storni insisted that his government had pursued an extremely benevolent neutrality toward the United States throughout the course of World War II. Argentine ships had operated exclusively in the service of Britain and the United States; Argentina had recognized its northern neighbor as a nonbelligerent immediately after Pearl Harbor; and both the Castillo and Ramírez administrations had restricted the secret communiques of Germany, Japan, and Italy, while other neutrals had permitted absolutely free use of their cables. In addition, Argentina had supplied the Allies with vital exports, the loss of which had seriously endangered Argentine security. Storni protested that America's demand for an immediate, unprovoked severance of relations was unreasonable. In the first place, the international situation could not be abruptly changed by a government that was attempting to reconstruct a land thoroughly corrupted in its educational, social, and political institutions by the former administration. In the second place, a rupture without apparent cause would recall Mussolini's dastardly attack on a prostrate France and would therefore offend world opinion. The foreign minister concluded by predicting dire consequences if the United States continued to deny material and equipment to Argentine industry. Unless the United States made a genuine gesture of friendship in the form of "airplanes, spare parts, armaments and machinery" and did everything in its power "to restore Argentina to the position of equilibrium to which it is entitled with respect to other South American countries," a wave of anti–United States opinion would engulf Argentina and would poison Argentine-American relations for years to come.[69]

Far from feeling threatened by Storni's charges, the internationalists, Welles, and Armour (who with the Radicals was now thoroughly disillusioned with the general-president) believed that the incident presented a unique opportunity to brand Argentina as a silent partner in the Axis conspiracy, to label the Ramírez regime as a threat to the peace and safety of the Americas, and to appeal to the Argentine people to rise up and restore their nation to the paths of righteousness.[70]

Hull's carefully prepared reply began with a review of the various inter-American resolutions that Argentina had allegedly violated by continuing to maintain relations with the Axis. He then cited statistics to prove that Argentina was enjoying a level of prosperity that it had not reached for twenty years. Wartime trade with the Allies in strategic materials and other commodities was at least as beneficial to Argentina, if not more so, as it was to Britain and the United States. Moreover, thanks to the efficiency of Allied military and naval operations, many of Argentina's markets remained open during a war that had wreaked economic havoc throughout most of the rest of the world. In a blatant appeal to the Argentine citizenry to repudiate the Ramírez regime and its policies, Hull asked rhetorically how long a people as devoted to democracy as were the Argentineans could continue to support a government that not only refused to recognize its hemispheric commitments but even lent aid to the Axis. The State Department concluded its rebuttal by flatly rejecting Storni's bid for arms aid. Denying that Washington had supplied Argentina's neighbors with arms for any other reason than hemispheric defense, Hull observed facetiously that for the United States to supply a neutral power such as Argentina with planes and munitions would be inconsistent with the inter-American doctrine of peaceful settlement of disputes.[71]

Press reaction to the Hull-Storni exchange, which was made public on September 7 simultaneously by the State Department and the Argentine Foreign Office, more than fulfilled the hopes of the internationalists. In Buenos Aires the great Argentine dailies blasted the Ramírez government for playing into Washington's hands and making the nation appear to be a selfish, militaristic power.[72] Indeed, so intense was domestic criticism that the Casa Rosada closed down a number of papers, including *Noticias Gráficas*.[73] Latin opinion outside of Argentina was no less distressing to Buenos Aires. Some *latinos* sympathized with Argentina as being a victim of Yankee imperialism, and some were even willing to tolerate Argentine nonalignment; but Buenos Aires's public appeal for arms aid to "restore Argentina to the position of equilibrium to which it is entitled" aroused fears of Argentine expansionism and militarism, thus canceling much of the sympathy that Ramírez had previously enjoyed.[74] Although Chile had been one of Argentina's strongest supporters, *La Hora* and *La Nación*, both of Santiago, attacked in no uncertain terms the Argentine position expressed in Storni's note.[75] *El Tiempo* and *Ultimas Noticias* of Caracas, which had previously displayed a tolerant attitude toward Argentine neutrality, condemned Storni's appeal and called upon the Ramírez government to make a full and immediate compliance with the Rio resolutions.[76] Not surprisingly, newspapers in Cuba and Panama, representing the two American republics that were perhaps most committed to the Allied cause, were thunderous in their denunciation.[77]

Response to the Hull-Storni affair north of the Rio Grande was even more critical of Argentina—a fact that was particularly gratifying to Hull, who had writhed under charges of appeasement stemming from the State Department's policies toward the Pétain and Badoglio governments.[78] Typical of the hundreds of laudatory telegrams that poured into the State Department was one that praised Hull's denunciation of the "balance of power concept" contained in Storni's appeal and declared that the exchange had restored the people's faith in America. Another pronounced the State Department's self-righteous rejoinder "one of the few real American statements that have come out of Washington in years." The *Washington Post*, which ran a front-page headline on the exchange, expressed the widely held view that Argentina was irrevocably committed to all inter-American resolutions and hence Washington should make no concessions whatever: "General Ramírez cannot expect the United States to kill any fatted calves on his behalf, regardless of what he does. . . . There can be no deals with him, as Secretary Hull's fine note makes clear."[79]

If the State Department's goals in the Hull-Storni affair were to further isolate Argentina within the hemisphere and to create support in the United States for a hard line toward the Ramírez government, its policy was a success. But if judged on its ability to produce an Argentine-Axis estrangement, arouse pro-Allied sentiment, and facilitate a return to constitutional democracy in Argentina, American policy in the Hull-Storni affair was an unqualified failure. United States intelligence reports had consistently indicated that Admiral Storni and Finance Minister Jorge Santamarina were the only two pro-Allied figures in the cabinet.[80] J. Edgar Hoover informed Harry Hopkins on June 12 that Storni, who had formerly been chief of the Argentine navy's general staff and who was an active Radical, was one of the most liberal of the "Argentine Naval Caste." Santamarina, a former director of the Banco de la Nación and brother of the pro-Allied Senator Antonio Santamarina, was reported to be definitely in the anti-Axis camp.[81]

In the wake of the storm of adverse publicity that broke after publication, Ramírez made a scapegoat of Storni and, on the evening of September 7, forced him to resign.[82] Santamarina's resignation a few weeks later left the integral-nationalist and anti-American elements within the cabinet virtually unopposed. Reflecting the changed situation within the cabinet and a general sense of humiliation felt at all levels of government, the Ramírez regime became far less willing to cooperate with the Allies and to tolerate domestic dissent than it had been during the first two months of its existence. To FDR's public request that all neutrals refuse asylum to persons accused of war crimes, the Argentine government responded that it reserved its right "to consider each individual case on its merits in the event that any fleeing Fascist or Nazi leader should seek sanctuary in Argentina."[83] Mid September saw the arrest of British and United States executives of the American and Foreign Power Company, thus increasing fears in Allied circles that restriction or even nationalization of foreign-owned businesses in Argentina was imminent. Later, when a petition demanding "effective democracy" and "loyal fulfillment of international obligation," which was signed by one hundred fifty prominent Argentineans, appeared in forty newspapers, Ramírez not only branded the protest as Communist-inspired and announced the discharge of all government and federal employees who had signed it, but he also used the incident to launch an intensive campaign to purge all antigovernment elements from Argentina's intellectual community.[84] Perhaps most important to the State Department, Argentina's position remained throughout the fall of 1943 one of unswerving neutrality. "The Argentine people firmly desire victory for the countries fighting for democracy," President Ramírez declared in an interview with *Mercurio* of Santiago, "but [they] do not want to break off with any nation in the world unless Argentina is offended by that nation . . . they are peace-loving people with no directly effecting reasons moving the citizens toward conflict."[85]

By the fall of 1943 Sumner Welles's position within the Roosevelt foreign-policy establishment had become completely untenable, and on September 16 the man who had been the principal architect of the Good Neighbor Policy for over ten years submitted his resignation to the White House. According to Hull, the undersecretary departed because the president realized that the continued existence of an independent, irresponsible organization within the State Department was intolerable. By the summer of 1943, Hull writes in his *Memoirs*, FDR had recognized the "impossible situation" that existed for the secretary of state and terminated it by forcing Welles out of the department.[86] The circumstances surrounding Welles's ouster were uglier and far more complicated than the secretary's account would indicate, however.

Sumner Welles was a man who made enemies easily. Aristocratic, acid-tongued, completely intolerant of incompetence, he swept away or by-passed everything and everyone who stood in his path. His enormous effectiveness, immense reputation, and particularly the power that Welles derived from his special relationship with Roosevelt aroused the enmity and jealousy of a host of lesser men. Perhaps the least of these was William C. Bullitt. Wilson's envoy to Lenin during the Paris Peace Conference, Bullitt had also been appointed by Roosevelt as the first American ambassador to the Soviet Union (1933–36). Later he was ambassador to France (1936–41), and in 1941 he was ambassador at large, a post without any real responsibility. Bullitt spent most of his time during the war years, in the words of John Morton Blum, "contriving unsuccessfully to obtain high office in the State Department and in gossiping with calculated malice about those whom he would like to have replaced."[87] The man whom Bullitt most wanted to supplant was Sumner Welles, and in the summer of 1943 he set about to do just that.

The tale that Bullitt told to bring the undersecretary low concerned an incident that allegedly took place in August 1940. According to Bullitt, during a return trip from the funeral of Alabama Congressman John Bank-head, aboard a train jammed with dignitaries, Welles got very drunk and repeatedly pulled the emergency cord in his sleeping compartment; and when various porters came to investigate, he propositioned them.[88] Welles never admitted that the story was true, and his supporters contended that it was a pure fabrication, manufactured by Bullitt with the aid of J. Edgar Hoover.[89]

Bullitt told the story to all who would listen, including, of course, Franklin Roosevelt and Cordell Hull.[90] Hull denounced Welles's actions as "worse than murder," but, typically, he refused to confront his rival with the charge.[91] Soon, however, the Bankhead story began to surface every-where. Felix Belair, a friend of Henry Wallace's, told the vice-president about the alleged incident and declared that the story had come to him from the sleeping-car porters themselves. Various senators began to mutter about moral decay in the State Department and the need of a full-scale investi-gation. Arthur Krock, an incorrigible gossip and a close ally of Hull's, began to print stories in the *New York Times* about certain dark deeds committed by the undersecretary, after which Tom Connally and James Byrnes, those two untiring Democratic watchdogs, went to Roosevelt and demanded that Welles be ousted.[92] During the second week in August, Breckinridge Long confronted the undersecretary—"something Hull would never do," Long wrote in his diary—and advised him to resign before the Republicans got hold of the story. Welles denied Bullitt's accusation but agreed to step down.[93]

Welles submitted his resignation to Roosevelt personally on Monday, August 16.[94] The president, who believed that Welles's departure was inevitable but who was immensely annoyed by it because of the undersecretary's enormous ability, accepted but asked him to head the American delegation to the Moscow Conference. Welles rejected the post, however, because, he said, he was leaving the department primarily at Hull's behest, and he would undertake a task as important as the Moscow mission only with the full support of the State Department. He wanted no repeat of the Rio donnybrook.[95]

Berle was apparently the last person to see Welles before he left the State Department's quarters at Foggy Bottom. On Saturday, August 21, a despondent Welles phoned Berle and asked him to come to the department the following afternoon at five o'clock. When Berle arrived, Welles was cleaning out his desk; he appeared exhausted. He told Berle of his resignation and asked him to take charge of the department until Hull returned the following Thursday. "And so I said farewell," Berle records in his diary, "and left him in a dusty, sunlit office, in an empty building, finishing, as he believed, his stormy but brilliant career."[96]

Personal animosity was no doubt the key factor in the undersecretary's denouement, but there were issues involved as well. Henry Wallace implies in his diary that Welles's downfall was caused not only by Hull's jealousy and Bullitt's innuendo but also by the undersecretary's position on Russian-American relations. To the dismay of Bullitt and other hard-line anti-Communists, Welles looked forward to Soviet-American cooperation in the context of a postwar collective-security organization. He believed, moreover, that Moscow would support the concept of regional organizations operating within a larger world body. This attitude, coupled with his distrust of Great Britain, which he identified with colonialism and the outdated "balance of power approach," had as much to do with Welles's ouster as the bureaucratic situation.[97]

Two final and often neglected factors that contributed to the undersecretary's departure were the "failure" of United States policy toward Argentina and his increasing exclusion from the decision-making process. At Rio he had won control of hemispheric policy for the Latin American coalition, but at the time it was clear to all concerned that the Latin Americanists' continued dominance depended upon their ability to secure a severance of relations between Argentina and the Axis. The policy of selective, covert pressure pursued by Welles, Bonsal, Duggan, and their associates during 1942 was designed to accomplish the primary goal without destroying hemispheric unity or offending Argentine sensibilities. By the fall of 1942, continued nonalignment by Argentina, together with mounting pressure from the American people on the one hand and bureaucratic rivals on the other, produced the Trade Convention speech. This tirade constituted a tacit admission by Welles that he could not achieve an immediate change in Argentine foreign policy within the framework of the Good Neighbor Policy. By undercutting the position long held by himself, Duggan, Bonsal, and the rest of the Latin Americanists, the undersecretary's new hard line destroyed the prestige of the entire group and paved the way for the ascendancy of the internationalists. Moreover, Welles's subsequent attempts to regain his influence in hemispheric decision-making by adopting a position more aggressive than even that of the internationalists created an ever-widening gulf between him and his colleagues in the Latin American establishment.

Welles's resignation was a clear victory for Hull and the internationalists—on September 7 Secretary of War Henry Stimson congratulated Hull on obtaining a "reorganization" of his department[98]—but the undersecretary's forced retirement hardly ended the feud between him and Hull. By the spring of 1943 the secretary of state was seeing potential rivals around every corner. Berle was forced to call off a planned trip to England in June because Hull became "very mournful" about it. "He is a little worried and afraid when anyone gets active," Berle confided in his diary.[99] During the course of their prolonged feud, Welles and Hull had enlisted the aid of two of the most famous and most feared members of the Washington press corps—Arthur Krock, who served Hull, and Drew Pearson, who represented Welles. As has been noted, Krock played no small role in the ouster of Welles. In turn, shortly after Welles left the department, Pearson opened up on Hull and the other "incompetents" and "reactionaries" in the State Department. Pearson, who on one occasion told Henry Wallace that he had coauthored the Good Neighbor Policy in 1932 along with Welles, even went so far as to try to organize a massive Latin American protest over Welles's departure. As the hated "left-wing press" also turned its guns on the department in connection with Welles's resignation, Hull and his colleagues convinced themselves that the undersecretary had become the head of the Communist conspiracy that was out to discredit the department.[100]

The man who was chosen to replace Welles as undersecretary was Edward R. Stettinius, Jr. Franklin Roosevelt's choice of this former GM executive signaled a change in the president's administrative philosophy that had been developing since the outbreak of World War II. Amid the stresses and strains of global war, the White House began to crave order and stability within the federal bureaucracy, and by 1943 Roosevelt believed that the country, the war effort, and his political reputation could not afford the waste and confusion caused by continued organizational and personal rivalry within the State Department.[101] In regard to this last consideration, Roosevelt was already looking ahead to 1944. He planned to run for an unprecedented fourth term, and he knew that he would need all the support he could get. As a result he began to cultivate "the Morgan banking crowd," as Vice-President Wallace referred to Bernard Baruch, Will Clayton, and other wealthy dollar-a-year men who had entered the federal bureaucracy in droves after 1940.[102] In short, the White House wanted to replace Welles with a man who was not only a competent and experienced administrator, a bureaucrat unencumbered by excess ideological baggage, and a reliable observer who would report to the White House everything that transpired at Foggy Bottom, but who would be a political asset as well.[103]

Born on 22 August 1900 in Chicago, Edward Stettinius, Jr., was the son of a partner in the firm of J. P. Morgan and Company. Despite his father's wealth and position, young Stettinius at first rejected a future in the business world and decided to go into the ministry instead. His four years at the University of Virginia were characterized by missionary work among the "hillbillies," active participation in the YMCA, and failure to gain enough credits for graduation. Sensing Stettinius's managerial ability, John Lee Pratt, a vice-president of General Motors and a family friend, persuaded him to reject the cloth and to carve out a business career on his own. Beginning in a stockroom of the Hyatt Roller Bearing division of GM at forty-four cents an hour in 1924, Stettinius rose to become chairman of the board of directors of United States Steel by 1938, with an annual salary of $100,000. Throughout his rapid climb to the top of the corporate heap, Stettinius managed to retain a deep sense of mission toward his fellow men, and as a result he was sympathetic to many of the Roosevelt administration's relief, recovery, and reform efforts. Due to his position in industry and his work in behalf of the NRA program, Stettinius was named to the Business Advisory Council (BAC), a group of businessmen who were not overtly hostile to the New Deal and who served as advisors to Harry Hopkins while he was secretary of commerce from 1938 to 1940.[104] While serving on the BAC, the thirty-eight-year-old executive caught Roosevelt's eye, and in 1939 he was brought to Washington to head the War Resources Board. In this and subsequent jobs, "Stet," as he was known to his colleagues, so impressed the White House, particularly Harry Hopkins, that he was named to head lend-lease in 1941—the job he held prior to entering the State Department. Because of Stettinius's gift for creating administrative efficiency and because of his devotion to the establishment of an orderly, prosperous world community in the postwar era, he was, in the view of the White House, not only a suitable replacement for Welles but the perfect heir apparent to Hull.[105]

It was not until he actually became secretary of state in the fall of 1944 that the man who one White House staffer described as a "curious blend of businessman and world reformer" left his mark on hemispheric affairs. Both the internationalists and the Latin Americanists sought to draw Stettinius into their respective camps. The former lend-lease administrator had settled into Welles's old office when Hull, who saw in the new undersecretary very little threat to his policy-making authority, warned him to beware of Duggan, Bonsal, and their subordinates; for, being protégés of Welles, they tended to operate "off the cuff."[106] Simultaneously, the Latin Americanists were working to commit Stettinius to their view of hemispheric affairs. Laurence Duggan told the new undersecretary that for many *latinos,* Welles had come to symbolize the Good Neighbor Policy, and naturally his departure had caused a good deal of uneasiness south of the Rio Grande. A word of reassurance to the American republics would be of inestimable value. Already deeply concerned that the internationalists might run roughshod over the principle of hemispheric solidarity in their drive to force Argentina to conform to the Rio resolutions, Duggan urged Stettinius to consult the other American republics in all important decisions, particularly those concerning postwar planning.

Stettinius was impressed with the Latin Americanists, especially Avra Warren, who was later to figure prominently in the rapprochement with Argentina, and he promised a continuance of the Good Neighbor Policy.[107] Nevertheless, at this point the new number two man in the State Department had neither the desire nor the presidential mandate to challenge the internationalists for control of America's Argentine policy. Indeed, he chose during his fourteen months as undersecretary to remain aloof from intradepartmental wars. Above all, this meant swimming with the tide on all matters relating to Argentina.

In taking unilateral action in the Transradio affair, in using the Montevideo Committee to depict Argentina as a tacit ally of the Nazis, and in invoking hemispheric opinion against first Castillo and then Ramírez, the State Department was reacting to public criticism that it was "soft on fascism"; to attempts by Treasury, BEW, and FEA to usurp its authority; to the backlash following the revolution of June 1943; and to the internationalists' perception of inter-American affairs. Implementation of these policies was made possible by (and reflected) a marked loss of power within the foreign-policy establishment on the part of the Latin Americanists. Welles's defection to the hard-liners during the spring and summer of 1943 and his subsequent resignation robbed the Latin Americanists of much of the leverage they had enjoyed during the previous decade. Although Duggan, Bonsal, and their subordinates shared Welles's frustration, they had continued to fight for a policy of selective coercion and struggle against those who advocated a direct frontal assault.[108] The latter course, they felt, would only drive the sensitive Argentineans to support whatever government happened to be in power. In addition, the Latin Americanists were fearful that the increasingly hard-line tactics being pursued by the State Department would rekindle Latin memories of the big stick and lead to the establishment of a postwar Inter-American System that would be limited to the Latin republics.[109] They urged the Roosevelt leadership to abandon divisive denunciations and blatant intervention and to rely on lend-lease aid to Argentina's neighbors, subtle economic pressure through restriction of certain United States exports, and selective distribution of newsprint. In virtually every case, except where their arguments were useful in fending off a bureaucratic challenger, the internationalists, with Welles in tow, dismissed their reservations and rejected their policy options. The Latin Americanists believed for a time that Edward Stettinius might be converted to the cause and used to regain lost leverage. When he rejected Duggan's and Bonsal's invitation to replace Welles as a "symbol of the Good Neighbor Policy," they were left without a spokesman in the top echelon of the State Department—a situation that augured ill for the Good Neighbor Policy and Argentine-American relations.

6

WILSONIAN DIPLOMACY
IN THE AGE OF ROOSEVELT

As the Roosevelt administration grappled with its personnel problems in the State Department in the fall of 1943, the Argentine foreign-policy establishment was itself undergoing a profound change, a change that produced a new, ominous set of objectives in the nation's foreign policy. From the GOU's inception, that organization had refrained from adopting expansionist slogans. Shortly after the June revolution, however, the "colonels" outlined their diplomatic goals in a public statement that seemed to bode ill for the independence of Argentina's neighbors:

> Once we have conquered power [in Argentina], it will be our mission to be strong—stronger than all the other (South American) countries together. We must arm ourselves and remain armed always, triumphing over difficulties, battling against internal and external conditions. Hitler's struggle in peace and in war will be our guide.
>
> Alliances will be the first step. We already have Paraguay; we shall have Bolivia and Chile, and it will be easy for us to put pressure on Uruguay. Then the five united nations will easily draw in Brazil, because of its form of government and its great nuclei of Germans. The South American continent will be ours when Brazil falls.[1]

As has been noted, however, the integral-nationalist and pro-Axis groups within the GOU constituted only one faction within the junta that overthrew Ramón Castillo. From June through September the pro-Allied clique

—headed by Foreign Minister Storni—and a pro-Axis and sometimes expansionist cabal—headed by Colonel González, Colonel Perón, and General Farrell—struggled for control of the government and its policies.[2] The Hull-Storni affair all but eliminated the pro-Allied faction from this political equation and paved the way for the ascendancy of the integral nationalists. Consequently, in the fall of 1943, the reorganized Ramírez government inaugurated a campaign to actually fulfill the expansionist pledges made by the GOU.[3]

The State Department responded to the attempts by Argentine ultranationalists to convert southern South America into an anti-American neutralist bloc by wielding virtually every diplomatic weapon short of a declaration of war with the object of forcing drastic changes in Argentine policy. Pressure from Washington not only deflated the expansionists but eventually produced the long-awaited severance of relations between Argentina and the Axis. Not satisfied with causing a basic reorientation in Argentina's posture toward the war, the internationalists decided to withhold vital intelligence information from the Ramírez regime, and in so doing, they contributed to the downfall of that government in early 1944. The department's tactics in this situation revealed a subtle shift in goals on the part of the internationalists. During the fall of 1944 Hull, Long, and their associates reached the conclusion that it was the duty of the United States to secure not only a pro-Allied orientation in Argentine diplomacy but a democratization of the Argentine political system as well. In pursuing this new objective the State Department was responding to developments in southern South America, to continuing attacks by Henry Morgenthau and the Treasury Department, and to the weakened condition of the Latin Americanists. The drive to restore representative government to Argentina also stemmed from the dichotomy inherent in the internationalists' Wilsonian view of foreign affairs and their conviction that totalitarianism and neutralism were but two sides of the same coin.

Hull, Long, and their associates were firmly committed to Wilsonian internationalism—that is, to the creation of an association of nations that would be dedicated to the eradication of aggression, the promotion of national self-determination, and the elimination of economic exploitation. Before a peaceful and law-abiding world community could emerge, however, democracy would have to prevail throughout the world. Thus, in the Wilsonian scheme of things, America had two mutually reinforcing roles to play. The republic must work to establish an international concert of powers devoted to the collective good and to foster democracy in every region of the globe. To Hull, Long, and their subordinates, World War II was being fought not only to preserve a balance of power in Europe and the Far East and to prevent foreign domination of the Americas but also to make the world safe for democracy. The internationalists disagreed violently with the Latin Americanists' contention that the nations of the world could be judged only on the basis of their international conduct. The Axis powers, for example, were proper subjects of a United States declaration of war not only because of their external aggression but because of the tyrannical and repressive nature of their domestic regimes. Like Wilson, Hull and his associates adhered to the view that a particular government's domestic policies and its foreign posture were inextricably intertwined. Argentine neutrality was both a reflection and an inevitable product of the philosophy that prevailed in domestic affairs.

Cordell Hull, taking full advantage of one of the few opportunities available to him to participate in the diplomacy of the Grand Alliance, attended the Moscow Foreign Ministers' Conference from October 19 through October 30. While he was absent, the State Department was innundated with reports from the American embassy in Buenos Aires and from other sources that the Ramírez government had become thoroughly Fascist and had dedicated itself to establishing Argentine dominance in southern South America. On the nineteenth, Ambassador Armour cabled Washington that President Ramírez, through cowardice or calculation, had gone over completely to the pro-Axis camp and had named a new cabinet composed of all the country's leading right-wingers. Gen. Alberto Gilbert was foreign minister, and Perón's stalking horse, General Farrell, assumed the vice-presidency.[4] To the Interior Ministry, Ramírez appointed the ultranationalist Gen. Luís Perlinger, who immediately initiated an effective campaign of political repression.[5] On September 24 Col. Charles Deerwester, chief of the United States Air Mission in Argentina, wrote his superiors in Washington: "Things have really changed. . . . The government didn't turn out as we thought it would. . . . The people are weary and sick of this government. . . . I can easily understand life in Germany now, for this country is just about as totalitarian as it can be."[6]

Only days later, American officials learned from the Polish government-in-exile in London that those who now dominated the Ramírez government were intensely nervous over Argentina's increasing isolation and therefore had established a secret fund within the Ministry of War to be used for the overthrow of neighboring governments. Heading the list of priorities was a plan to penetrate the Bolivian government and help Fascist elements stage a right-wing insurrection in that country.[7]

So alarmed was the American embassy at the political situation in Buenos Aires that on October 20 Armour cabled Washington, urging the freezing of all Argentine assets in the United States. His proposal unwittingly opened the door for another major clash between the State and Treasury departments for control of Argentine-American policy.[8] When a copy of Armour's advisory reached the Treasury Department on October 25, Morgenthau was out of the country, touring military installations in North Africa and Italy. His zealous subordinates—White, Randolph Paul, John Pehle, and Herbert Gaston—believing that they could exploit Hull's absorption with the Moscow Conference and the recent shake-up in the leadership of the State Department, decided to use the Armour recommendation to press once again their antagonists at Foggy Bottom to support a freeze on all Argentine funds in the United States. On the morning of the twenty-fourth, officials of the State and Treasury departments held a lengthy meeting to discuss Armour's suggestion. White, Paul, and Pehle argued both on economic and political grounds that freezing was essential. In the first place, Argentina was commonly recognized as the "base from which the Axis conducts its operations throughout the Western Hemisphere," and in the second place the Ramírez regime was thoroughly Fascist and a threat to the peace and safety of surrounding republics. Stettinius, who admitted that "he was just learning about such matters,"[9] deferred to his subordinates, who once again argued that freezing would be counterproductive both economically and politically. Emilio Collado and Dean Acheson, of the Division of Economic Affairs, pointed out that while such a move would have no immediate impact on Argentina or on Axis activities there, it would threaten the Allied procurement program, which was absolutely vital to the war effort. Speaking for the Latin American establishment, Duggan and Bonsal insisted that the matter be viewed from the perspective of the entire hemispheric community and that freezing be placed in the context of the Good Neighbor Policy. *Latinos* everywhere, they declared, would regard freezing

as designed to alter the domestic and foreign policies of the present government: "The foundation of hemispheric solidarity that has been achieved is
due to the conviction that we should not use our superior strength, political
or economic, no matter how plausible or noble the motive, to interfere with
the right of the peoples of the other American republics to enjoy or to suffer
any government which they might tolerate."[10] White and his colleagues
were no more willing to accept this view than they had been in the summer
of 1942. The Treasury Department attributed Acheson's objections to his
well-known pro-British bias, and the Latin Americanists' objections to their
parochialism.[11] Thus, the two groups of rival policy-makers found themselves at an impasse over Argentina for the second time, and as before, they
turned to the White House for a final decision.

The Treasury Department's bid for control of Argentine policy once
again drove the Latin Americanists and the internationalists into a momentary alliance. On the afternoon of the twenty-fourth, Stettinius cabled the
American embassy in Moscow to inform Hull of the Treasury Department's
new campaign in behalf of all-out economic coercion and to recount the
State Department's objections as articulated by the Latin Americanists. The
undersecretary's note stressed particularly that the Treasury Department's
goal was the overthrow of the Ramírez government.[12] However much Hull
may have hoped for just that event, he deeply resented the Treasury's in-
trusion into what he considered to be the State Department's area of responsibility. Therefore he cabled Stettinius, saying that he was as adamantly
opposed to freezing as ever and ordering him to communicate those views
to the president.

The following morning Stettinius made the trip to 1600 Pennsylvania
Avenue and laid the two diametrically opposed memoranda, one from the
State Department and one from the Treasury, together with Hull's cable, in
Roosevelt's lap. Once again, "the Great White Father,"[13] as Morgenthau
frequently referred to him, ordered that the freezing idea be tabled.[14]
Hoping to appease Treasury Department officials, however, he suggested
that a story be leaked to the press to the effect that Washington was con-
sidering the idea of freezing controls.[15]

White, Paul, and Pehle saw in the president's suggestion more than a
compensatory crumb, because they perceived correctly that rumors of an
impending blockage would cause Argentina's financial community to panic
and to withdraw their assets from the United States. If they could prove that

much of this money belonged to "pro-Axis" firms, they believed they could use acts of withdrawal very effectively in arguing for an immediate freeze. Consequently, on the twenty-sixth, not only did Treasury Department officials endorse Roosevelt's suggestion, but Paul and Gaston actually planted the leak themselves. As a result, on the twenty-seventh the *New York Times*, the *New York Herald Tribune*, the *Washington Times-Herald*, and UPI in Buenos Aires carried stories to the effect that Washington was seriously considering freezing controls.[16] The threat of seizure brought not only the hoped-for withdrawals[17] but a dividend in the form of a renewed plea for freezing from Armour.[18]

The American embassy's insistent messages and the outflow of Argentine gold produced some concessions by the Latin Americanists. The State Department agreed to the blockage of the funds of Banco de la Nación and Banco de la Provincia on the twenty-eighth, but Stettinius, on the twenty-ninth, once again secured a thumbs-down decision from the White House on general freezing.[19] Stettinius subsequently reported to Hull, who was still in Moscow, that FDR was quite irritated at White and his colleagues over the whole affair. According to the undersecretary, Roosevelt had labeled the Treasury Department's recommendations as "imprudent" and had ordered him to keep a lid on things until Hull and Morgenthau could be consulted.[20]

No one was more aware than Henry Morgenthau that power within the federal bureaucracy depends on credibility. Upon his return to Washington the secretary realized instantly that the State Department had used his subordinates' impetuosity to undermine the Treasury's influence in hemispheric policy-making, and he was, to say the least, furious. The departmental meeting on November 2 was not a pleasant one for Paul, Pehle, and Gaston. "I think the Treasury is in an absolutely false position," raged Morgenthau. "We were outsmarted, or something." Whatever its political objectives in Argentina, the secretary declared, the Treasury Department must not appear to be concerned with the domestic policies of the ruling clique. The department would have to base is recommendations on economic-warfare grounds only.[21]

Although stung by Hull's and Roosevelt's rebuff, Morgenthau by no means believed that his department had lost the war for adoption of freezing controls. On the same day that he berated his subordinates, the secretary informed Stettinius that the Treasury Department continued to regard freezing as imperative.[22] Morgenthau's persistence was to be rewarded more quickly than he had dreamed. The growing threat of Argentine expansionism in southern South America, the internationalists' response to that threat, and Morgenthau's personal influence with FDR led in late December to a reversal of the State Department's position toward the ultimate economic sanction.

Cordell Hull returned to Washington on November 12. His pleasure at having bested Morgenthau in the latest bureaucratic encounter between the State and Treasury departments was quickly replaced by concern over the rapidly deteriorating political situation in southern South America. Continuing reports from the American embassy and from Polish operatives concerning the imperialistic aims of the new Ramírez cabinet were supplemented by complaints throughout November and December from Argentina's neighbors that Buenos Aires was employing a combination of material concessions and economic coercion in order to maximize southern South America's economic dependence on Argentina. In mid November the Paraguayan ambassador notified the State Department that a trade treaty had been signed between his country and Argentina and that the Ramírez government was pressing for creation of a customs union.[23] Soon thereafter, Argentine spokesmen announced the conclusion of such a pact and described it as a step leading toward the establishment of a regional customs association that would be open to all South American countries.[24] Finally, during an interview with Ambassador Armour on December 18, former Argentine Finance Minister Jorge Santamarina confirmed that Buenos Aires was threatening neighboring capitals with economic sanctions and military intervention in order to mold them into an anti–United States bloc, and he urged the State Department to take a much stronger line against the Ramírez government.[25]

Public utterances by various Argentine officials throughout the fall of 1943 only served to reinforce Washington's fears that the Ramírez regime was bent on absorbing Argentina's neighbors. In November, Ramírez, in an interview with *El Mercurio* of Santiago, and Perón and Gilbert, in similar articles in *La Hora*, appealed to neighboring states, in the name of both principle and self-interest, to align their foreign policies with that of Argentina by declaring neutrality. Reaffirming their country's intention to pursue an absolutely independent course in international affairs, all three made an impassioned plea for Chile, Paraguay, Uruguay, and other nearby states to join with Argentina in combating North American imperialism.[26]

On 22 December 1943 right-wing revolutionaries in Bolivia overthrew the pro-Allied government of Gen. Enrique Peñaranda. Argentina watchers in both the United States foreign-policy establishment and the press corps immediately pointed an accusing finger and declared that Bolivia constituted the first step in a chain reaction. There was evidence to indicate that the revolutionaries had used Argentine arms and money and that Berlin had encouraged the coup, but there was little to show that the new government was Nazi- or GOU-dominated.[27] Actually, the forces responsible for the revolution were complex and had more to do with the domestic situation in Bolivia than with international affairs. While the Peñaranda government had cooperated with the United States from 1941 through 1943 in supplying tin and tungsten for the war effort, it had at the same time pursued an increasingly repressive socioeconomic policy. Labor disturbances in the tin mines had been crushed with ruthless brutality. Labor leaders had accused the government of exploiting Bolivian workers for the benefit of the giant tin companies. When, in December, Peñaranda closed newspapers representing his political opposition—the Movimento Nacionalista Revolucionario (MNR)—a group of young army officers together with the chief of the MNR, Victor Paz Estenssoro, deposed the general and seized power.[28]

Despite the fact that various Bolivian labor leaders announced wholehearted support for the new government and despite the fact that Paz Estenssoro, now minister of finance, assured Washington that Bolivia would continue to honor the commitments made at Rio, the Roosevelt administration insisted on viewing the new government of Major Gualberto Villarroel as Fascist, pro-Axis, and Argentine-dominated. Berle, for example, repeatedly referred to the MNR as "the Bolivian equivalent of the Nazi party."[29] Writing in the *Nation*, Manuel Seaone declared: "What has happened in Bolivia has been a triumph for Hitler and a defeat for the puerile policy of 'non-intervention' of the United States State Department."[30] While convinced that Paz Estenssoro was a "sincere friend of the workers in Bolivia," Henry Wallace had no doubt that the "Argentine Nazis" were behind the coup.[31] Indeed, Wallace viewed the Bolivian revolution as doubly alarming, because he believed that it indicated that the pro-Axis Fascists in Latin America were successfully exploiting labor grievances. The really great danger in Latin America was Argentina, Wallace told President Isaias Medina Angarita of Venezuela. The situation in Bolivia was greatly confused, and thus the most important thing was to pursue a strong policy toward Argentina.[32]

To the various groups within the Roosevelt foreign-policy establishment, including the Latin Americanists,[33] and to the vast majority of the American people,[34] revelations concerning Argentina's plans to subvert the independence of her neighbors, in addition to the belief that Buenos Aires was responsible for the Bolivian revolution, served once and for all to identify the Ramírez government with the Nazi and Fascist regimes that were then enslaving Europe. Had not the military junta in Buenos Aires exhibited each of the three faces of fascism—totalitarianism, racism, and, most recently, imperialism—since its takeover in June 1943? Reaction to the Bolivian coup and Argentina's alleged involvement in it was particularly strong, moreover, because these developments were seen as part of a much broader and far more ominous movement. By late 1943 and early 1944 both conservatives and liberals within the Roosevelt foreign-policy establishment were articulating a strikingly similar world view. Men with very diverse philosophies such as Henry Stimson, Adolf Berle, and Henry Wallace agreed that world peace, democracy, and free enterprise were currently being threatened by two rival totalitarian systems—fascism and communism—with Berlin at the head of one and Moscow directing the operations of the other. While the two competing ideologies warred openly in Europe, their representatives in Latin America were engaged in feverish preparations for the ultimate takeover of the Western Hemisphere.[35] The Bolivian revolution was undoubtedly the work of the "Berlin–Buenos Aires Axis."[36] Indeed, many believed that the Bolivian uprising marked the beginning of a "year of revolution" in Latin America which would pit the "Franco type South American activities dictated from Berlin" (i.e., the Bolivian revolution) against a "counter-offensive of Leftist forces dictated from Leftist Europe," whose New World center of operations would be in Mexico City. The Communists might eventually pose the greatest threat to peace, democracy, and free enterprise in the Western Hemisphere, but in 1943–44 the Fascists were the most immediate, and hence most dangerous, enemy.[37] Thus, virtually everyone in the State, Treasury, and War departments and in the intelligence community agreed that the United States had to take immediate steps to contain Argentine expansion.[38] As Norman Armour put it, the question was no longer one of the relative dangers of neutrality but of the absolute and unquestioned danger of direct Argentine aggression.[39]

The overthrow of the Peñaranda government provided the State Department with the occasion to revive a coercive tactic pioneered by Woodrow Wilson during his altercation with the Mexican government of Victoriano Huerta in 1913. During the formative years of the Good Neighbor Policy, the State Department had agreed to accept Latin America's contention that the withholding of diplomatic recognition from a particular government on the basis of its internal policies constituted a form of intervention, and it had scrupulously refrained from passing judgment in this form on new administrations.[40] Nevertheless, not only the internationalists but also the Latin Americanists believed that the Bolivian coup would appear to Latin America as a sufficient excuse for resurrecting nonrecognition as a pressure technique.

Not coincidentally, Dr. Alberto Guani, chairman of the Montevideo Committee, notified Hull on December 24 that the delegates (the Argentine member being absent) had voted to recommend that those American states that had declared war on, or broken relations with, the Axis should consult before recognizing any government instituted by force in order to determine if it had complied with the inter-American agreements for defense of the continent.[41] Washington immediately made use of this resolution in an attempt to secure hemispheric support for its nonrecognition policy. No matter how the nations of Latin America felt about United States imperialism and insensitivity to their problems, at this point their fear of Axis subversion and Argentine expansion outweighed virtually every other consideration. Thus, when the State Department announced that it was not entering into relations with the new regime in Bolivia, every American state except Argentina either followed suit or announced its support of the United States position.[42] It should be noted that Hull, Long, Spaeth, and their colleagues hoped to derive other benefits from hemispheric nonrecognition of the Villaroel government. Once the Americas agreed to withhold recognition from Bolivia because of its attitude toward the Rio and Washington resolutions, a precedent would have been established for possible use against Argentina.

The State Department next moved to strengthen those governments in Latin America that were most susceptible to Argentine pressure. In early January the Brazilian ambassador called on the secretary of state to say that he and his government were convinced that German money and the pro-

Axis clique in Buenos Aires were responsible for the Bolivian coup d'état. He demanded increased military aid for Brazil and her neighbors, slyly pointing out that it would be unfortunate if the Argentineans and Germans were able to say that the United States was failing to support its ally.[43] The secretary immediately had President Roosevelt approve increased arms shipments from lend-lease stocks to Brazil in order, as he said, to reassure Paraguay and Uruguay as well as Rio de Janeiro. The military "gang" in Buenos Aires would understand this type of diplomacy.[44] The final step in the plan to quarantine Bolivia and Argentina consisted of the transfer of powerful units of the South Atlantic Fleet, under Adm. Jonas Ingram, into the mouth of the River Plata, just across the estuary from Buenos Aires.[45]

For the internationalists, diplomatic and military isolation was not enough, however, because it posed no threat to Argentine neutrality or to the Fascist government responsible for it. As Hull and his associates assembled the facts relating to Argentine imperialism in December 1943 and as they gauged the temper of domestic opinion in the United States, they saw an opportunity to move beyond the mere containment of Argentina and to do nothing less than topple the government that had been responsible for that nation's refusal to join with the Allies. In so doing, they once again threw into sharp relief the differences between their approach to inter-American affairs and that of the Latin Americanists. As previously noted, both factions viewed the Ramírez regime as thoroughly Fascist, and by the closing weeks of 1943 both ardently hoped for its fall. The Latin Americanists believed, however, that given the Good Neighbor Policy and the United States' long-range interests in the Western Hemisphere, Washington would have to wait for the Argentine people to lose patience with their rulers and, of their own volition, cleanse the Casa Rosada.[46] Bonsal, Duggan, and Collado had even convinced themselves that a spontaneous revolution lay in the not-too-distant future:

> In recent months, the repressive measures of the government, including closing of universities, press and radio censorship, the ban on certain Jewish newspapers, arrests of labor leaders and the cancellation of elections have alienated large sections of the Argentine people. . . . There have been signs that the repressive measures above described have tended to shake the prosperous apathy of the Argentine people. Student riots have caused the closing of universities. Labor is unsettled with a general strike being agitated.[47]

Long and Spaeth did not share their adversaries' optimism, however, and they believed that it was Washington's duty to act upon the assumption that a basic reorientation of Argentine foreign policy could be achieved only after the democratization of its political system.

By late December, Hull and his hard-line assistants had concluded that nonrecognition and military encirclement were tactics that would at best only preserve the status quo and that, short of all-out war, the most promising methods for bringing about the collapse of the Ramírez regime, and thus a pro-Allied change in Argentine foreign policy, lay in the economic and propaganda fields: specifically a total embargo of Argentine trade and a publicity campaign linking high-ranking Argentine officials with the Bolivian coup.

In late December 1943 Hull asked the department's economic experts for an analysis of the probable effect that an embargo would have on Argentina and on United Nations' stockpiles of raw materials. E. G. Collado reported that: (1) assuming that the liberated areas of Europe made no great new demands, the Allies could go for all of 1944 without Argentine exports, provided Great Britain switched to pork and Brazil did without wheat; (2) a continuance of the embargo for more than six months would cause severe civilian rationing in the United States; (3) in view of these two considerations, withholding purchases from Argentina for three to six months would be admissible if Argentine supplies would then become fully available.[48] Hull was certain that this was more than enough time for a policy of economic constriction to destroy Argentine prosperity and provoke the populace to replace the Ramírez government with an administration that would join wholeheartedly with the Allies.[49] Hull's advisors had warned him repeatedly, however, that any measure of economic warfare that did not include Great Britain would be virtually worthless.[50] Here too the secretary was quite sanguine. If shown the moral and practical necessity for taking economic measures against Argentina, the British would surely go along.

In view of past Anglo-American diplomacy, the secretary's optimism was a bit unrealistic. In the fall of 1943 officials of the Treasury and State departments had approached the British about cooperating in Washington's plans to freeze the funds of Banco de la Nación and Banco de la Provincia. The British embassy rejected the suggestion out of hand, arguing that the value of Argentine aid to the Allies far outweighed any possible danger resulting from assistance which that country might be furnishing to the Axis.

And too, as G. F. Theobald, counselor of the embassy, remarked, the British "were not anxious to do anything which would decrease Argentine enthusiasm for sterling."[51]

As Hull quickly discovered, new revelations concerning Argentine expansionism had done nothing to alter Whitehalls' opinion. With evidence of present and future Argentine aggression in hand, the secretary approached Lord Halifax, the British ambassador to the United States, in late December and requested cooperation in a drive to oust the reigning coterie in Buenos Aires. He wanted the United Kingdom, he told Halifax, to move against Argentina like a "battering ram," and he demanded that His Majesty's government desist from all acts that would be helpful to the Ramírez government. If Washington and London worked in harness, the militarist-nationalists who were in control of Argentine foreign policy could be brought down within thirty days.[52]

The British were convinced that the vital force behind America's animosity toward Argentina was Buenos Aires's challenge to United States supremacy in the Western Hemisphere. Whitehall believed that it was being asked to help restore Washington's authority in South America—a cause that British diplomats were not at all sure was in their nation's interest.[53] For one thing, despite the war in Europe, the economic rivalry in Latin America between Britain and the United States intensified markedly in 1943. Moreover, Britain was even more dependent on Argentine meat than it had been in 1942. Consequently, in response to Hull's increasingly insistent demands for support, Halifax replied that His Majesty's government would be more than willing to back the United States provided Washington could explain how Britain was to replace foodstuffs that it would lose in case of a breach with Argentina, foodstuffs amounting to one-fourth of the nation's consumption.[54] Whitehall also pointed out that because the British Ministry of Foods had been designated as the procurer of meat for all Allied forces in Europe, the problem was not merely a domestic one. In view of Argentina's agreement to sell virtually her entire meat surplus to Great Britain on credit, the British government claimed to see relatively little danger in either Argentine expansion or neutrality.[55]

During discussions with the British in late 1943 and early 1944, Hull was forced to stop using the war as justification for coercing the Ramírez government, and in offering new rationales, he provided further insight into the assumptions that underlay the internationalists' view of "the Argentine problem." Whitehall rejected the secretary's contention that the ruling faction in Buenos Aires posed a threat to Allied military operations and argued that the Bolivian coup was the work of a handful of misguided ultranationalists in Buenos Aires. Once Bolivia and Argentina had been isolated, the threat to the South American members of the Grand Alliance, and thus to the war effort, would be removed. Further intervention would be pointless and even dangerous, given Argentina's value as a supplier of raw materials.[56] The Joint Army and Navy Advisory Board inadvertently supported Britain's contention that Argentina was relatively harmless when, in late December, it informed the State Department that under present strategic conditions, the Axis threat to the security of the hemisphere had been largely removed.[57] For Hull, however, the Argentine affair was more than just a matter of logistics, German espionage, or even Argentine expansion. Neither Argentina's contribution to the Allied war machine in Europe nor reports of a declining Axis threat to the Western Hemisphere could alter his conviction that the Ramírez government, by rejecting United States leadership as embodied in the various inter-American security pacts, was refusing to reciprocate American "sacrifices" made during the 1930s.[58] The secretary more and more frequently expressed a view that he had held since 1942, namely, that Argentine neutrality signified an affiliation with world fascism.[59] The Ramírez government's refusal to adhere to the Rio and Washington resolutions on combating Axis influences in the Western Hemisphere, its policy of neutrality, and now its expansionism were all evidence that a foreign ideology was flourishing in southern South America and was threatening to infect the entire hemisphere like a "cancerous growth." If the United States failed to remove this malignancy (and to reconstruct Argentine politics and diplomacy), Hull declared to Halifax, not only would the free institutions of the New World be endangered but Washington would be forever discredited in the eyes of its neighbors.[60]

Whitehall's rejection of Hull's plans for joint economic sanctions, plus the internationalists' overriding determination to find a solution to the Argentine problem, led the Treasury Department leadership to believe that at long last the State Department was prepared to endorse freezing as a coercive technique. And, indeed, these factors, coupled with renewed pressure from Morgenthau, White, Pehle, and the vice-president, prompted the State Department in late December to abandon its long-held opposition to a freeze and to make a general blocking order the key to the economic phase of its anti-Argentine campaign.

Although Morgenthau continued to bombard the State Department with demands for an immediate freeze, he decided, in the wake of the October fiasco, that in order to avoid another presidential rebuff the Treasury Department would have to apply both direct and indirect pressure on Hull and his subordinates. Therefore, from early November to late December, Treasury officials conducted a dual campaign in behalf of the freeze: one, which was aimed at the State Department, based on the requirements of economic warfare; the other, which was directed at the White House, emphasizing the political situation in southern South America. After Hull returned from Moscow on the twelfth, he and Stettinius received almost daily memos from the Treasury Department, indicating that by December 9 the Banco Central would have withdrawn $10 million in gold from the United States and thus would have removed the object of any freezing order. According to Morgenthau, not only were these shipments eliminating a potential source of leverage to be used against the Ramírez government, but much of the money being withdrawn belonged to Axis collaborators.

Meanwhile, Morgenthau, using information derived from an independent intelligence source, urged President Roosevelt to approve a general freeze on the basis of the Fascist nature of the Argentine government and the threat that Argentina posed to her neighbors. On December 21 he persuaded FDR to convene a conference immediately at the White House, with Hull and Gen. George Strong in attendance. Strong, chief of army intelligence and the source of the Treasury Department's information on much of what went on in Argentina, would naturally present a damning indictment of the Ramírez government, and this in turn, the Treasury Department hoped, would prompt the president to call for a new, tougher line and to direct Hull to consult with Morgenthau. "You know . . . on the Argentine thing," Morgenthau told Roosevelt during their conference on the twentieth, "Cordell is taking an interest but he's awful slow. . . . (It) looks as though there had been an overthrow in Bolivia as a result of scheming from Argentina. . . . If you want to get the lowdown on it, why don't you send for General Strong and he will give it to you."[61] As he left, he asked the president to "please use Bolivia as an excuse [for a meeting] so Hull won't smell Morgenthau."[62] Later in the day, Strong called at the Treasury Department and notified Morgenthau that the briefing session with FDR had turned out exactly as anticipated.

This elaborate maneuvering was largely unnecessary, for unbeknownst to the Treasury, the State Department had come to the conclusion that freezing was necessary, whatever the bureaucratic cost. In early January, reports flowed into the department indicating that the Argentine cancer was spreading. A distraught L. S. Rowe, head of the Pan American Union (PAU), dropped by Foggy Bottom and told a group of officials that Argentina was doing everything in its power to destroy the Inter-American System. The head of the Chilean Federation of Labor had informed the PAU that Argentine officers were filtering into Chile in the guise of tourists. Rowe declared that the time had come for the United States to take "drastic action."[63] The internationalists agreed. "We are rapidly coming to grips with Argentina," Berle recorded in his diary on January 10. "Evidence is now conclusive that the Army crowd there headed by Perón financed and handled the plot to take over the Bolivian government and proposes to execute another, similar plot in Chile and Peru, and probably also in Paraguay.... They are working hand in glove with the Germans in all this. We are convinced that the Argentine government does not represent the bulk of the people and the problem is to stand up to the Argentine buccaneers.... By consequence the Secretary is prepared to go to the ultimate."[64] Two days earlier, Berle had notified FDR that Hull was attempting to commit the British to a far-reaching program of sanctions which had as its heart the freezing of all Argentine assets in the United States.[65]

Seizure of Argentine holdings was to be only the economic phrase of the broader offensive, however. Hull, Long, and Spaeth were well aware that the State Department files contained numerous military intelligence reports (furnished by both Polish sources and the FBI) linking certain Argentine officials with the Bolivian uprising, and they believed that publication of these reports would further their objectives in two ways. Although the Montevideo Committee's revelations on Axis espionage activities within Argentina had had minimal effect on hemispheric opinion, Hull anticipated that linking the Ramírez government with the Bolivian uprising would stimulate Latin fears of Argentine imperialism and hence would prompt the republics to support a harsher line toward Argentina. Simultaneously the Argentine citizenry would be so shamed, or outraged, or both, that they would purge the Fascist clique then ensconced in the Casa Rosada. After outlining his plans to FDR, Hull in mid January prepared a press release denouncing Argentina for enriching itself from World War II while subjecting its neighbors to the danger of Nazi enslavement. The statement not only charged that Argentine had become a haven for Nazi agents but explicitly accused Buenos Aires of playing a decisive role in the overthrow of the pro-Allied government in Bolivia. The release was to be accompanied by documentary evidence intended to prove these charges and by an announcement that all Argentine holdings in the United States were henceforth frozen.[66]

The British, who were as opposed to freezing as they were to an embargo, joined with the Argentineans in an attempt to forestall Washington's offensive. On January 23, the day before the State Department was to publish the incriminating documents and implement the freezing order, Lord Halifax called on Hull and implored him to withhold sanctions against Argentina. Simultaneously, Prime Minister Churchill cabled FDR in connection with the Argentine affair: "Before we leap, we really must look."[67] Hull refused to change course, however, and was preparing to fire his broadside, when, on the morning of the twenty-fourth, Argentine Foreign Minister Gilbert promised Armour that his country would break relations with the Axis nations. It seemed, said Gilbert, that the Ramírez government now had proof that Germany had grossly abused Argentine hospitality by operating at least three spy rings within her borders. The agitated foreign minister assured Armour that the break would come no later than noon on Saturday, January 26, provided that there was no action in the meantime that could be interpreted as external pressure.[68] Roosevelt and Hull decided, to the immense relief of both Britain and Argentina, that they would issue, at a specially called press conference, a simple statement announcing that the United States was withholding recognition from the new regime in Bolivia.[69] On January 26 Ramírez proclaimed that in light of the recent discovery that a widespread Axis espionage network headed by the former naval attaché to the German embassy was operating in Argentina, his government was severing relations with Germany and Japan.[70]

It quickly became clear that the internationalists, unappeased by the diplomatic rupture, intended to press their advantage and force the Ramírez government to assume the duties of a full-fledged member of the inter-American collective-security community. On January 26 Ambassador Armour cabled the department and asked for room to maneuver, declaring: "I am optimistic. I have always felt that when we have once broken the dike a lot of things might happen." He urged that the assets of Banco de la Nación and Banco de la Provincia be unfrozen at once so as to prevent the forthcoming United States–Argentine discussions on the implementation of the Rio and Washington agreements from beginning on a discordant note.[71] But Hull refused, observing that past concessions had made not a dent in Argentine neutrality; firmness alone would produce results. While expressing appreciation to Buenos Aires for its decision to break with Germany, Japan, and Italy, Hull made it clear that he regarded this as merely a prelude to further action. Indeed, even before President Ramírez officially announced the severance of relations, the United States had begun prodding the Argentine Foreign Office to conduct a complete housecleaning. On Hull's instructions, on January 25 Armour informed Buenos Aires that it could demonstrate a real reorientation of policy only by (1) eliminating those influential groups within the government that had been active in trying to establish pro-Axis regimes throughout the hemisphere; (2) turning over all information relating to Axis espionage activities in the Western Hemisphere to United States intelligence; (3) living up to commitments made at the Rio and Washington conferences; and (4) severing telecommunications with Germany and its allies.[72]

Ironically, the internationalists created pressures that contributed directly to Argentina's rupture with the Axis and then rejected the severance of relations as meaningless because it was the product of those outside pressures. No sooner had Buenos Aires broken with the Axis, than Hull, Long, Spaeth, and their associates began to question the integrity of the Ramírez government's decision because it was not based on overall inter-American collective-security agreements;[73] by severing relations over a specific offense committed by Germany, Argentina was still denying its "pledges" and was implicitly defying United States hemispheric leadership. To be redeemed, Argentina would have to abandon neutrality and autocracy and accept belligerency and democracy. It was a matter of principle.

Meanwhile the Ramírez government was in desperate straits; the threatened State Department revelations and the subsequent suspension of relations had placed it in an extremely vulnerable position. In breaking with the Axis, the chief executive had alienated the integral nationalists within the officer corps and thus knocked away his main political prop.[74] Waiting in the wings were Farrell and Perón, who hoped to step into the breach between the integral nationalists and the president and to form Argentina's third wartime government.[75] At this point it was to Ramírez's advantage to reveal as much information about Axis activities within Argentina as possible so as to justify his new policy. Given the forces arrayed against him within his own administration, the president's only hope for political survival was to provoke a ground swell of anti-Axis feeling among the citizenry and to link his enemies with German intelligence agents operating in Argentina. In early February, official sources announced that the rupture was due solely to Axis espionage within Argentina and denied that there had been any hint of foreign (i.e. North American) pressure.[76] The federal police submitted a report confirming that German and Japanese rings were operating inside Argentina.[77] But due to the fact that all information-gathering agencies were under the control of the ultranationalist minister of the interior, Gen. Luís Perlinger, those in the army and the government who had facilitated Axis activities and who were now attempting to destroy Ramírez politically escaped the revelation unscathed. To ensure its own survival, the regime had to make a clean sweep, but Ramírez needed help in eliminating the very elements that theretofore had formed his base of support. The Office of Strategic Services and the Federal Bureau of Investigation, as the United States agencies most active in assembling data on Axis operations in Argentina, were in a position to furnish the Argentine government with invaluable aid. In addition, the State Department could offer the Casa Rosada the devastating material supplied by its Polish sources. When the Argentine Foreign Office, in order to give a cutting edge to its disclosures, requested the evidence held by the United States, Hull turned its request down flatly, declaring that Washington had to protect its sources.[78]

Despite strenuous objections from Armour, who pointed out that the Foreign Office was trying to gather as much material as possible in support of a break and that Washington's refusal to help would defeat its own objective, the secretary of state remained adamant. In February, Ramírez was still in control; he had no place to turn except to Washington, and he was in a position to hold his enemies at bay with the aid of North American intelligence. By the end of the month the president's position was untenable, and he was ousted by a nationalist clique devoted to nonalignment with the Allies.[79]

The expansionist schemes of the GOU provided the Hull internationalists with the opening for which they had been waiting, and in late 1943 and early 1944 Washington acted first to halt Argentine aggression and then to force abandonment of neutrality. Hull's decision to proceed with coercion of the Ramírez government—despite notification by the Joint Army and Navy Advisory Board in December 1943 that the Axis had virtually ceased to be a military threat in the Western Hemisphere and warnings by Whitehall that Argentine strategic materials were vital to the functioning of the United Nations war machine—left little doubt as to his motives. Washington moved beyond the eradication of pro-Axis activities in Argentina, not in order to facilitate Allied military operations, but to destroy a government that, to the internationalists' way of thinking at least, had become unalterably tainted by its resistance to United States hemispheric leadership, its collaboration with international fascism, and its refusal to submit to constitutional restraints.

7

THE POLITICS OF CONFRONTATION

Argentine-American wartime relations reached their nadir in 1944. When the Ramírez government gave way to another clique of officer-politicians in February 1944, Washington used the occasion to initiate a policy of unilateral nonrecognition. In succeeding months, State Department officials denounced the new government in ever-harsher terms, attempted to isolate Argentina within the hemisphere, and steadfastly refused to state the terms by which Argentina could rejoin the inter-American community. For their tactics as well as their objectives during this the decisive year of World War II, Hull and his associates continued to draw on their Wilsonian heritage. They refused to accept the severance of relations between Buenos Aires and the Axis capitals as placing Argentina in compliance with the Pact of Rio, and they remained convinced that only a fundamental reordering of Argentina's political processes would produce solidarity with the Allies. Inevitably, the result was blatant coercion of the Argentine government conducted in the name of freedom, democracy, and the Argentine people. Although their mental make-up determined the broad outlines of the internationalists' policy, developments within the bureaucratic and international milieu often determined the type of tactic selected as well as the timing of its implementation.

Contributing to the internationalists' intransigence and affecting the formulation of their stratagems was the continuing rivalry with the Latin Americanists, on the one hand, and the Treasury Department and its allies on the other. While Hull and his colleagues managed during the year to completely eliminate the first group from the formal decision-making process, this group's sympathizers outside the governmental hierarchy, led

131

by Sumner Welles, continued to hammer away at the hard-liners. Simultaneously, Henry Morgenthau and his aggressive underlings, aided and abetted by Henry Wallace, used every device known in bureaucratic warfare to gain control of Argentine policy through persuading the White House to approve sweeping economic sanctions. All the while, Cordell Hull and the State Department were being excluded from the decision-making process as it related both to World War II and the postwar order. Their increasing isolation within the administration and the continuing rivalry with the Latin Americanists and the Treasury Department created intense pressure on the internationalists to bring the Argentine affair to a "successful" conclusion.

It was inevitable, however, that the internationalists' attempts to bring Buenos Aires to its knees would alienate groups whose power transcended that of the Latin Americanists. By the end of the year a number of nations and organizations that felt their interests threatened by the Argentine-American feud began to challenge the validity of the policies being pursued by Hull and his associates.

In Argentine politics the year 1944 began with the fall of Pedro Ramírez and ended with the rise of Juan Perón. Between October and December 1943 the Ramírez regime had become increasingly autocratic and nationalistic. The general-president continued the state of martial law, which had been proclaimed under Castillo, and erected an elaborate federal bureaucracy dedicated to suppression of domestic dissent. This authoritarian trend culminated on 31 December 1943, when the Casa Rosada promulgated two decrees, one establishing obligatory religious education and the other dissolving all political parties "for not responding to the political reality of the nation."[1] Despite the fact that the administration established a Secretariat of Labor Planning, which Juan Perón utilized to appeal to certain sectors of organized labor, Ramírez did not look favorably upon the general objectives of Argentine workers, and he was not tolerant of strikes and other direct-action tactics.[2]

By January 1944 Ramírez's domestic policies had created a ground swell of public discontent among workers and middle-class Argentineans, while his pursuit of neutrality in international affairs continued to alienate the small but vocal group of interventionists centered in Buenos Aires. To undermine the rising tide of opposition, Ramírez in January 1944 initiated a highly publicized program of reform. During the opening weeks of 1944, Argentineans were deluged with some twenty thousand decrees designed, according to the Casa Rosada, to achieve social and economic justice and to pave the way for eventual return to constitutional government.[3] Then, on January 26, Ramírez made the decision to sever ties with the Axis (a stratagem that he apparently thought would win the support of the pro-Allied element in Argentina), end the nation's growing isolation within the hemisphere, attract arms aid from the United States, and, as we have seen, forestall publication of information linking high-ranking Argentinean officials with the Bolivian coup.[4]

Unfortunately for Ramírez, the rupture with Germany, Italy, and Japan alienated the one group in Argentina that was still firmly committed to him—the integral nationalists. Many within the GOU were simply angry because they believed that the Casa Rosada had buckled under to pressure from Washington. Others, who looked to Nazi Germany for inspiration and who had been responsible for Argentina's aborted program of expansion in late 1943, feared that Ramírez had indeed turned the nation toward a pro-democratic, pro-Allied course. Last, but most important, were the political opportunists headed by Gen. Edelmiro Farrell and Col. Juan Perón. This group was motivated less by ideology and principle than by the desire to use the resentment of other Argentineans in order to further their own political ambitions.

As these diverse factions once again coalesced in opposition to the existing regime, Ramírez acted to preempt the coup that he knew was coming. On 24 February 1944 he requested the resignation of General Farrell as minister of war and vice-president.[5] Farrell responded by summoning the commanders of surrounding army installations and, of course, Perón to a secret conference. Once assembled, the conspirators quickly agreed that Ramírez must go, and they settled upon Farrell as their leader. That same day the minister of war, buoyed up by the vote of confidence from his fellow officers, ordered units from the Campo de Mayo to surround the Casa Rosada. Finding himself a virtual prisoner, Ramírez capitulated and subsequently submitted his resignation to the Supreme Court.[6] The more astute of Farrell's advisors quickly realized that a simple resignation carried with it ample opportunity for nonrecognition by hostile nations. Thus, on February 25 the junta pressured the docile former president into changing his resignation to a delegation of authority to the vice-president, thus, they hoped, ensuring the continuity of the existing government and thereby fore-stalling the question of recognition.[7]

It quickly became apparent that Edelmiro Farrell was but a figurehead in his own government. The administration was dominated in its early stages by a bitter struggle between the ultranationalists, headed by the min-ister of the interior, Luís Perlinger, and the new minister of war, Juan Perón. Perón's failure to use sufficient vigor in opposing Argentina's rupture with the Axis had alienated the ultras and convinced them that the colonel knew no god but ambition.[8] A number of factors, both historical and con-temporary, combined to tip the balance of power in favor of Perón during the course of the year. Historian Joseph Barager has succinctly summarized the forces and conditions that the young colonel was to parlay so brilliantly into a nationalist dictatorship. Argentina's newest man on horseback was able to profit from "a constitutional system tailored to exploitation by a dynamic leader; a new class of economic interest groups and entrepreneurs whose needs were ignored by the old power elite representing the great land-holders; an amorphous lower class neglected by the existing labor organiza-tions and political parties; a military establishment divided over its attitude toward the world conflict whose final outcome was still in doubt; and a middle class . . . which was resentful of more than a decade of corrupt, reactionary rule, but whose elements showed little ability to subordinate their individual group interests in a common effort."[9] Soon after becoming head of the nation's armed forces, Perón assumed the duties of minister of labor and then, in July, those of the vice-president.[10] From this bureaucratic vantage point he was able to utilize his luck, charisma, and incomparable political sensibilities to become, by the fall of 1944, the dominant political force in Argentina.[11]

Because the officers in charge of the February coup wanted to deflect possible questions from the international community about the legality of its succession to power, the new government immediately sought to reassure the world as to its diplomatic posture. On February 28 the acting foreign minister, Gen. Diego Mason, held a press conference and declared that there was to be absolutely no change of foreign policies under General Farrell. As always, the policy of the republic would be based on "loyalty and respect towards the governments of friendly countries."[12]

American public opinion was far less favorably inclined toward the February coup than it had been toward the revolution of June 1943. Continuing reports of imperialism, pro-Axis activity, and totalitarianism—juxtaposed with news of the blood and treasure being expended by the Allies on the battlefields of World War II—caused many Americans to demand nothing less than democratization of the Argentine political system and active participation by that nation in the war against the Axis. Most journalists saw the change of government in Buenos Aires as just a shift from one group of power-hungry militarists to another. The *St. Louis Post-Dispatch*, which had reacted to the Ramírez government's severance of relations with the Axis by berating the State Department for "accepting Argentina's hasty about face without applying pressure to bring about its downfall,"[13] informed its readers that nothing had really happened in Buenos Aires in February; the new regime, like the old one, was still "a gangster government that must so rule to thwart the will of the people for membership in the U.N."[14] Others, instead of linking the Farrell government with its predecessors, regarded the new regime as a distinct turn for the worse. In the aftermath of Ramírez's downfall the *New York Times* announced that the president was forced to resign under extreme pressure by the ultranationalist GOU, just as he was preparing to announce the formation of a liberal government.[15] An editorial, closer to the truth but equally as damning to the new junta, contended that the coup had been staged in order to prevent publication of the full details of German espionage in Argentina, a move that would have implicated many high-ranking officials. Even conservative oracles such as the *Chicago Tribune*, the *Los Angeles Times*, and the *Saturday Evening Post*, which were usually opposed to interference in the affairs of "stable" Latin republics, concluded that the United States had to be increasingly concerned over internal developments in Argentina.[16]

Congressional opinion accurately reflected the prevailing mood. Congressman John Coffee of Washington berated the State Department for pursuing much too soft a line toward Argentina. To America's shame, he declared, Caribbean leaders had been far more outspoken on the matter than had been the Roosevelt administration.[17] In a major radio address, Congressman Emmanuel Celler of New York lashed out at the State Department's handling of the Argentine affair: "You cannot confine or isolate fascism any more than you can confine a stink in a closet. . . . Our own freedom is correspondingly contaminated with Franco flourishing to our east and Farrell to our south."[18]

A great many Americans demanded that the State Department wield one of the oldest diplomatic weapons known to the international community —nonrecognition. Finding the Bolivian government a "paragon of virtue" in comparison to Farrell and his colleagues, the *Washington Post* maintained that

> there would seem to be no reason why the Farrell regime in Argentina should be recognized and every reason why recognition should be withheld from it. The fresh coup gives this country a chance to bail out of the recognition that was so hastily given to Ramírez.[19]

The internationalists had no intention of struggling against the popular demand for a severance of diplomatic ties. On the day following Farrell's assumption of the presidency, Armour reported to the State Department that Farrell and Perón had put pressure on Ramírez to term his abdication a delegation of power rather than an outright resignation. The new regime had simultaneously ordered a series of nighttime police raids on various newspapers to confiscate copies of the original resignation message. Armour concluded that the whole thing was a poor attempt at forestalling the question of recognition. Armour, Hull, Long, and Spaeth all agreed that there had been a coup d'état and that Washington should call upon the Montevideo Committee to initiate the procedure that had been established in the wake of the Bolivian coup for consultation in case of the forceful overthrow of an American government.[20]

In spite of Washington's campaign to persuade the other hemispheric republics to view the Farrell regime as pro-Axis and totalitarian and to isolate Argentina as completely as possible, some Latin governments indicated that they intended to adhere strictly to a de facto recognition policy. On March 3 the Chilean Foreign Office notified the United States that it regarded Farrell's assumption of power as entirely legal and that, in view of the new government's publicly announced policy of continental solidarity, it would be impossible to delay a vote of recognition.[21] That same day the Paraguayan ambassador, stressing the danger to his nation's national existence if his government were to take any extreme measures against Argentina, informed the department that Asunción would continue its relations with Argentina without interruption.[22]

On March 4, in the midst of the hemispheric discussions that it had initiated, Washington subverted its attempts to multilateralize coercion of

Argentina and prejudiced any further consultation by unilaterally announcing its position. At a specially called news conference Undersecretary Stettinius informed reporters that because it appeared that a group not in sympathy with President Ramírez's policy of joining in the defense of the hemisphere was now in control of Argentina, the State Department would refrain from entering into relations with the new government. "In all matters relating to the security and defense of the Hemisphere," he declared, "we must look to the substance rather than the form."[23] The United States would not recognize the Argentine government, or any other for that matter, as long as it contained elements inimicable to the United Nations. The internationalists persuaded the White House to reinforce its proclamation of nonrecognition by dispatching to Montevideo Adm. Jonas Ingram and a naval squadron from the South Atlantic fleet.[24]

Unilateral nonrecognition promised to satisfy a number of needs for the internationalists. First of all, it would vitiate some of the election-year criticism that was being leveled at the Roosevelt administration for its failure to bring Argentina into line. Hull and his associates had become increasingly despondent over the secretary's exclusion from the decision-making process during 1943. By relieving pressure on the White House over the Argentine affair, Hull hoped partially to regain the confidence of the president and to become once again a member of FDR's inner circle. In addition, the internationalists were determined to facilitate a return to constitutional government in Argentina, a development that they viewed as a precondition for Argentine-Allied solidarity.

In withholding vital intelligence data from the Ramírez government, the State Department believed that it was aiding a broad prodemocratic, pro-Allied coalition which was headed by former finance minister Jorge Santamarina and Gen. Arturo Rawson and which included the navy and the Radical party. Reports from the FBI during February 1944 indicated that Santamarina, Rawson, and their partisans were pressing the Casa Rosada for free elections, a return to constitutional government, and complete cooperation with the Allied nations; and if the government did not comply, a popular uprising would surely follow.[25] When, instead, Ramírez was ousted via a coup engineered by Farrell and Perón, a man whom Adolf Berle characterized at the time as "the particular and putative Mussolini" within the GOU, Washington's disappointment was intense.[26] The coup merely hardened the internationalists' determination to restore the blessings of liberty and democracy to Argentina; they hoped that nonrecognition would either bring down the Farrell government or force the president to call elections. As the end of the war approached, democratization of the Argentine political system assumed an even higher priority than before because the hard-liners were determined that a totalitarian state not be allowed to participate either in the Inter-American System or the proposed worldwide collective-security organization.[27]

Because they were willing to settle for nothing less than the destruction of the Farrell government, the internationalists refused to make explicit the steps that Argentina must take to end her isolation. Thus, in one of the most bizarre interludes in United States–Argentine relations, from March until December 1944, Washington steadily increased pressure on Buenos Aires, all the while refusing to state the grounds for reconciliation. At one point the secretary advised Armour, in the strictest confidence, that recognition would never be forthcoming until certain key cabinet changes were made. On March 6 Armour rejected a proposal by the Argentine Foreign Office for a secret meeting between him and Perón to iron out the differences between the two nations. After conferring with Washington the ambassador informed the Foreign Office that there was no need for a conference because Argentina well knew what she had to do for recognition.[28]

Finally, nonrecognition appeared doubly attractive as a coercive technique to the internationalists in general and to Cordell Hull in particular because it promised to alienate the Latin Americanists so completely that they would leave the department. The secretary was convinced that Sumner Welles, though he no longer held an official position in the diplomatic hierarchy, still commanded Duggan, Bonsal, and their associates and that the entire group was plotting to replace the internationalists at the top of the State Department hierarchy as soon as FDR was elected to a fourth term.[29] Consequently, early in 1944 Hull began to lay plans to force the Latin Americanists out of the foreign-policy establishment altogether.[30] The internationalists were familiar enough with their adversaries' views to know that a unilateral severance of relations with Argentina would more than likely drive Duggan, Bonsal, Collado, and the other top men in American Republic Affairs to resign.

The Latin Americanists were not long in assuming the position that Hull had anticipated they would. On March 22 Bonsal suggested an "informal interview" between Hull and Argentine ambassador Adrian Escobar, during which the secretary could deliver a brief *aide-mémoire* covering the various Argentine activities that the United States considered inimicable to hemispheric security. According to the director of ARA, Hull should limit himself to activities that would help the Axis in the war and should exclude "broad allegations as to what we think the GOU and other Argentine nationalist groups believe should be Argentina's role in South America." Such a move, Bonsal advised, "would produce an atmosphere in which the friends of continental cooperation in Argentina would be assisted rather than hindered by our attitude."[31] In early June, Bonsal notified Hull through Duggan that, in his opinion, nonrecognition was reducing the State Department's flexibility and was destroying its ability to influence events in Argentina. Moralistic denunciations only strengthened the hand of the rabidly anti-American elements. If Washington continued on its present course, it would have to rely on "good luck" rather than "good management" for success. "We and the other United Nations need Argentina and she needs us. Only Germany is the gainer from any real rift with us."[32]

It remained, however, for Laurence Duggan to render the definitive criticism of diplomatic nonintercourse. On June 22, some three weeks before his departure from the department, he submitted a long memorandum to Hull in which he traced the internationalists' policy to its historical roots and restated the basic assumptions behind the Good Neighbor Policy. Terming the "reactionary political cycle that began in 1930" in Argentina an aberration, Duggan insisted that "Argentine evolution has been towards democracy" and not away from it. The United States should not expect a sudden reversal in the political situation, however: "What is more likely is the beginning of a gradual return to the country's democratic institutions. . . . Several years, even a decade might be required." Arguing that "the present Argentine military regime does not have its roots dug deep into Argentine tradition and life" and that it faced increasing opposition from the liberal middle class, the leader of the Latin American establishment concluded that the Farrell government was holding its own by "waving the banner of outside interference with Argentine sovereignty—in other words, nonrecognition."[33]

When these and numerous other remonstrances failed to alter American policy, the Latin Americanists, as they had done so many times in the past, cited the need to preserve the credibility of the Good Neighbor Policy. Quite simply, if the State Department continued to repeat the mistakes of the past, it would destroy the rapprochement between the United States and Latin America that Washington had worked so hard during the 1930s to create. The United States, Duggan declared, had achieved the trust of the Americas "by openly and frankly laying the Big Stick on the shelf and relying instead upon the development of a community of interests that would produce common attitudes and unity of action." All the republics save one responded by rushing to the defense of the United States after Pearl Harbor. If the United States destroyed the good faith upon which the Good Neighbor Policy was based, as it was doing by its unilateral policy toward Argentina, it could not expect cooperation and support in any future crisis.[34]

Hull, Long, and Spaeth responded to these charges in two ways. Their rhetorical rebuttal consisted of another attempt to link the Farrell regime with the Axis. "It is a travesty on the doctrine of nonintervention," the secretary declared during a heated interview with Duggan and the Chilean ambassador, "for any Government or group of military officials who are the real power behind it to deny all their sister nations the right of self-defense by attempting to shield behind the doctrine of nonintervention a notorious state of pro-Axis activities within their boundaries."[35] Or as he put it in a draft of a speech on the Argentine matter some two months later: "To aid the Argentine government is to aid the Axis powers in the present war."[36]

As they rejected the Latin Americanists' arguments, the internationalists simultaneously moved to eliminate their dependence on Duggan, Bonsal, and their subordinates for information on day-to-day events in the hemisphere and for implementation of policy toward Latin America. To do so, they by-passed the top echelon of the Latin American establishment and worked through the Division of River Plata Affairs (RPA), a component of ARA.[37] The officials in RPA, which was headed by Eric Wendelin, did not possess wide experience in hemispheric affairs, had not participated in the development of the Good Neighbor Policy to any extent, and were used to dealing with the Argentine problem to the exclusion of all others.[38] Hull, Long, Spaeth, and their associates were able to obtain all needed intelligence and to enforce complete nonintercourse with Argentina without consulting ARA.[39] Because Duggan and Bonsal no longer wished to be associated with a policy that they believed was destroying hemispheric solidarity and because they were by now completely excluded from the decision-making process, the two career diplomats resigned in mid July. From then until the close of the year there was not a significant dissenting voice left within the State Department to challenge the internationalists.[40]

There was, nevertheless, continuing bureaucratic competition from the other extreme. As with virtually every other coercive technique employed by the State Department, unilateral nonrecognition did not go far enough to satisfy the Treasury Department. It did not produce an instantaneous change in Argentine domestic and foreign policies, and it did nothing to increase the Treasury's control over Argentine-American relations. Convinced that the State Department was appeasing an obviously Fascist state either out of sympathy with its anti-Semitic policies or out of simple weakness, Morgenthau, White, Paul, Pehle, and their associates not only redoubled their efforts to have FDR approve a comprehensive freeze of Argentine assets but demanded that the State Department institute an absolute embargo. Hull chose once again to oppose a freeze, primarily because he perceived this to be a threat to his and the State Department's position in the bureaucratic hierarchy; but he decided to support commercial nonintercourse, a tactic that could be implemented with a minimum of Treasury interference.

The Treasury Department's approval on January 14 of the decision to suspend the order freezing Argentine assets in the United States did not signal a reversal of its hard-line approach but rather a momentary hope that the break with the Axis was a prelude to a declaration of war. On February 2, however, White and his subordinates informed the Economic Division of the State Department that the Argentine decree severing financial relations with the Axis was proving to be totally ineffective. When Armour requested that the Banco de la Nación and the Banco de la Provincia be taken off the list of blocked nationals as a sign of good will toward Buenos Aires, the Treasury Department refused to do so. J. K. Bacon, an officer in ARA, reported to Duggan and Bonsal that the Treasury Department still had a chip on its shoulder as far as Argentina was concerned and was not willing to give an inch to demonstrate America's trust in the present Argentine government.[41]

Just as the hard-liners within the State Department used the transfer of power from Ramírez to Farrell as an occasion to institute nonrecognition, Treasury Department officials attempted to utilize the coup once again to persuade Hull—and, failing that, Roosevelt—to impound all Argentine assets in the United States. Through their confidential sources in military intelligence, the department was able to follow developments in Argentina quite closely. Reports received from General Strong seemed to confirm the suspicions of Treasury officials that Argentina was a thoroughly Fascist state and a potential successor to the Third Reich.[42] By the first week in March, Morgenthau faced a virtual rebellion among his subordinates concerning his inability to persuade Hull to approve a general freeze.[43] As a result, Morgenthau brought up Argentina during a conversation with Roosevelt on March 7. "This [Argentine fascism] is going to spread all through South America and what you have accomplished in the last eleven years is all going up in thin smoke," Morgenthau declared. "Yes," Roosevelt replied, "but we can't prove anything on the Argentines." Morgenthau was incredulous at the response, but FDR refused to approve any further action.[44] At a departmental meeting on the ninth the secretary tried to placate Pehle and White by threatening to deliver a "show cause" order to the State Department as to why freezing controls had not been imposed.[45]

The secretary's resort to legal action remained merely a threat, however, and by late April, Morgenthau, stung by continued criticism both implicit and explicit from his subordinates, decided that it was time once again to force Hull to make a decision, even if that necessitated going directly to the White House. Morgenthau was at first unsure as to exactly what approach he should employ. On the twenty-seventh he called Dean Acheson, who was in overall charge of financial and economic matters in the State Department, and informed him that he was bringing Leo Crowley, head of the Foreign Economic Administration, to the State Department within the next day or two and that they would jointly recommend the freezing of Argentine assets.[46] "I've just gotten to the point," Morgenthau told Acheson, "where I don't feel that I'm living up to my responsibility if I don't make a firm recommendation."[47] Later in the day, in consultation with his subordinates, the secretary, obviously agitated, dropped the Crowley plan and briefly considered bureaucratic blackmail as a device to achieve his objectives. He proposed going to Hull with a copy of a memorandum containing a scathing indictment of Argentine domestic and foreign policies and recommending a freeze. At the projected confrontation, Morgenthau would tell Hull that unless the State Department authorized a complete blockage of Argentine funds, the Treasury would once again take the matter into the inner sanctum of the Oval Office.[48] The record is unclear as to whether Morgenthau actually visited the State Department. Late on March 27 he did send a written note to Hull, citing numerous anti-Argentine statements made by the secretary of state in the past and urging an immediate freeze.[49]

As in the past, Treasury officials were aided and abetted in their struggle with the State Department by Henry Wallace. Although BEW had been abolished in July 1943, Wallace remained deeply interested in the Argentine situation. He continued to refer to the Argentine government as a "nest of fascists" and as a tool of Nazi foreign policy. The ultimate objective of Argentine expansionism, he told President Alfonso López of Colombia in January 1944, was the acquisition of the raw materials of southern South America for the Third Reich.[50] Wallace and his advisors were convinced that the State Department's soft line toward Argentina was due in part to its sympathy with the military-Catholic-landowner coalition which dominated Latin American politics and which was now throwing its support to Farrell and Perón, just as "conservative Germany and conservative Italy" had opted for Hitler and Mussolini.[51] Revelations in early 1944 that Breckinridge Long had been blocking efforts to rescue Jewish refugees from occupied Europe aroused suspicions that anti-Semitism might also have something to do with America's "appeasement" of Argentina.[52] Thus, alarmed at the state of affairs in South America, certain that the State Department leadership was thoroughly reactionary, and still smarting over Jones's and Hull's successful vendetta against BEW, Wallace throughout 1944 harangued Chief of Staff George Marshall, President Roosevelt, and other administration figures about the dangers of Argentine expansionism, the impotency of State Department policies, and the need for an immediate freeze.[53]

The most the State Department would agree to do was to invite an opinion from Armour.[54] The ambassador's views on freezing had changed since 1943. Prompted in large part by continuing interference with embassy operations on the part of officials from the Treasury and FEA, Armour was once again adamantly opposed to a total blockage of funds. His views were, no doubt, well known to Hull and his associates. On May 5 the secretary cabled Buenos Aires "that the Secretary of the Treasury has again urged, and I am seriously considering, the desirability of subjecting Argentina to a general Treasury freeze similar to the one proposed last January."[55] The next day, Armour flatly rejected the scheme, terming it superficial and counterproductive.

Morgenthau brought the simmering feud between himself and Hull, the Treasury and State departments, to a head on May 10 by announcing to

Hull that he had a responsibility to communicate his views on freezing in writing to the President. As Morgenthau put it in a subsequent conversation with one of his subordinates, that "was like lighting a match to a powder keg."[56] Freezing, declared Hull, who had for one of the few times in his life lost complete control of himself, was an obsession with Morgenthau, an obsession that had gotten the United States into trouble more than once in the past:

> That is the trouble with you. You always want that [freezing]. That is what you wanted in the case of Japan. You are completely wrong. If we had followed what you had done, we would have been in the war right away. . . . You wanted to freeze the Japanese. It is going to come out in the future! You were all wrong. The Army wasn't ready, and the Navy, and we have been called, and that is going to come out.[57]

Morgenthau, who never needed an excuse to bait Hull, retorted by accusing the State Department of supplying the Japanese with the scrap iron and aviation fuel with which to fight the war.[58] On the afternoon following this stormy interview, the Treasury Department officially requested the White House to intercede and to allow it to freeze Argentine assets in the United States. "We can win the battle of Europe and the Pacific," Morgenthau wrote to FDR, "and find that we have lost the war, or what we were fighting for, in our own backyard, i.e., a Fascist Latin America."[59]

Roosevelt responded to the Treasury Department's request during the cabinet meeting of May 18. To Morgenthau's chagrin, FDR rejected a freezing order on the grounds that Argentine shipments of raw materials were too vital to the war effort to endanger and that Brazil was strong enough to contain Argentine expansionism. Humiliated, Morgenthau withdrew.[60] This marked both the last attempt by the Treasury Department to leapfrog the State Department and the last serious effort to obtain a comprehensive freezing order. From the summer of 1944 on, Morgenthau was preoccupied with plans for postwar Germany, and he wanted to do nothing that would reduce his influence in this area.[61]

Despite their adamant opposition to confiscation of Argentine assets in the United States, the internationalists were not opposed to economic sanctions per se. As has been noted, their objections to freezing stemmed both from fear that, if implemented, it would give the Treasury Department a large degree of control over Argentine policy and from resentment over the fact that Morgenthau had twice gone over Hull to the White House.[62] An economic embargo of Argentina offered no such bureaucratic threat. Moreover, to their minds, economic nonintercourse appeared to be consistent with nonrecognition; it promised to exert a great deal more pressure on the Farrell regime than freezing would; and it enjoyed a precedent in the diplomacy of Woodrow Wilson.

In their attempt to interdict all Allied trade with the Argentine, the internationalists enjoyed—perhaps "endured" would be more apt—the support of their principal bureaucratic rivals. The Treasury Department and Vice-President Wallace were strong backers of an embargo. Wallace, who had taken a much-publicized tour of Latin America in 1943, told Treasury officials in March 1944 that, given the threat to peace and democracy in Latin America posed by the Farrell-Perón regime, the Allies should make whatever sacrifices were necessary in order to isolate Argentina economically.[63] Morgenthau was in wholehearted agreement. Over lunch with Marvin Jones, the war food administrator, who adamantly opposed sanctions for fear they would eliminate Argentina as a source of food, and Wallace, the secretary of the treasury expressed disgust with those who were not willing to pull in "our protruding belt one little notch" and declared that if "the President gave him the job of seeing this thing through [the embargo] he would see to it that the British stopped shipping food from Argentina, even if he had to blockade Argentine ports."[64] Jones, whose primary concern was supply, was not enthusiastic. Shortly thereafter, the vice-president proposed buying up British investments in Argentina—all $1.3 billion worth —and reselling them to the Argentineans in return for concessions in the political and diplomatic sphere.[65] Because they believed that Hull was dragging his feet on the matter of an embargo, Wallace and Morgenthau at one point schemed to have Tom Connally, chairman of the Senate Foreign Relations Committee, "put a little heat on the Secretary of State."[66]

In addition, congressional and public support for sanctions increased markedly during 1944. Emanuel Celler of New York proclaimed: "We should blockade the ports of Argentina, embargo essential gasoline, and terminate a most lucrative export trade of hides, corn, meat, and wheat. The Farrell-Peron militarist-Fascist government would then collapse." Even the usually cautious *New York Times* was calling for all-out economic warfare by July. Added belt-tightening, according to the editors, would surely result in the calling of elections and the turning out of the Farrell government.[67]

In opposition, however, were a wide variety of organizations and agencies whose sole concern was Allied victory on the battlefield. Not the least of these was the Combined Chiefs of Staff. As early as 1 February 1944, this highest of Allied military bodies notified the State Department that the cessation of purchases of meat, wheat, and leather from Argentina would have "serious military implications."[68] Military authorities remained adamantly opposed to sanctions throughout the remainder of the war, and despite Morgenthau's comment that the Chiefs of Staff were totally incompetent when it came to economic warfare, their views carried a great deal of weight with FDR and Harry Hopkins.

Adding their voices to those of Allied military authorities were various combined boards that were responsible for fueling the Allied war effort in Europe. The State Department began a drive to gain the support of these agencies as early as January 1944, when Hull and his associates were considering a cessation of trade in connection with the Bolivian coup. At that point and periodically throughout the rest of the year, the State Department asked what and how much the United Nations proposed to buy from Argentina in 1944, how the liberated areas would figure in such purchases, what foregoing Argentina as a source of raw materials would cost Allied civilian populations and military forces, and how long the Allies could endure without Argentine products.[69]

Replies from the combined boards gave no encouragement whatsoever to advocates of an embargo. The United Nations' dependence on Argentina was high, reported the Combined Food Board in January 1944, and of so vital a nature that the Board "would regard with the gravest apprehension the cessation of Argentine supplies." The agency's recommendation was unambiguous: "We know of no political possibility of meeting the position which would be created by their withdrawal."[70] Submitting a supplementary report in April, the food authorities noted that two conditions had changed: world food demands had increased, and the United Kingdom had undertaken new commitments to the Supreme Commander of the Allied Expeditionary Forces, General Eisenhower. As a result, (1) food consumption was at a level in Great Britain below which the British government would not allow it to fall; (2) there could be no further cuts in United Kingdom quotas if commitments to the Supreme Commander were to be met; and (3) the United States members had received specific instructions from the president to use the board's resources to meet the heavy relief demands from devastated areas.[71]

The Combined Raw Materials Board was equally as pessimistic. Rationing of boots and shoes was in effect in both the United States and Great Britain; loss of the Argentine supply would result in an end to domestic supplies in both nations. The agency's objections to an embargo became even more strident in March when the White House notified United States delegates to the raw-materials agency that relief and rehabilitation requirements were to be regarded as equally important with maintaining the economies of the other members of the United Nations and the Associated Nations.[72]

Shipping authorities asserted that the balance between the requirements of the European theater and the tonnage that was available did not leave a sufficient margin to take care of the increase in distances that would result if purchases from the Argentineans were cut off. The board informed Acheson that it refused to assume responsibility for any resulting shortages.[73]

All relevant inter-Allied agencies, in short, judged that Argentine exports were essential to the Anti-Axis Alliance's war effort, vital to the British economy, and extremely important to United States consumers. With the steady increase in wartime devastation and with the expansion of the area of liberation, the situation could only worsen.

As in 1942 and 1943, however, Great Britain was the chief impediment to the imposition of economic sanctions. Typical of British arguments in favor of restraint toward Argentina was that put forward by Neville Butler, undersecretary for North and South America, in a conversation with a member of the United States embassy in London. Using language reminiscent of Welles and Duggan, Butler asserted that the current Argentine regime was an extreme nationalistic-militaristic government rather than Fascist in the commonly accepted sense. Extreme pressure from abroad would only accentuate this nationalism and "make heroes of certain individuals." He predicted that if the Farrell regime were overthrown, it would surely be replaced by a more intransigent one.[74] The British generally agreed with this point of view. A July editorial in the *Economist* blasted the idea of Anglo-American cooperation in economic sanctions. United States–British collusion in a drive to topple the present Argentine regime would "greatly antagonize the Argentines who are rightly sensitive about their sovereignty."[75]

The key commodity in Anglo-American discussions concerning economic sanctions was meat. Britain's desire to augment its political influence in South America and a determination to protect British investments in Argentina were the prime considerations behind British policy; but Whitehall, for obvious reasons, chose to center its arguments on the importance of Argentine beef to the British public and to Allied armies in Europe. When Whitehall was pleading with Washington to forego economic sanctions in connection with the Bolivian coup, Churchill cabled Roosevelt: "I beg you to look into the formidable consequences which would follow our losing their hides, meats, and other supplies. We get from them one-third of our meat supply. If this is cut out, how are we to feed ourselves plus the American Army for Overlord?"[76]

The internationalists accepted beef as the most important consideration in any program of economic sanctions, not because of its importance to the Allied war effort or to Britain's nutritional well-being, but because it was Argentina's chief export. Hull, Long, Spaeth, and the other hard-liners suspected throughout the war that Whitehall was overstressing Britain's dependence on Argentine meat and that that nation was quite capable of enduring any shortages that might result from a cessation of trade with Argentina. In March 1944, officials of the United States Mission for Economic Affairs in London advised the secretary of state that Whitehall had been underestimating its meat stockpiles to the amount of some 300,000 tons and that, in their opinion, British attitudes toward a beef embargo were at best "cautious."[77] On March 5, Stettinius told Morgenthau that the State Department had found that the statistics that the combined boards had given to it regarding supply reserves were generally inaccurate.[78] Thenceforth, the internationalists operated on the assumption that British representatives had hopelessly prejudiced the findings of the Combined Boards and that the United Kingdom could reasonably be expected to forego Argentine meat for a period necessary to bring the Farrell government down.

Hull and his associates decided to use the Anglo-American diplomatic conferences scheduled for April to approach the British once again. When, at that conclave, Stettinius pressed Foreign Secretary Anthony Eden to commit the Churchill government to an embargo, Eden informed the undersecretary that the imposition of sanctions would be very difficult for his country but that Britain would go along if the United States would give the proper guarantees on shipping and supply problems. These the State Department simply could not provide.[79]

Morgenthau and Wallace urged the State Department to appeal to FDR to exert pressure on the British, but Hull, Stettinius, and their associates believed that the opponents of an embargo both in London and Washington were still too strong to risk a direct confrontation. The State Department's estimate of the situation proved to be entirely correct. At the May 18 cabinet meeting at which FDR quashed the Treasury Department's request for a freeze, the president also shunted aside Morgenthau's demand for an embargo. "Henry wants to apply sanctions," Roosevelt told Stettinius, "but you can't do that on account of the English, and the food. . . . Ed, you make a bad face at the Argentineans once a week. You have to treat them like children."[80]

By the summer of 1944, however, Hull and his colleagues believed it was pointless to wait any longer. It was obvious that the British were not going to accept Washington's view of the Argentine affair voluntarily. More importantly, by mid 1944, State Department officials were convinced that London was plotting to incorporate Latin America into its strategic defenses as well as make it the cornerstone of its postwar economic empire. For example, beginning in June, Washington frantically sought comprehensive airbase agreements with the Vargas regime and other American governments. "The necessity for covering the situation," Berle told Hull, "is increased by the very active British operations now going forward for surveying bases and routes allegedly for use by the R.A.F. in transporting men and material to the Far East after the war, but which are very obviously undertaken with longer range objectives in mind."[81]

In addition, Britain was in the midst of negotiating a long-term meat contract with Argentina which, if concluded, would end any chance of instituting an effective program of economic nonintercourse. On July 15 the secretary of state called at 1600 Pennsylvania Avenue and urged Roosevelt to persuade Churchill to use Britain's buying power in the Argentine export market "to let Argentina know beyond a doubt that we are all fed up with the pro-Axis sentiments and practices of her government."[82] The president refused to ask Churchill to forego a meat agreement[83] and would consent only to request the British to show their disfavor in some manner that would not threaten the Allied war effort or Anglo-American consumers.[84]

In frustration the internationalists decided to implement a unilateral intensification of economic warfare against the Farrell-Perón government. In August, Hull ordered a reduction of forty to sixty-five percent in all United States imports from Argentina. At the same time he refused a request from the Caribbean Defense Command that United States export policy toward Argentina be revised in order to allow airplane parts to be shipped to that country. Later in the month the State Department established the Inter-Departmental Economic Committee on Argentina, which had as its primary objective the coordination of economic sanctions against that country.[85] Protests from sectors of the American business community that were dependent on Argentine trade had no impact whatsoever on Hull and his colleagues. As a memorandum from Spaeth to Long on the subject clearly indicates,[86] preservation of America's economic empire in Latin America did not at that point top the State Department's list of priorities:

> There is a disposition to resist an affirmative stand, to seek to carry on "business as usual," and to be governed primarily by the possibility of postwar trade benefits in Argentina. Such thinking recalls only too clearly the attitude toward Germany and Italy in the months before the War.[87]

Unilateral attempts at economic constriction proved as fruitless as they had in 1942 and 1943. Argentina continued to prosper. Consequently, as Anglo-Argentine meat negotiations drew ever closer to a successful completion, Hull became desperate. In mid September he informed Lord Halifax that if the Fascist threat in Argentina grew and began to threaten the rest of Latin America, the repercussions could be quite severe for Great Britain. If worst came to worst, the United States would feel compelled to publish all the facts about Britain's reluctance to cooperate in bringing Argentina into line. FDR, Hull informed the ambassador, felt that His Majesty's government could furnish full cooperation without endangering their meat supply and that they could exert great influence as the purchasing party in a buyer's market. He concluded the talk with the gratuitous observation that British officials were unduly apprehensive about the loss of Argentine beef because they had made only a superficial study of the matter.[88] Shortly thereafter, the United States embassy in London informed Whitehall that until the United States could discern more clearly Britain's export-import policy toward Argentina, the State Department would feel obligated to withhold equipment needed to facilitate Argentine exports to the United Kingdom.[89] Finally, on October 10, Hull instructed Ambassador Winant to make it clear to Eden that the United Kingdom was contributing to the survival of a state that was "working feverishly" to subvert the independence of its neighbors, while at the same time it served as a New World refuge for Nazi technicians, economists, and military personnel.[90]

At the last possible moment an extremely annoyed Churchill capitulated by agreeing to delay six months before signing a comprehensive meat contract with Argentina. Nevertheless, he warned Roosevelt and Hull, Whitehall would honor this pledge only on the condition that the United States keep all other buyers out of the Argentine meat market.[91]

Actually, Churchill's pledge was meaningless, because British purchases in Argentina not only continued but increased. Moreover, London let Buenos Aires know that it would resume negotiations on a comprehensive agreement at the earliest possible date.[92] As a result, phase two of Washington's trade-restriction offensive was no more effective than the 1943 campaign had been. The *Wall Street Journal* ran an extensive survey of South America in late 1944 which reported that Argentina was the best-fed country in the world. Clothing was plentiful, housing was adequate, transportation was good, and prices were low. "There have been fewer interferences with the individual's freedom to move from place to place," the *Journal* reported, "to buy what he wants when he wants it; to work when and as he pleases. . . . There has been less interference in the conduct of private business, and there have been fewer labor altercations and disturbances."[93] Argentina was definitely not in a revolutionary state of mind.

In retrospect, one of the key factors in the State Department's failure to persuade Britain to cooperate in economic sanctions was Roosevelt's consistent refusal to make up Britain's loss of meat supplies out of stockpiles earmarked for consumption in the United States. Nineteen forty-four was an election year, and the White House was convinced that the electorate would retaliate against the administration at the polls for the ten percent cut in meat rations which any diversion to England would necessitate. Ironically, the internationalists' program of economic coercion against Argentina, motivated in part by a desire to reduce domestic criticism of the White House, was sabotaged by a president who was convinced that the political cost of such a program would be prohibitive.

All the while that Hull, Long, Spaeth, and Wendelin were maneuvering to avoid one kind of economic sanction and to implement another, the State Department continued to avoid formal diplomatic contact with the Farrell government. As the Latin Americanists had predicted, nonrecognition did not weaken the Farrell regime in Argentina, and more importantly, it hindered Washington in its pursuit of America's long-range goals in the hemisphere. The internationalists believed that in announcing nonrecognition on March 4, they would create irresistible pressure on the other states of the hemisphere to join in isolating Buenos Aires. It quickly became apparent that Hull and his colleagues had sadly miscalculated. By March 9 Chile, Paraguay, and Bolivia had established relations with Argentina. Of those who agreed to support the North American position, only Costa Rica, the Dominican Republic, El Salvador, Haiti, Nicaragua, and Panama assented to Washington's request that they make public statements denouncing the Farrell regime. Uruguay, the object of intense pressure from her neighbor across the Plata, notified the State Department that she could not hold out for long.[94] Brazil, which welcomed as a sign of weakness every new change of government in Buenos Aires, perceived no threat in the Farrell regime. While Foreign Minister Oswaldo Aranha fended off United States demands that Rio join the nonrecognition front, leading Brazilian newspapers abounded with expressions of friendship for Argentina.[95] Typical of these journals was *O Globo*, which repeatedly voiced its desire that the "recent misunderstanding" between the United States and Argentina could soon be resolved.[96] Even Mexico, certainly one of America's staunchest wartime supporters, refused to lend unconditional support. On March 7 Foreign Minister Ezequiel Padilla informed Washington that because of a lack of information, he could not make a public statement denouncing the Farrell government. The longer the difficulties with Argentina dragged on, he warned the United States ambassador, George Messersmith, the harder they would be to resolve.[97]

Argentine propagandists proved quite successful in 1943–44 in exploiting popular discontent within various pro-Allied republics that resulted from rationing, shortages, and various other material discomforts caused by the war. Argentine prosperity was much on the minds of his countrymen, Brazil's Ambassador Carlos Martins told Berle in January 1944. Argentines had made steady capital out of the "ease and luxury of their own life . . . and ascribed it to the fact that they were neutral while others had been fools enough to join the war effort." Martins complained bitterly that Washington was taking its Latin allies for granted. The United States was refusing to provide the steel, tin plate, and machinery necessary to maintain Brazil's economy at merely prewar levels and, in so doing, was contributing to Argentina's drive to win the hemisphere to neutrality. During 1944, then, the Vargas regime and a number of other Latin governments were beginning to question whether blind acquiescence in Washington's anti-Argentine campaign really served their interests. A more "independent" course might compel the Roosevelt administration to be more sensitive to the needs of its cobelligerents.[98]

Too, many *latinos* believed that both the objectives and the tactics of America's Argentine policy represented a throwback to the not-so-distant past, when the United States treated the hemispheric republics as retarded wards. In the first place, Latin America had historically defined the withholding of recognition from an existing government as diplomatic intervention into the affairs of another state. In 1930 Mexico's foreign minister, Manuel Estrada, announced that henceforth Mexico would simply "maintain or recall, when it is deemed appropriate, its diplomatic officials in other countries, and accept . . . the diplomatic officials accredited in Mexico, without passing judgment . . . on the right which other nations have to accept, maintain, or replace their government or authorities."[99] The Estrada Doctrine was, of course, a reaction to the then prevailing United States policy of refusing to recognize other American governments which, in its opinion, were not legally constituted, and it was designed to provoke Washington into foreswearing the use of such a coercive tactic. After the inauguration of the Good Neighbor Policy, New Deal diplomats accepted the Estrada interpretation and assured the hemispheric community that henceforth America would recognize New World governments purely on a de facto basis.[100] Not surprisingly, a number of Latin states believed that Washington's nonrecognition of the Farrell regime constituted a repudiation of the Estrada Doctrine, a change of policy that was not justified by a threat to the peace and security of the hemisphere. Perhaps even more offensive to the *latinos* than the policy of nonintercourse was the fact that Washington had proceeded unilaterally, thus vitiating the principle of consultation upon which the Inter-American System rested. Finally, during 1944 most Latin Americans came to the conclusion that the Farrell government posed no threat to the Allied war effort and that the State Department's primary objective was democratization of the Argentine political system, a goal that they believed to be beyond the proper scope of United States foreign policy. Increasingly, the Latin republics saw in North America's coercion of Argentina the setting of a number of precedents that would pose a potential threat to their own national sovereignty.[101] These considerations, voiced frequently by prominent *latinos* and, before their departure in July, the Latin Americanists, had no impact on the State Department's leadership.

In view of the pervasiveness of Argentine nationalism and the presence of such ultranationalists as Perlinger in the cabinet, Farrell and Perón could hardly have moved toward a more conciliatory position after the State Department instituted its policy of denunciation and nonrecognition, even if they had wished to do so. Instead, Argentina began to retaliate. In early March the minister of the interior demanded of All-America Cables—the Anglo-American company that provided Argentina with international cable service—that all communiques from the United States embassy be delivered first to the Argentine Foreign Office. When the company refused, the government closed All-America for twenty-four hours and imposed an embargo on AP and UPI for sending uncensored dispatches.[102] The government began disseminating rumors that it was going to nationalize foreign interests as a penalty for nonrecognition, rumors that soon became reality.[103] After expropriating a portion of the American and Foreign Power Co., Perlinger ordered seizure of the East Argentine Electric Company.[104] By preying on unprotected American and British interests, the government hoped to bring home to the State Department the disadvantages of nonrecognition.

Instead, these and other acts of economic retribution, coupled with two events that transpired in June, prompted the State Department to withdraw its ambassador from Buenos Aires, further reducing the opportunity for communication and thus reconciliation. The first of these events concerned a secret meeting between Armour and key figures in the Farrell regime. By mid May the Latin American states within the nonrecognition camp began to grow extremely restive. A number of republics let the State Department know that they wanted to establish relations with the Farrell government before May 25, Argentine National Independence Day.[105] Pointing out that the United States still recognized such neutrals as Iceland, Switzerland, and Spain, they questioned the validity of continued nonintercourse with the

Farrell government and warned that it would be a grave insult to the Argentine people not to attend the official functions scheduled in connection with the nation's birthday. The State Department's refusal to consent intensified hemispheric demands for a rapprochement. Complaining that pressure from the other American representatives in Buenos Aires was growing stronger, Armour cabled Hull on June 16, asking for permission, for appearance's sake if nothing else, to enter into secret talks with Orlando Peluffo, the Argentine foreign minister. When Hull reluctantly agreed, Armour proceeded with the covert conference.[106] The ambassador was received not only by Peluffo but by Perón and the former ambassador to the United States, Felipe Espil, as well. The Argentineans opened the discussion by accusing the United States of employing crude pressure tactics, citing Admiral Ingram's trip to Montevideo as an example, and they warned that the government could cope with any economic sanctions that Britain and the United States might impose. On the positive side, Perón, Peluffo, and Espil promised that in return for normalization of relations, the Casa Rosada would cut off all aid to pro-Axis firms and newspapers and would fully implement a break in relations with the Axis.[107] The meeting came to an abrupt halt, however, when Peluffo informed Armour that to avoid the appearance of foreign pressure, the United States would have to recognize Argentina before Argentina would take any further steps to comply with Washington's wishes.[108] The entire episode infuriated the State Department, which regarded it as a ploy designed to create the appearance of recognition.

No less upsetting to the internationalists than the Armour-Peluffo encounter was a highly publicized, ultrachauvinistic speech delivered by Juan Perón at the University of La Plata on June 10. Although it did not become apparent until late 1944, Perón favored a rapprochement with the United States. As World War II ground toward a successful conclusion, the colonel saw that if the nation were to break out of its existing isolation and were to play an active role in the postwar world, Buenos Aires would have to seek accommodation with Washington.[109] In June, however, the man who was to dominate Argentina politics for a generation had not yet regained the confidence of the integral nationalists, a group that he felt he had to win over before he could embark on any new, dramatic schemes or international initiatives. Many of his former colleagues in the GOU distrusted his ties with organized labor and his views on international affairs. Argentina, he proclaimed to the graduating class at La Plata, had to rededicate itself to the principle of national defense. The victorious powers in the present conflict, whoever they might be, would surely fall out among themselves and would probably "attempt to establish in the world an odious imperialism which will obligate the oppressed to rebel." The power of Argentina's armed forces must be increased, he asserted, "in order to ensure the respect and consideration it [Argentina] deserves in the world concert and in the family of nations."[110] He called for long-range planning and total mobilization to prepare the nation for the coming struggle. The speech was a political gambit. Industrial and military leaders welcomed Perón's theme of ensuring peace by preparing for war, while the integral nationalists were gleeful over what they perceived to be a veiled threat to the United States.[111]

Analyses of the address by military intelligence, as well as the speech itself, confirmed the Hull group's conviction that the Farrell government represented the same faction that had plotted the overthrow of the Bolivian government in the last days of 1943. A report from the Office of Strategic Services entitled "The Significance of Perón's Speech of June 10" stated that the minister of war and labor had called for

> the scrapping of the present hemispheric system of peaceful consultation and the substitution of power politics based on armed force. It also confirms . . . that the guiding principle and major factor holding the Farrell regime together had been preparation for military action in support of a program of economic and territorial expansion aimed at giving Argentina political and economic control of its neighbors and eventual hegemony over the entire South American continent.[112]

This document, given wide credence by the internationalists, even hinted that the author of the La Plata address was not Perón but a highly placed Nazi official.[113]

In response to the abortive Peluffo-Armour talks, to Perón's speech,[114] and to the demands made by Morgenthau, Wallace, and Crowley, the State Department persuaded the White House to recall Armour, pressured the British into withdrawing their ambassador from Buenos Aires,[115] and delivered the tirade against Argentina that had been planned for release on January 25. On June 22 the secretary of state announced to all diplomatic representatives of the United States in the Western Hemisphere that since the Farrell government had continually denied the relevance of hemispheric defense commitments and since, by repeatedly insisting that the rupture was due to foreign pressure, it had implicitly disavowed any intention to honor its obligations, Ambassador Norman Armour was being recalled.[116] Meanwhile, the president, at the behest of the State Department, ordered the Joint Chiefs of Staff to make all necessary preparations to defend Paraguay, Uruguay, or any other state that was vulnerable to an attack by Argentina.[117] On July 26 the secretary of state delivered one of the strongest verbal blasts ever leveled at a nation with which the United States was not at war. It was abundantly clear, he proclaimed in a press release, that Argentina "has deliberately violated the pledge taken jointly with its sister republics to cooperate in support of the war against the Axis . . . and has openly and notoriously been giving affirmative assistance to the declared enemies of the United Nations." Turning to United States policy, he declared that to recognize Argentina then would be "seriously to damage the Allied cause" and would undermine hemispheric and wartime principles. What was more, the pro-Axis and totalitarian elements that dominated Argentina had thoroughly suppressed the basic civil rights of the Argentine citizenry. On the basis of both its domestic and foreign policies, therefore, the clique then holding forth in Buenos Aires was beyond the pale.[118]

As had been true so often in the past, those in control of Argentine affairs were able to use the State Department's intemperate blasts to rally public support for the government and to create a ground swell of anti-Americanism. Government censors permitted domestic papers to carry full texts of the press release, while Buenos Aires recalled Ambassador Escobar from Washington.[119] *La Nación* and *El Mundo* ran editorials on June 27 in support of the government in general and Perón in particular. Claiming that Argentina had steadfastly supported the Allies, they argued that their country, by standing up to the United States, was defending not only its own sovereignty but that of free states everywhere.[120] *La Prensa*, the great prodemocratic and pro-Allied daily of Buenos Aires, scored Hull's indictments as unfounded and denounced his habit of discussing weighty international problems in "impromptu declarations to the press." With America's entire policy of nonintercourse no doubt in mind, the editors advised Washington that diplomacy should be conducted by direct personal contact between diplomats, not by means of news releases.[121] Not since the war began had the Argentine nation been so unified.

Increasingly convinced that the Argentine problem was simply a bilateral squabble between Washington and Buenos Aires, a number of Latin American states attempted during the summer and fall of 1944 to mediate between the two. In July the Paraguayan and Uruguayan ambassadors called on Hull and urged him to outline publicly the steps that Argentina must take in order to elicit recognition.[122] Shortly thereafter, the Peruvian representative in Washington arranged an interview at the State Department, during which he asked what he and his country could do to bring Buenos Aires and Washington closer together.[123] In early September the foreign minister of the Dominican Republic, a nation that was virtually immune to direct pressure from Argentine, called on Breckinridge Long and pushed for the presentation of specific terms to Buenos Aires. The present situation, he declared, was only strengthening the hand of the extreme nationalists within Argentina.[124]

Although it did not dare offer its services as an intermediary, Whitehall tacitly supported the Latin drive to break the Argentine-American impasse. The British had agreed to withdraw their representative from Buenos Aires, but they did so grudgingly. United States policy had caused great "anxiety" in the War Cabinet and the Foreign Office, Churchill wrote Roosevelt after an appeal for Ambassador Kelly's recall. Asserting that he could not see where United States tactics were leading or what Washington hoped to gain, the prime minister expressed the hope that coercion of Argentina would not injure either vital Anglo-American interests in Argentina or the war effort in Europe. What was more, he complained, "This American decision [has] placed us in an invidious position, having been taken without consultation with us. . . . We were faced with a *fait accompli*."[125]

Latinos who were disgusted with the State Department's hard-line approach to inter-American affairs also received vigorous support from Sumner Welles. By January 1944 the former undersecretary's columns on foreign affairs were appearing not only in papers across the United States but in journals throughout Latin America, including *La Nación* of Buenos Aires.[126] In late May he came out strongly for recognition of the Farrell regime and told his readers that attempts to change existing Latin governments through nonrecognition would inevitably stimulate the nationalist movements that were already burgeoning south of the Rio Grande. The State Department's attempts to establish a pro–United States puppet regime in Buenos Aires, he warned, would only earn the unremitting hostility of the Argentine people.[127] As of 25 June 1944, the Casa Rosada required all federally subsidized newspapers and radio stations to carry Welles's re-marks.[128] In September the former undersecretary presided over a secret meeting of Latin American officials at his home in Bar Harbor, Maine. The discussion centered on the need for an inter-American conference on postwar problems and on the state of Argentine-American relations. News of the conclave prompted Hull to complain bitterly to Stimson and Morgenthau that Welles "seemed to be operating a second State Department."[129]

In the face of this criticism and the attempts by various Latin republics to mediate, Hull and his associates clung ever more firmly to nonrecognition and attempted to coerce into submission those states that objected to Wash-ington's tactics.[130] Both the pressure applied to dissenting members of the hemispheric community and the rhetoric that accompanied it once again revealed the degree to which the Argentine problem had come to over-shadow all other considerations. Chile, which had steadfastly refused to sever relations with the Farrell government, hoped, despite its refusal to join in the nonrecognition front, to improve relations with the United States during 1944. The State Department responded to Chilean initiatives by denouncing that nation's "collaboration" with Buenos Aires. When, in March, Chilean officials inquired about the possibility of having President Rios visit the United States, Hull indicated that he would be welcome only after his country had reversed itself on the Argentine matter. Shortly thereafter the secretary confided to the United States ambassador to Chile: "While the Chilean people have given constant indications of their wholehearted sym-pathy for our cause . . . I cannot honestly say that the record of the Chilean government impresses me in an equally favorable light."[131]

Other states that urged Washington to settle its differences with Buenos Aires encountered threats of economic coercion. When on July 12 the Bolivian chargé d'affaires, whose government still maintained relations with the Farrell regime, offered Bolivia's services as mediator, Hull blew up. If La Paz equivocated much longer, the secretary declared, the United States would make permanent arrangements for acquiring its tin supplies from Indochina rather than from the mines of Bolivia.[132]

Just as they had come to equate Argentine neutrality with a pro-Axis posture, the internationalists in the summer and fall of 1944 began to view diplomatic intercourse with the Farrell government as a form of aid to the Rome-Berlin-Tokyo coalition. On July 1, State Department officials told the Chilean representative in Washington that if the republics then abjuring relations with Buenos Aires were to reverse themselves and recognize the Farrell regime, then they would be "paying her a premium for her desertion and treason." "It is manifestly impossible," he continued, "to give full support to the Allied cause while at the same time giving strength and vigor to the Argentine Government while it supports the cause of Hitler and Germany. . . . Thus to aid the Argentine Government is to aid the Axis powers in the present War."[133] Moreover, Washington argued that to enter into diplomatic relations with Argentina would be to reward a state for violating its international obligations and thus would undermine the principle of collective security upon which the peace and security of the postwar world was to rest. Now was the time, Hull told Halifax in late August, "to develop a tradition of respect for such obligations among civilized nations. . . . Only by persisting in a firm collective policy can we develop a real and practical sense of international responsibility, not only among governments but also among peoples."[134]

The Argentine-American dispute was only one of a number of problems that Latin diplomats believed the hemisphere needed to solve before the end of World War II. The Latin American republics were disturbed about being excluded from the major diplomatic conferences of the war, particularly the meeting held at Dumbarton Oaks in the fall of 1944 to discuss the creation of a world organization.[135] An increasing number of *latinos* hoped to strengthen the Inter-American System in order that it might serve as a bastion against communism,[136] a restraint on North American imperialism, and a device for enhancing the hemisphere's unity and influence within the new world organization.[137] In addition, a majority wanted to commit the United States to a transition from wartime to peacetime purchasing programs in Latin America that would not disrupt the fragile economies of the region. As always, they looked to North American capital and technical assistance to facilitate industrialization and thus to drive living standards upward.[138] The desire south of the Rio Grande for a general inter-American conference to solve these and related problems was, by late 1944, virtually universal.

Hoping to take advantage of the rising discontent in Latin America and the widespread desire for a hemispheric conference, on October 30 the Farrell-Perón government officially requested the Governing Board of the Pan American Union to hold an inter-American meeting in order to consider Argentina's situation in relation to the rest of the hemisphere. While emphasizing the righteousness of its cause, Buenos Aires proclaimed that Argentina was willing to go an extra mile to achieve reconciliation. The Farrell government maintained that the systematic consultation outside a formal conference engaged in by the rest of the hemisphere in connection with nonrecognition would constitute a violation of Pan-Americanism as defined at Lima, and it argued that only a full-dress consultative meeting of the PAU was qualified to formulate policy for all the Americas. The only reason that Argentina was so unselfishly submitting her international conduct to Pan-American scrutiny, declared the Foreign Office, was a desire to see that the postwar world would be established on a foundation of unity and harmony.[139]

As Buenos Aires had hoped, a number of Latin American states literally leapt to the support of the Argentine proposal. Several governments, including those of Colombia, Venezuela, and Ecuador, indicated their immediate approval of Argentina's request, arguing that Argentina could not really be denied such a meeting under the rules of the PAU.[140] Venezuela declared that Argentina was sincerely trying to make honorable amends and should be respected for subjecting itself to the judgment of the other American republics.[141] On November 6 Ezequiel Padilla of Mexico pressed the attack by suggesting to Washington that when Argentina's request came before the Governing Board, the Mexican ambassador would propose a foreign ministers' meeting to discuss general subjects. At the same time he would also move a delay of two or three months during which Argentina would have an opportunity to reincorporate itself into the hemispheric family. Asserting that he was speaking not only for his own government but for the ambassadors of Brazil, Cuba, and Uruguay, the Mexican foreign minister implied that reincorporation of Argentina into the hemispheric fold should be the goal of each member of the American community. He made it clear that if Buenos Aires were to comply with conditions to be established by the nonrecognizing governments, then the Farrell government should be accorded recognition and a seat at the forthcoming meeting of foreign ministers.[142]

The Argentine initiative and Latin America's response threw the State Department into a momentary state of confusion. There was no question as to what attitude to adopt toward the Farrell government's proposal. Throughout 1944 the internationalists had adamantly opposed the calling of an inter-American meeting. Not only had it been a pet project of the Welles-Duggan-Bonsal group,[143] but more importantly, Hull and his associates feared that Argentina would be able to use any such conclave to escape from its diplomatic isolation without having to institute the proper "reforms."[144] Furthermore, the internationalists, in addition to a number of others within the Roosevelt foreign-policy establishment, opposed the holding of a hemispheric conference prior to the United Nations Conference of International Organization (UNCIO), scheduled for April 1945, for fear that the Latin American republics would insist on amending the Dumbarton Oaks proposals so as to preserve the sanctity of regional arrangements such as the Inter-American System.[145] Such reservations would, United States diplomats feared, hamstring the unborn world organization by making it less than a collective-security system or by alienating the Russians, or both. The way in which the State Department reacted to the Argentine request indicates that of these factors the most important to the internationalists was the possibility that Argentina might secure readmittance as a full-fledged member of the hemispheric community.[146] Hull was absent from the State Department due to illness—the secretary was sick and away from the department between 30 and 40 percent of the time in 1943 and 1944—when Padilla's suggestion was received.[147] Nevertheless, Long, Spaeth, and Wendelin were present to combat any attempt at "appeasement."

The State Department sought to foil the Farrell government's machination by first giving way on the issue of a foreign ministers' meeting to discuss general problems and then holding fast against reincorporation of Argentina into the hemispheric fold. The immediate problem, however, was to prevent any additional Latin American republics from publicly declaring their support for the Argentine proposition. On October 28 Washington reminded the Latin American governments that the states of the hemisphere must reach a consensus before an answer could be given to the Farrell government.[148] The next day the internationalists expressed their view of the Argentine initiative in no uncertain terms. "It is our judgment," RPA informed the United States chargé d'affaires in Mexico City, "that the Argentine proposal is a brazen and insincere move which does not deserve consideration on its merits." The Farrell regime was well aware of what it needed to do to regain grace. A conference on Argentina would only provide Buenos Aires with another opportunity to make meaningless pledges, and "the American republics would certainly not accord recognition at a meeting on the basis of a mere promise of future performance."[149] By November 11, however, Stettinius, Long, Spaeth, Armour, and their subordinates had decided that they were going to have to make some concessions lest a full-scale revolt should erupt.[150] After Padilla put forth his proposal on November 6 and again on the ninth, Breckinridge Long, with White House approval, suggested to the foreign minister that he push for a consultative meeting on war and postwar problems, including the creation of a hemispheric collective-security organization. If they wished to do so, the Argentineans could send a representative to appear at the conclusion of the regular meeting and to present the Farrell-Perón government's case for the holding of a conference to hear its problems. Under no circumstances, however, would the United States consent to the creation of a formula by which Buenos Aires could gain recognition.[151] "There is grave danger," Stettinius asserted, "in the creation of a façade of unity behind which hostile forces can work to undermine and destroy everything for which we have been fighting."[152]

Latin America was hardly placated by Washington's "compromise" plan. On November 14 Padilla called a meeting of the American ambassadors in Mexico City to discuss the Argentine situation. Ambassador Messersmith was conspicuously absent from the conference. In his report to the Latin American diplomatic corps, Padilla termed the State Department's reply to the Latin American proposals "a harsh and peremptory repetition of the irreconcilable United States position." The Peruvian ambassador spoke for many of his colleagues when he remarked that it was all very well for the United States to treat Argentina as it had, but Latin America would have to live with the Argentineans after the war was over. The group, clearly in a rebellious mood, decided that the best approach would be to take the position that the Argentine problem was a "temporary divergence" within the hemisphere and to try to solve the matter with the help of Buenos Aires.[153] Later that same day, acting as spokesman for the insurgent republics, Padilla relayed the views of his colleagues to Messersmith. There were those in the hemisphere, he declared, who felt that the United States might not be really interested in bringing Argentina back into the American fold. When the ambassador denied that such was the case, Padilla retorted that Washington could hardly object, then, to a procedure that would end Argentina's isolation.[154]

To compound the State Department's problems, the Farrell government initiated an intensive public-relations campaign both inside and outside Argentina in behalf of ending its quarantine. Government propagandists did an excellent job of creating the impression that United States attempts to exclude the Argentine from any inter-American meeting was destroying "continental solidarity."[155]

As consultations concerning the Argentine initiative proceeded during November, it became increasingly clear to all concerned that the State Department viewed the ouster of the Farrell-Perón government as an absolute prerequisite to recognition. On the seventeenth, Padilla suggested two sweeping conditions, which, if met to the satisfaction of the nonrecognizing American republics, would lead to the reincorporation of Argentina into the hemispheric fold. They were, simply: "1. The fulfilling of the commitments by the Argentine not complied with, and 2. The calling of elections." Even though the latter point would create an opportunity for a return of constitutional government to Argentina, Messersmith, reflecting the views of the hard-liners and not his own, rejected the foreign minister's terms out of hand. The United States, announced the ambassador, would insist on the holding of a foreign ministers' meeting without Argentina "as long as the present people remained in control of the government."[156] On November 21 Spaeth reiterated this view. Once again describing the Argentine government as Fascist, pro-Nazi, anti–United Nations, and expansionist, he declared that the United States would never accredit an ambassador to Buenos Aires and that it would prevent all Argentine-American commercial intercourse as long as the Farrell-Perón regime remained in power. Diplomatic and economic sanctions had "hurt and hurt badly." Recognition would only solidify the domestic power of this odious regime, and readmission to the Inter-American System would provide it a façade of unity behind which it could proceed with its plans to dominate South America. Buenos Aires, according to Spaeth and his colleagues, was trying to engineer "a Western Hemisphere Munich" and had to be stopped at all costs.[157]

Washington's unwillingness to support a hemispheric conference on war and postwar problems before the convening of the UNCIO and to at least discuss the Argentine matter at such a meeting finally persuaded the insurgent Latin American states to drop their demand for a procedure that could lead to the immediate recognition of Argentina. Colombia and Ecuador informed the State Department that while they favored a prompt public hearing for Argentina, they would gladly go along with the majority of republics which had declared in favor of the American plan.[158] Padilla, suddenly compliant again, told Messersmith that his country would formally issue a call for a conference based on the United States agenda.[159]

Although they had staved off open rebellion within the Latin American community for the moment, the hard-liners still faced a procedural problem that, if not solved, threatened to lead to inadvertent recognition of the Farrell regime. Those who had framed the charter of the Pan American Union had operated on the belief that while administrations were transitory, peoples were not. Thus, they had established a community of nations, not of governments. It was commonly accepted among experts on inter-American law that because the Union was composed of Brazilians, Mexicans, Guatemalans, and other national groups, membership was permanent and could not be affected by the policies of particular governments that might rule the peoples of the hemisphere.[160] Argentina, which was well aware of the terms of the charter, had deliberately applied to the Governing Board for a hearing, knowing that it could not refuse and that Argentina would have to be seated as a full member at any conference of Union members. Washington, however, managed to shunt Argentina's initiative aside and to turn the procedure for the calling and holding of an inter-American meeting into another channel. Conforming closely to the "suggestions" of Carl Spaeth, the Governing Board, which met on December 6, chose to defer action on the Argentine question to a later date, citing the small number of replies that had been received from the other republics. On December 11 the United States suggested to the hemispheric states that the meeting of foreign ministers be called through regular diplomatic channels, rather than by the Governing Board, so that there would be no juridical requirement that Argentina be present throughout the meeting.[161] The Latin American republics proved to be amenable, and as a result, Foreign Minister Padilla formally issued invitations to the Inter-American Conference on Problems of War and Peace to be held in Mexico City in February 1945. The Argentine request for a hearing was to be discussed under the last point on the agenda, entitled "Other Matters of General and Immediate Concern."[162]

The internationalists succeeded during 1944 in eliminating their arch rivals from the State Department, in fending off the threat to their control of policy mounted by the Morgenthau-Wallace group, and in implementing an ever-tougher approach toward Argentina. Their victories, as it turned out, were pyrrhic. Preoccupation with the Argentine affair on the part of Hull and his colleagues both reflected and contributed to their isolation within the Roosevelt foreign-policy establishment. That the internationalists would agree to an inter-American conference, which they believed to be a potential threat to the UNCIO, in return for the continued diplomatic isolation of Argentina indicated the degree to which the Argentine problem had come to dominate their thoughts. By the end of the year, Hull and his associates were completely cut off from policy-planning for Europe and the Far East. Meanwhile, the period of unilateral nonrecognition left the Americas divided and uncertain as to the direction that the hemispheric policy of the United States would take in the postwar world. Nor did Washington's Argentine policy contribute to Anglo-American cooperation. The Churchill government viewed nonrecognition and coercion as needless threats to the war effort and to Britain's ravaged economy. Finally, the diplomatic and economic policies of the hard-liners produced a reaction against United States policy toward Argentina among important groups both inside and outside the foreign-policy establishment, a reaction that, in conjunction with the advent of a new group of policy-makers in the State Department, led to a redefinition of the Good Neighbor Policy and to a sharp reversal in Argentine-American relations.

8

TWO CONCEPTS OF COMMUNITY:
THE ARGENTINE-AMERICAN RAPPROCHEMENT

For America, 1945 was simultaneously a year of triumph and tribulation. Allied air attacks and amphibious assaults steadily eroded Japan's vast Far Eastern empire. By June the lightning thrusts of Patton's armored units in the west and the relentless pressure of the Red Army in the east had reduced the legions of the Third Reich to impotency. While the warriors of the Grand Alliance struggled to bring hostilities to a successful close, the Big Three met first at Yalta and then at Potsdam to hammer out the shape of the postwar world. In May, representatives of the United Nations convened in San Francisco and attempted once again to breathe life into Woodrow Wilson's dream of a world organization. Despite the illusion of unity created by the impending victory over the Axis and by the various conferences, Russia, Britain, and the United States were deeply divided over the shape of the postwar world, and they maneuvered throughout the closing months of the war to advance their respective economic and strategic interests.[1] In the midst of these momentous events there occurred a dramatic reversal in Argentine-American relations, during the course of which the United States agreed to Argentina's reincorporation into the hemispheric community and supported her bid for a seat at the United Nations Conference on International Organization.

In essence the rapprochement between Washington and Buenos Aires was the result of collaboration between a new group of Latin Americanists who assumed control of hemispheric policy during the last days of 1944 and a new coterie of internationalists that was brought together by the White House to supervise implementation of America's United Nations policy. The hemispheric experts who took over ARA during the closing days of

1944 were convinced that the Good Neighbor Policy as defined by Welles, Duggan, and Bonsal was the best possible method for achieving the traditional goals of the Latin American policy of the United States—stability, security, and commercial intercourse. As a result they attempted to reintroduce the principles of nonintervention and consultation into hemispheric matters in general and Argentine-American relations in particular. In their drive to reverse the policies of the Hull group, this new contingent of decision-makers enjoyed the support of several powerful organizations and pressure groups within the Roosevelt foreign-policy establishment, most notably the United States military and a portion of the American business community. Far more important to the eventual success of the Latin Americanists than these allies, however, was a new clique of internationalists brought into the State Department by the White House to preside over the creation of a world organization. Because the new leadership in the State Department eventually concluded that Argentine-American rapprochement would facilitate the establishment of a viable, effective United Nations—which was regarded by both Presidents Roosevelt and Truman as the key to peace and security in the postwar era—they supported the Latin Americanists' drive to normalize relations with Buenos Aires.

By the end of 1944 Cordell Hull's physical and emotional resources were virtually exhausted. His dozen years as secretary of state had taken a toll on his health, especially in light of his advancing age. Contributing to Hull's physical decline was the mental anguish produced by the rivalries with Welles and Morganthau and the ever-wideing gulf between him and the president.[2] When in November 1944 Morgenthau asked his colleague what he was going to do about the "State of Germany," by far the most compelling diplomatic question of the day, Hull replied: "I don't have any chance to do anything. . . . I am not told what is going on. . . . That's on a higher level. . . . I have consultations with the War Department every day on the immediate objectives, but when they talk about the State of Germany I am not even consulted."[3] Hull was particularly upset by White House neglect in connection with the Quebec Conference held in October 1944. After assuring the secretary that he would call on the State Department if political questions arose, FDR instead summoned Morgenthau to Canada, accepted his plan for postwar Germany, and, in so doing, completely undercut Hull and the State Department.[4] Moreover, Hull was not at all sure that his exclusion from the circle of postwar policy-planners did not portend his ouster in favor of Sumner Welles after the November presidential election. Embittered, Hull submitted his resignation on December 2, and the president accepted it the following day.[5]

Hull's departure precipitated a wholesale personnel change in the State Department, which placed the Latin American policy of the United States in the hands of an organization whose techniques and goals differed radically from those of the Hull internationalists. To fill the newly created post of Assistant Secretary for Latin American Affairs, Roosevelt chose Nelson Rockefeller, who in turn brought with him virtually all of his top advisors in the Office of the Coordinator of Inter-American Affairs. The young New Yorker and his subordinates had been fighting for organizational survival since early 1944, when Henry Morgenthau and a number of other veteran bureaucrats had attacked the OCIAA as a "functional mishmash" and had demanded that it be dismantled.[6] Although many of the economic functions of the agency had gone to the Foreign Economic Administration in mid 1944, it had managed to stay afloat largely because of Rockefeller's success in building a personal reputation as a skilled administrator and a devotee of the Good Neighbor Policy.[7] After his appointment as assistant secretary on December 5 and his subsequent confirmation by the Senate, Rockefeller named John McClintock, one of his trusted OCIAA lieutenants, as special advisor on economic matters to the assistant secretary. John Lockwood, who had formerly been the general counsel of OCIAA, became deputy director of ARA. There were, however, two significant individuals in the new Latin American establishment who had not been connected with the OCIAA. Avra Warren, Armour's replacement as chief of ARA, was a career foreign-service officer and a veteran Latin Americanist. A disciple of Welles, the new chief of the Latin American desk had presided over the normalization of relations with Bolivia in June 1944.[8] The second, another old Latin Americanist, was Dudley Bonsal, veteran diplomat and brother of Philip Bonsal.[9]

Rockefeller's selection of Warren to command the Division of American Republic Affairs and of Bonsal to be a special assistant to the assistant secretary was not an aberration but rather a culmination, for ties between the old Latin American establishment and the new were quite close. The OCIAA had been created under Welles's auspices and was designed to forge cultural and economic links between the United States and Latin America and generally to undo the damage done to hemispheric relations during the first quarter of the twentieth century. Rockefeller and Duggan corresponded frequently, even after the latter's influence had all but evaporated in the State Department. Both agreed that the Latin American policy of the United States must be based on nonintervention and recognition of the juridical equality of all states.[10] The new group of Latin Americanists, like the old, recognized how sensitive *latinos* were concerning even the hint of North American coercion. In March, Rockefeller wrote Duggan: "In a sense the Western Hemisphere has been a laboratory for possible world collaboration. . . . It would help to reassure our neighbors of the permanence of our Good Neighbor Policy, not as a wartime measure alone but as a continuing factor in our foreign policy."[11] Throughout its existence the OCIAA went to great lengths to assure the Latin American republics that the Good Neighbor Policy would indeed survive World War II. "None of the transitions from war to peace will be easy," proclaimed Rockefeller in an article that appeared in the *Saturday Evening Post* in November 1943, "but they will be much less difficult if we keep in mind that the problem of one is the problem of all, if we attempt to solve each in the spirit of mutual self-interest and hemisphere co-operation, if we give practical proof that we mean what we say when we speak of the Good Neighbor Policy."[12] Franklin Roosevelt clearly perceived an ideological affinity between Welles and Rockefeller. This perception, together with the president's conviction that Rockefeller was the only man in Washington who could match the former undersecretary's knowledge of Latin America and his skill in handling Latin American diplomats, was primarily responsible for his appointment.[13] Rockefeller, Warren, and Lockwood, like Duggan, Welles, and Bonsal, believed that consultation was essential to the maintenance of good relations between Washington and capitals of the other American republics. They were ardent advocates of an inter-American conference to deal with war and postwar problems.

The neo–Latin Americanists emphasized to a much greater extent than their predecessors, however, the economic phase of the Good Neighbor Policy: that is, the assumption that not only the United States business community but the hemisphere as a whole would benefit from the freest and fullest exchange of goods and industrial technology. That the new group in charge of hemispheric affairs should view economic aid, both public and private, and unlimited commercial intercourse as the most effective means of promoting hemispheric harmony and of furthering United States interests south of the Rio Grande is not surprising, given their backgrounds. Rockefeller, McClintock, and Lockwood, like Stettinius, were corporate executives who had proved themselves acceptable to the Roosevelt administration by combining faith in capitalism with a social conscience. Moreover, the coordinator's office had been created for the express purpose of implementing the economic facet of the Good Neighbor Policy. The primary function of the OCIAA, wrote Lockwood to D. B. Johnstone in 1944, was "to formulate, recommend, and execute programs in the commercial and economic fields which, by effective use of government and private facilities, will further the commercial and economic well-being of the Western Hemisphere."[14] That the advent of industrialization, mass production, and free trade in Latin America would put an end to class warfare, political polarization, and anti-Americanism seemed self-evident to the New Deal businessmen within the State Department.[15] As David Green points out in *The Containment of Latin America*, Rockefeller and his associates were fearful that south of the Rio Grande there would be a trend toward economic nationalism.[16] But their anxieties stemmed not only from a desire to maintain an open door for American goods and capital, as Green implies, but from a belief, shared by liberals and conservatives alike, that economic nationalism in the form of high tariff barriers, refusal to share technology, and a dearth of foreign investment had been prime causes of both the Depression and World War II.[17]

While the neo–Latin Americanists had no sympathy whatsoever with Argentina's diplomatic posture during the war or with the repressive tactics of her several military governments, they were convinced that further attempts at coercion would not only be futile but, in terms of America's long-range interests, counterproductive. Rockefeller had concluded, before assuming his new post, that even if one shared Hull's assumptions and objectives, further coercion was pointless in view of the United States' demonstrated inability to bring effective economic pressure to bear on Argentina. He was well aware of Britain's opposition to sanctions of any type, of the views of the combined boards, and of the political impossibility of diverting United States meat and leather supplies to Great Britain. "By condemning Argentina and doing nothing," he later wrote, "we were losing the respect of the other American republics and her power and influence were growing in the southern part of the hemisphere."[18] More importantly, the new group in charge of hemispheric affairs rejected Hull's intransigent policies because they had destroyed the trust built up in Latin America from 1933 to 1941, had aided Argentina in her desire to create an anti–United States bloc in southern South America, and had immeasurably strengthened Great Britain's influence in Argentina and throughout the Western Hemisphere.

In seeking a rapprochement with Buenos Aires, Rockefeller, Warren, McClintock, and Lockwood were able to count on the support of perhaps the most influential organization in the Roosevelt foreign-policy establishment—the United States military. Attempts to coerce Argentina into the proper diplomatic and political posture had encountered stiff resistance from virtually every branch of the armed services, particularly when the techniques employed bore directly on relations between the American and Argentine armed services.[19] Throughout the period from 1942 to 1945, United States military planners had opposed the withholding of military hardware as a coercive technique.[20] During the Argentine-American staff talks that took place in the aftermath of Pearl Harbor, military negotiators stubbornly resisted the State Department's attempts to intervene and use essential war materials to bargain for a softening of Argentina's position toward the United States. The officers in question demanded the right to be free from outside pressure while negotiating agreements, which they would then submit to the State Department for approval or disapproval.[21] Despite the determination of the hard-liners to block the shipment of as many strategic items as possible to Argentina, the navy and the air force insisted in December 1943 that the United States provide replacement parts to their corresponding services in Argentina. What is more, the Caribbean Defense Command successfully resisted the efforts of the hard-liners during 1943 and 1944 to have the United States Air Mission in Argentina withdrawn.[22]

Not only did the army, the navy, and the air force seek to be free from diplomatic interference while continuing their relations with their Argentine counterparts, but various representatives of the military establishment argued throughout the war that America's get-tough posture was politically and strategically impolitic. Gen. George Brett and his subordinates in the Caribbean Defense Command (CDC) steadfastly maintained that the primary goal of the Argentine people was to remain neutral and that Washington's antagonism of the Castillo, Ramírez, and Farrell governments was not only pointless but counterproductive.[23] Economic sanctions, both actual and proposed, drew the fire of the CDC and particularly the Joint Chiefs of Staff, who feared that retaliation by Argentina would leave Eisenhower without the supplies needed to bring the war in Europe to a successful conclusion.[24]

Finally, American military planners argued that needless coercion of Argentina was undercutting the Good Neighbor Policy and destroying hemispheric solidarity. In late 1944 the Joint Chiefs of Staff submitted a comprehensive memorandum to the State Department, expressing their views on Argentine-American relations. The "political moral" to be drawn from the whole situation, declared America's top military planners, was that the stamping-out of minor enemy activity in Argentina must not take priority over the Good Neighbor Policy. After all, the Latin American republics had supported the United States during the war not because Washington had raised a menacing fist but because these countries felt it in their national interest to do so. "We have, beginning with the Rio Conference, created an Argentine bogey," warned America's military leaders, "which is now returning to haunt us. . . . If we are not careful we will dissipate our energies in chasing this phantom and thereby waste our strength needed in the creation of a decent postwar order." Their policy paper concluded by advising the State Department to call immediately a conference on postwar problems and to include Argentina in such a conclave. Such a step would restore Latin America's faith in the Good Neighbor Policy and would assuage the feelings of those who felt that the United States was ignoring the other American republics in the formulation of plans for the postwar world.[25]

The American military welcomed the changes that took place within the State Department in December 1944. During a luncheon conversation with Henry Wallace, Gen. George Marshall, chairman of the Joint Chiefs of Staff, had expressed the utmost confidence in Nelson Rockefeller. Rockefeller's appointment, he said, would immediately straighten out the Latin American situation.[26]

Joining the military in urging a thaw in Argentine-American relations were those American investors and traders who had real or potential interests in South America.[27] United States firms, including such giants as International Harvester, Ford, Armour, Swift, and International Telephone and Telegraph, had invested over $570 million in Argentina prior to 1942.[28] After every blast at Buenos Aires by the State Department, the Treasury, BEW, or FEA, these companies had faced the threat of expropriation. American exporters and importers who traded with Argentina were hurt by Washington's hard-line policies no less than were those with direct investments. The State Department's various attempts to strangle first the Ramírez and then the Farrell government by forbidding the issuance of export licenses to United States shippers caused them to add their voices to those of Armour, ITT, and Ford in insisting on a normalization of relations between the two nations.

Originally, among United States businessmen there were two sets of opinion regarding Argentine-American affairs. One group, probably the larger, equated Argentina with Nazi Germany and argued for vigorous sanctions against the recalcitrant republic.[29] In April 1942, Armand May, president of the American Associated Companies and American Factors Company, commended the State Department's stand against Argentina and advocated an even harder line in the future. A pro-Allied posture by Buenos Aires would surely emerge, he proclaimed, "if we and the balance of the United Nations refuse to support Argentina in her every day life."[30] Another sector of the business world believed that the matter was simply a dispute between two headstrong groups of officials and claimed that a dynamic American executive could settle the dispute in a matter of days.[31] In May 1943 Alfred H. Benjamin, an official of the Anglo-American Trading Corporation and a close friend of FDR's, wrote to the president, warning that Argentine-American relations were getting out of hand. Requesting prompt action by the White House to end discrimination by the Export Control Division of the State Department in the granting of export licenses for steel, tinplate, and other products that were vital to the Argentine economy, he argued that America's present course would cut off the Allies from their best source of strategic raw materials, would alienate all of Latin America, would deprive Great Britain of her beef supply, and would drive Argentina into the hands of the Nazis.[32]

As it became obvious that the United Kingdom would not participate in sanctions against Argentina and that the State and Treasury departments' campaign of economic coercion was not affecting either Argentina's prosperity or its policies, the hard-liners began to defect to the group that was urging détente. In late 1943, officials of Buenos Aires branches of the National City Bank of New York and the First National Bank of Boston called on the American embassy to protest the freezing of the assets of Banco de la Nación and Banco de la Provincia. Arguing that Argentina was actually providing as much support for the war effort as were such nations as Bolivia or Peru, they suggested that sanctions against Argentina would only be justified if they were total and if they were supported by the British.[33]

Great Britain's attempts to use the Argentine-American rift to improve their economic position in southern South America were particularly important in crystallizing sentiment within the business community for a rapprochement. The continuance of British commercial activity in Argentina produced a wave of protest that swelled into a mighty flood by the end of the year.[34] By July, FEA and the State Department were being swamped with bitter complaints from United States businessmen who felt that they were losing their competitive advantage in Argentina to the British.[35] Typical were the officials of Gilbarco, a subsidiary of Standard Oil that manufactured gasoline pumps. They informed the department that because export licenses had been denied to them for two and a half years, the State Petroleum Monopoly in Argentina was buying large quantities of British pumps at about one-third more than the American price.[36] One group of United States exporters became so angered at what they considered the irrationality of Hull's policies that in the summer of 1944 they urged the State Department to dispatch an unofficial yet authoritative mission of businessmen to Buenos Aires to seek a complete understanding with the Farrell government. Charging that Washington's approach had been at best muddling, the would-be diplomats maintained that they could achieve complete inter-American unity if authorized to "in a business-like way talk over advantages that would accrue to both sides if Argentina were to take a few more steps away from the Axis."[37]

So that United States exporters and investors would increase their pressure on the State Department, the Farrell-Perón government shrewdly tempted American businessmen with visions of an enormous postwar market in Argentina. Officials in Buenos Aires let North American manufacturers know that the government was establishing a National Council of Postwar Planning to conduct a complete survey of Argentine needs for replacement, renovation, and extension of industry, agrictulture, and transportation services during the first five postwar years; and they implied that United States businessmen would have an excellent chance of satisfying those needs if there were a normalization in relations between the two countries.[38] American businessmen could discern the economic opportunities present in Argentina even without the aid of the Casa Rosada, however.[39] In February 1945 the *Wall Street Journal* published the first in a series of

175

front-page promotional pieces on Argentina which depicted an investment area that was attractive almost beyond belief:

Argentina needs immediately some $1.2 billion of automobiles, machinery, electrical equipment, and other durable goods to bring her economy up to pre-war functioning standards and to provide for normal growth. . . . This calculation does not include rehabilitation or extension of the Argentine Railways, which require a minimum of $200,000,000 or direly needed materials. . . . This together with consumer demands indicates the staggering size of the potential market . . . viewed in terms of need and the desire to buy.[40]

Armed with itemized five-year requirements, $478 million in balances, and an impeccable credit rating, Argentina constituted an almost irresistible area for investment. Lest American businessmen become overconfident, however, Buenos Aires was careful to let them know that there were other interested sellers. In March the Argentine government announced that Perón, as head of the Council on Postwar Planning, was meeting with representatives of the British Chamber of Commerce to clarify Argentina's future needs, especially in the area of transportation, industrial machinery, and armaments. Actually, the Farrell-Perón government was quite candid with the State Department about its intention to use the American trading community to facilitate de-isolation.[41] In November 1944 Alejandro Shaw, a prominent Argentine industrialist who was frequently employed as an unofficial emissary by Buenos Aires, informed Norman Armour that Perón firmly believed that, once the war was over, United States exporters would force Washington to change its policy toward Argentina.[42]

By early 1945 United States business and financial chronicles were engaged in a continuous diatribe against Washington's Argentine policies. *Business Week* denounced Hull's coercive tactics and called for a rapprochement to protect United States economic interests.[43] The *Wall Street Journal*, declaring that Argentina had the right to choose her own political forms and diplomatic policies, called for a resumption of relations. The United States, declared the *Journal*, must always realize that North and South America emanated from two different cultures, each with separate traditions. "Our neighbors do not conceive 'liberty' and 'democracy' in quite the same terms as we do."[44] The conservative *Saturday Evening Post* proved to be equally understanding. John Lear, in an article entitled "The Truth about

Argentina," argued that if the Good Neighbor Policy were amended to allow the United States to intervene to establish democracy, Washington would have to begin with Brazil. Why couldn't we be practical like the British, he pleaded. Argentina was going to have millions in credit in the United States after the war, and it would want, above all, industrial machinery. This was just what we would want to sell to keep our factories going and our people at work.[45] The message to the Roosevelt foreign-policy establishment concerning Argentina was quite clear. Accept that nation for what it was, and get down to business.

Most of the business figures arguing in behalf of a rapprochement were internationalists, men who believed that their own economic interests, as well as the peace and security of the world, would be served by lowered trade barriers and increased United States investment, both public and private, in the developing areas of the world.[46] This philosophy and the trading community's specific views on the Argentine matter corresponded quite closely with those of the neo–Latin Americanists.[47] Thus, business pressure in the winter and spring of 1945 impelled Rockefeller, Warren, and their subordinates in the direction that they were already headed.

Even more important to the fulfillment of the Latin Americanists' goals than support from the military and business communities was the fact that their desire for rapprochement complemented the objectives of a new group of internationalists which was in charge of America's United Nations policy. According to historian Thomas Campbell, Presidents Roosevelt and Truman were both committed to the creation of a viable international collective-security organization that would prevent future wars, raise living standards, and facilitate the spread of democracy. So great was their faith that such a body could solve most major international problems that Roosevelt, and to a lesser extent Truman, postponed pressing political and economic questions in 1944–45 until the world organization could get off the ground.

The man who was chosen to oversee America's United Nations policy was Edward Stettinius, Jr. FDR, after consultation with Harry Hopkins, decided to promote Stettinius to secretary of state in December 1944, not only because of his administrative ability and political clout among conservatives, but also because his one identifiable principle was Wilsonian internationalism. One of the new secretary's first duties was to oversee creation of a task force on "International Organization and Security Affairs" within the department, under Leo Pasvolsky.[48] Like Hull and Long, members of this new group of internationalists were not experts on Latin American politics and culture, nor did preservation and perfection of the Inter-American System top their list of priorities. Theirs was a world view, and they were determined to subsume all other considerations to the triumph of Wilsonian internationalism.

Although this new group of internationalists was at first mildly negative about rapprochement with Argentina, it became increasingly apparent to them that Argentina's reincorporation into the hemispheric family and her participation in the UNCIO were vitally important to the success of America's postwar policy.[49]

To the neo–Latin Americanists, the first logical step toward the solution of the Argentine problem was to articulate the terms by which that nation might be readmitted to the hemispheric family of nations—a step that was bitterly opposed by the residue of hard-liners remaining in the State Department.[50] Rockefeller and Warren believed that a return to constitutional government, elimination of Axis influences, and a declaration of war were real possibilities. Reports from the United States embassy in Buenos Aires during the fall and winter of 1944 indicated a growing split in the Argentine government between Perón and the other leaders of integral nationalism, as well as mounting dissatisfaction among the populace with Argentina's international position. On October 7, in a comprehensive analysis of the political situation in Buenos Aires, the United States chargé d'affaires reported that Perón appeared to have broken the extremists' power within the government, and as a result the prospect for a return to constitutional normality and international cooperation was within sight.[51] As Perón sought during November and December to augment his support among Argentine civilians, rumors abounded that a return to constitutional procedures, specifically presidential elections, was imminent.[52] On December 11 Stettinius ordered the Latin American section to prepare a comprehensive memo for FDR on the Argentine situation "in view of Mr. Perón's recent speeches . . . and the indication that there had been a change of sentiment recently."[53] The note, which reached the White House on January 2, envisioned two possible courses of action by Argentina: (1) aggression against the other nations of southern South America or (2) a drastic change in internal policy, followed by steps by Argentina to reintroduce itself into the American community. Rockefeller and his colleagues proposed that if the Farrell-Perón regime were to pursue the first option, the United States should be prepared to render all necessary aid to Argentina's neighbors. If, however, Buenos Aires were to adopt the second, Washington should initiate consultations with the other American republics, looking toward recognition. If matters were to reach this point, it would be Washington's position that Argentina could achieve recognition by reaffirming the rupture with the Axis, ridding Argentina of all Axis organizations and influences, abolishing the state of siege, calling general elections, and guaranteeing full exchange of information with the other American republics concerning Axis espionage activity.[54] Although Spaeth and Wendelin, who were still ensconced in the Division of River Plata Affairs, denounced the proposal as the beginning of a sellout and refused to initial it, Stettinius forwarded the memo to FDR, who endorsed it enthusiastically.[55] The schedule of demands to be made on Buenos Aires differed little from those made by Hull and his associates in 1943, even to the point of requiring elections, but it was highly significant that the State Department had agreed to lay down conditions—a step that Latin America had been urging on the State Department unsuccessfully throughout 1944.

As the opening date of the Mexico City Conference approached, however, it became obvious to Stettinius and the Latin Americanists that normalization of relations with Argentina would be far from a simple matter. Despite their desire for a rapprochement, both the internationalists on the one hand and Rockefeller, Warren, and their colleagues on the other were determined to secure complete Argentine solidarity with the Allies and, if possible, a modification of the totalitarianism that had gripped the nation since the proclamation of the state of siege in 1942.[56] The signs from Buenos Aires were difficult to interpret. Hoping to make as favorable an impression as possible before representatives of the other American republics who were gathered at Chapultepec Castle, Perón, using the Chilean chargé d'affaires as an intermediary, contacted the American embassy in mid January and submitted a comprehensive report on the state of Argentine affairs. Through his emissary, the vice-president advised the United States that, among other things, his government had eliminated all pro-Axis personnel from the administration, had closed permanently *El Cabildo* and *El Federal,* and had established supervision over all important German firms. Perón politely but firmly rejected American demands concerning democratization of the Argentine political system. While attributing Washington's concern over the state of political and personal liberty in Argentina to the best of motives, he asserted that the matter of elections was entirely an internal affair.[57] (The

Casa Rosada subsequently announced, however, that the republic had entered a preelection phase.)[58] Yet information from other quarters seemed to indicate that conditions in Argentina had not really changed at all.[59] The American embassy reported in mid January that despite official assurances to the contrary, the press continued to labor under censorship and that real freedom of expression was nonexistent.[60]

Then, during the first week in February, news reached the State Department that Perón had finally and completely resolved a power struggle within the Argentine government between himself and a virulently anti-American clique headed by Foreign Minister Orlando Peluffo. This resolution, coupled with a growing realization that Perón would be able to win any national election that might be held and would probably dominate Argentina for years to come, did much to convince the leadership in the State Department that the charismatic young colonel was the best that could be had. Unless the United States wished to resort to massive intervention, it would have to work with the existing regime. Military intelligence and FBI reports had consistently portrayed Peluffo as the most anti-American and pro-Fascist member of the Farrell administration. In early January 1945 the foreign minister attempted to blame Perón for Argentina's failure during the previous fall to break the nonrecognition front. The vice-president's bellicose speeches and armaments program had frightened away nearly all of Argentina's potential Latin allies. Perón responded to this attack by seeking and gaining the personal allegiance of Gen. Eduardo Avalos, the powerful commander of the Campo de Mayo garrison, and then forcing Farrell to choose between him (Perón) and Peluffo. Farrell deferred to Perón. The foreign minister's subsequent resignation in the last part of January was viewed by Washington as a qualified victory for the Allies.[61] Shortly after Peluffo's ouster on February 7, Perón and Avalos held a highly secret interview with a member of Adolf Berle's staff. (Berle had become ambassador to Brazil on 23 December 1944.)[62] Perón insisted that Washington no longer needed to distrust Argentina. Peluffo and his satellites were gone forever. "In October at the latest we shall call the people to democratic, honest elections. . . . We have sworn to return this republic to its constitutional and democratic life, and we will do it. . . . The United States and other sister nations of America can depend on that." Regarding collaboration with the United States and the other republics on war and postwar matters, Buenos Aires, Perón announced, was ready to do everything needed or desired, provided that there was no attempt to humiliate the government or the nation. Argentina's "friends" in the United States Army knew that well. Argentina's alleged expansionist program was a pure myth. Deprived of nickel, steel, and aluminum, the armament industry was at a standstill. "All we can do and must do now is to train future pilots and equip decently our army which has been for years in a state of complete neglect."[63]

The American embassy in Rio was impressed with the aura of permanency if not sincerity that infused the interview. In their report to the State Department, Berle and his staff concluded that "hopes expressed by some people in Buenos Aires that something is brewing that will finally oust the present government are entirely unfounded." Perón and Avalos had gained complete control, even winning the grudging support of the conservative, landed classes. Elections would soon be held in which the vice-president would be chosen president for a six-year term. "It is important," Berle's report advised, "to be realistic about this well-defined situation."[64]

In developing a rational, "realistic" policy toward Argentina during the opening weeks of 1945, the State Department had to maneuver between two conflicting bodies of opinion concerning Argentina's fitness to reenter the hemispheric family. There was in the United States a large degree of residual hostility against Argentina which prevented any abrupt change in American policy whatever the department's conciliatory intentions. America's sense of moral outrage was well expressed by the *New York Times*:

> A Government that has sinned as grievously as has that of Argentina against the spirit, if not all the letters, of previous Pan-American commitments and certainly has been the major disruptive element in hemisphere understanding and solidarity, hardly can expect to regain good standing merely by asking for it.[65]

In the House of Representatives, Congressman Jack Z. Anderson of California urged that the Americas take strong action at the Mexico City Conference to bring Argentina into line. Arguing that "nonrecognition by the United States and verbal brickbats" were not enough, he addressed a public letter to Stettinius, demanding an immediate embargo. In his reply, Stettinius felt compelled to assure the congressman that the administration would take no action to benefit or strengthen the Farrell-Perón regime "until it is conclusively demonstrated by unequivocal acts that there has been a fundamental change of Argentine policy in favor of the cause against the Axis and in support of inter-American unity and common action."[66]

At the same time, editorial opinion throughout Latin America was demanding, in ever-more-strident tones, that Argentina be reincorporated into the Inter-American System immediately. Expressing its hope that the blunders of Secretary Hull would be rectified under Stettinius, *La Noche* of La Paz asserted that nonrecognition and other coercive policies directed against Argentina, however justifiable during the previous year, were now indefensible and repugnant to all South America.[67] *La Razón* and *El Tiempo* noted that it would be impossible to exclude Argentina from the postwar world, and they urged the hemispheric nations to permit the Farrell government to state its case.[68] *O Globo, Diario Carioca,* and *A Manha* of Rio de Janeiro lamented the fact that Argentina would be absent from the forthcoming conference and predicted her quick return to the fold as a result of consultation.[69] *El Mercurio* of Santiago challenged Washington to show its good faith in the Argentine matter by scheduling a discussion of the problem at the beginning of the conference.[70] On January 15 *La Noche* issued an eloquent plea in behalf of a hearing for Argentina:

> Even those of us who believe that Argentina's international policy is erroneous have an obligation to listen to her representatives, and to bend all of our energies to free that government from its error, if they are proved to be such. The exclusion of Argentina does not appear to us to be a good step toward complete reestablishment of concord and unification.[71]

The American republics had pressed for the holding of an inter-American conference on war and postwar problems in part to ensure the survival of a strong Inter-American System that would provide the hemisphere with a voice in the postwar order.[72] Still chafing at their exclusion from the Dumbarton Oaks Conference, they were not at all sure that Washington would not sacrifice the Inter-American System on the altar of internationalism.[73] Those Latin American diplomats who were anxious over the question of what role the Americas would play in the postwar world believed that any effective hemispheric organization must include Argentina, one of the strongest and most influential of the Latin American republics.[74] Representatives of the Lopez government in Colombia told the United States ambassador in Bogotá that Colombia considered it extremely important to draw

Argentina back into the hemispheric family in order to preserve solidarity and increase American effectiveness in the proposed world organization. It was undeniable, they asserted, that the Latin American bloc would be immeasurably stronger with Argentina than without her.[75]

Argentina's inclusion in a regional collective-security system would not only strengthen the hand of the Western Hemisphere in its struggle to be heard in the postwar world but would also calm the fears of those Latin American states that were anxious about future Argentine aggression. A number of governments were convinced that Buenos Aires would prove more tractable inside rather than outside a strong collective-security organization. The Bolivian, Paraguayan, and Uruguayan foreign offices informed Washington that in their opinion the best way to control Argentina was to bind her tightly to the hemispheric system and then develop effective peace-keeping machinery within that context.[76] In early February, Getulio Vargas of Brazil pressed the United States to allow Buenos Aires to send an official delegation to Mexico City. This, in his opinion, would be the best possible method of suppressing latent Argentine aggression.[77] Shortly before the opening of the Chapultepec Conference, former President Eduardo Santos of Colombia visited the United States and met with FDR. In a lengthy interview the former chief executive first described a widespread fear of aggression in South America which had led to a monumental arms race, some nations allocating up to one-third of their budget for arms, and then he pressed Roosevelt to support a strong collective-security pact that would put an end to such waste and to the fears that were responsible for it.[78]

Finally, as mentioned previously, not a few Latin Americans viewed Washington's willingness to halt its coercion of the Farrell-Perón government and to negotiate with Argentina concerning recognition as a test of the Good Neighbor Policy. Quite simply, *latinos* demanded that Rockefeller, Warren, Bonsal, and Lockwood match their rhetoric with action.[79]

Caught between a continuing ground swell of anti-Argentine feeling in the United States and increasingly insistent demands from Latin America for an immediate rapprochement, the Latin Americanists rightly perceived that they would have to walk a tightrope at Mexico City. The problem was how to negotiate with Buenos Aires for proper guarantees without, on the one hand, giving the appearance of undue haste or, on the other, seeming to be unreasonable.[80]

The State Department's strategy for Mexico City, developed primarily by Stettinius and Rockefeller, was an attempt to satisfy simultaneously all the various forces and groups that were seeking to shape American policy.[81] As to economic matters, it was decided that United States representatives would work for the adoption of resolutions that would reassure Latin America regarding Washington's interest in its economic well-being. Specifically, United States officials envisioned agreements that would provide for a gradual end to huge American purchasing programs in South America rather than an abrupt halt, which would disrupt the region's war-inflated economies. In addition, the United States would promise long-term credits through the International Monetary Fund and would work for lower tariffs in order to stimulate inter-American trade.[82] Secondly, American diplomats would advocate a mutual guarantee of boundaries and would seek, as they had throughout the 1930s, to formalize the process of consultation. Indeed, the United States had already put Latin America on notice that it would once again seek to multilateralize the Monroe Doctrine. During the Santos-Roosevelt talks, the president had urged Colombia to propose a collective guarantee of borders and had promised that the United States would support such a guarantee even to the point of a treaty.[83] Not only would such a move placate the Western Hemisphere's fears of being ignored by the great powers in the postwar period and of being submerged in the United Nations, but it was hoped that it would mollify anti-Argentine opinion within the United States if rapprochement became a reality. The State Department could argue, as many Latin American nations had already done, that an aggressive, Fascist Argentina would be easier to control inside a collective-security organization.[84] Thirdly, in regard to the Argentine question per se, Stettinius and Rockefeller decided to respond to Latin American pressure grudgingly, to secure the most far-reaching pledges possible from Buenos Aires, but above all, to preserve inter-American unity on the matter. At the very least, American officials hoped to put off settlement of the Argentine question until the end of the conference.[85]

No sooner had President Manuel Ávila Camacho of Mexico delivered his welcoming address to the delegates gathered at Chapultepec Castle than various Latin American delegations launched a campaign to have the Argentine problem settled immediately. Their objective was nothing less than full Argentine participation in the meeting. When the chiefs of delegation met to organize the conference, the United States was barely able to defeat a Paraguayan motion to have the delegations deal with the Argentine problem at once.[86]

It was not Paraguay but Colombia, however, that was to be Argentina's chief advocate at Mexico City. As the Chapultepec Conference opened, officials of the Lopez government in Bogotá informed the United States ambassador that Buenos Aires had reexamined its position and that all it desired was a formula whereby Argentina could obtain recognition. Simultaneously, at Mexico City, members of the Colombian delegation apprised United States representatives that Perón had notified their government that Argentina was willing to accept any conditions without restriction in order to be reconciled with the United States, "provided only that Argentine decorum was protected." If "decorum" were violated, the Colombians recalled Perón as saying, then the world would see "his comrades from the Campo de Mayo marching in and cutting him to pieces." In urging the United States to back an immediate hearing for Argentina, the Colombians declared that chaos would be the inevitable result in Argentina if its case were not settled at Mexico City, chaos that would result in a Communist takeover and in Argentina's becoming a base for the subversion of the entire hemisphere. Although the North Americans continually rejected Colombian arguments, that nation served throughout the remainder of the conference as "Godfather to the Argentine attempt at rehabilitation."[87]

Stettinius and Rockefeller quickly concluded that if the United States were to avert a premature discussion on the Argentine situation, it would, unofficially at least, have to lay down the conditions upon which Washington would agree to reincorporation of Argentina into the hemispheric family. Consequently, on February 22 Stettinius cabled the White House, asking in effect for permission to come to terms. He reported that upon his arrival in Mexico City, he had found the mood within the nonrecognition camp to be quite volatile, and it was becoming more so every day as agents of the Farrell-Perón government spread the word that Argentina was prepared to desert the Axis. Although the United States delegation had managed, despite Latin American support for Argentine maneuvering, to hold the line, it was imperative that it take the initiative. On behalf of himself, Rockefeller, and Warren, the secretary strongly suggestd that as Argentina met certain conditions to be agreed upon at Mexico City, it should be readmitted to the American family. Otherwise, any unity achieved at Chapultepec would be superficial, and the lack of real cohesion would undermine

Washington's position within both the hemispheric and the world communities. Actually, a careful review of the department's records had revealed that there was little substance to the Argentine-Axis relationship. Such connections had been largely imagined and were, according to the secretary, due more to "an emotional feeling on the part of the American people and within our own government" than to a rational evaluation of the situation. In view of the facts that the current government showed no signs of collapsing and that Argentina was likely to legitimately elect Perón president, "much on the Vargas pattern," the secretary requested White House approval of the following formula: Argentina should (1) immediately declare war on the Axis; (2) announce its desire for the formation of an inter-American committee with United States and Argentine membership to design practical measures of continental defense, including control of subversive activities; (3) reduce troop concentrations along the Chilean and Brazilian borders; and (4) adhere to all resolutions passed at Mexico City. After these conditions had been fulfilled, the head of each American delegation could announce recognition. Stettinius pressed Roosevelt to reply quickly, as the Argentine government was moving swiftly to condition its people for a declaration of war on Germany. If this should happen before the Mexico City Conference could take action on the problem, the Farrell government might elicit public support from various European nations, thus drastically reducing Washington's control over the Argentine matter.[88]

White House approval of the memorandum the following day substantially lessened pressure on the United States from the Latin American community.[89] Although Perón subsequently refused to declare war and although Argentine agents worked assiduously from February 24 through February 26 to splinter the nonrecognition front, the lines held firm.[90] Washington's willingness to establish terms and to refrain from commenting on the domestic political situation in Argentina momentarily restored Latin American confidence in the Roosevelt administration.[91]

Meanwhile, the United States contingent had joined with the delegations of the other republics to implement the Roosevelt-Santos agreement concerning a collective-security pact. Although the internationalists and the Latin Americanists had previously agreed to support a mutual guarantee of boundaries, they had not come to terms on the question of the relationship between a hemispheric security organization and the proposed world body.[92] Pasvolsky and his subordinates took the position that an American collective-security organization operating independently of the United Nations not only would violate the Yalta and Dumbarton Oaks accords but would hamstring any global government that might be created. They demanded that all sanctions voted by the inter-American community be subject to approval by the "world council," as they referred to the organ that subsequently became the United Nations Security Council.[93] Rockefeller and his associates were sympathetic not only to Latin America's desire for an ironclad security pact but also to its wish to create an inter-American body that would be free from outside interference. Joined by the delegation's military advisors and by Adolf Berle and George Messersmith, the new Latin Americanists argued that nothing less than the Monroe Doctrine and United States leadership in the hemisphere were at stake. It was obvious that the other republics were united in their desire for establishment of a tightly knit organization.[94] If Washington completely rejected this "outstretched hand,"[95] then Latin America would form its own union, possibly with one of the European powers as sponsor. If the United States agreed to join a hemispheric organization but insisted on subsuming it to the world council, then Britain and Russia would be able to interject themselves into every inter-American dispute. Either course would open up the New World to European interference and would jeopardize the United States' ability to protect itself and its neighbors from the forces of international fascism and world communism. And, of course, there was the matter of containing Argentina.[96]

Pasvolsky, with half-hearted support from Stettinius, attempted to use the two congressional representatives on the delegation, Senators Warren Austin and Tom Connally, to block approval of a strong agreement. The internationalists argued with some success to the two politicians that the Senate would never agree to a pact providing for the commitment of American troops unless it had congressional approval.[97] They withdrew, however, when the Latin Americanists persuaded Walter Lippmann and other members of the press to write a series of articles strongly supporting hemispheric collective security and attacking those within the United States delegation who opposed it. When Austin framed a provision that would allow President Roosevelt to authorize United States adherence to the Act of Chapultepec based solely on his wartime power as commander-in-chief, thus vitiating the necessity of Senate ratification, the American delegation unanimously voted its approval.[98]

The Act of Chapultepec was designed to protect all American states from aggression of any sort, whether continental or extracontinental in origin. The key provision, which was authored jointly by the Americans and the Colombians, defined aggression as the invasion of one state by the armed forces of another and stipulated that an act of aggression against one American state would be considered an act against all. The signatories agreed that when violation of territorial boundaries occurred, they would consult in order to settle on appropriate measures of retaliation. In addition, the contracting parties proclaimed that they would regard such acts perpetrated during the remainder of World War II as interference with the United Nations war effort, and as such, these acts would elicit responses ranging from the recall of diplomatic chiefs to the use of force.[99] A concluding clause recommended that upon the termination of World War II, the states of the hemisphere convene in order to translate the agreement into a treaty.[100]

With the conclusion of the Act of Chapultepec, both those Latin American states that feared Argentine expansionism and those American officials who feared anti-Argentine sentiment in the United States felt free to turn to the question of the status of the Farrell-Perón government within the American community. On March 6 Stettinius, Rockefeller, and Warren presented to Argentina the plan that Roosevelt had earlier approved. When Perón rejected the United States conditions for readmission to the hemispheric system, Stettinius cabled the White House that the American delegation would now opt for a resolution regretting the unfortunate but necessary absence of Argentina and urging it to implement the declarations of Mexico City "while qualifying for membership in the United Nations."[101]

The efforts of those who were seeking an Argentine-American rapprochement culminated on the last day of the meeting when the delegates unanimously adopted a resolution that threatened, on the one hand, and cajoled on the other. The declaration, while it recognized the indivisible unity of the American people and the continuity of Argentine membership in the PAU, "deplored" that Argentina had not taken the steps that would have allowed it to participate in the Inter-American Conference. In the strained prose of yet another inter-American compromise agreement, the declaration expressed the wish of the delegates that Argentina "may put herself in a position to express her conformity with and adherence to" the principles of Chapultepec. After reaffirming inter-American solidarity in the event of aggression "by any state," the conference invited Argentina to "implement a policy of co-operative action with the other American Nations . . . so that she may achieve her incorporation into the United Nations as a signatory to the joint declaration entered into by them."[102]

With the final business of Chapultepec completed, the secretary set about telling each group that had divergent views on the Argentine matter what they wanted to hear. The non–State Department members of the American delegation, who had not even been told of the Roosevelt-Stettinius interchange of February 23/24, had bridled at the fact that the Argentine resolution did not contain, as a *sine qua non*, an Argentine declaration of war. Rockefeller barely averted a rebellion by arguing that it would be unfair and inconsistent to require an immediate declaration by Buenos Aires, since there were a number of other American nations that were simply in a state of belligerency. In his opinion the final statement on Argentina should be firm but not so harsh as to preclude her joining the inter-American fold.[103] On the final day of the meeting, Stettinius congratulated the delegation on its firmness in the Argentine matter and promised that "we should not even open the door a crack" until Argentina declared war and lived up to her obligations. By contrast, his concluding statement to the conference itself lauded the Argentine resolution as one of the six major achievements of the meeting. "It is our common desire," he proclaimed to the weary delegates, "that Argentina be able to resume her traditional place in the family of the American nations and restore in full measure the solidarity of this hemisphere."[104]

Reaction to the achievements of the Mexico City Conference proved extremely gratifying to Stettinius and the Latin Americanists.[105] In the first place, there was good reason to think that their diplomacy had restored Latin America's faith in the United States. The Colombian foreign minister heaped praise on the United States delegation for its willingness to cooperate with the other American republics, while Uruguay expressed its pleasure over the Act of Chapultepec. *El Mercurio* and *La Nación* of Santiago described the Argentine resolutions as the first great step toward the restoration of continental unity.[106] Even the anti-Argentine Central American states were optimistic. The *Star and Herald* of Panama termed the chances for Argentina's quick return to the fold quite good. In view of this resurgence of good neighborly spirit, the United States felt assured of Latin American support at San Francisco and beyond.[107] In the second place, newspaper reaction and official statements emanating from Buenos Aires seemed to indicate that Argentina was ready to put itself "in a position to express her conformity with and adherence to" the principles of Chapultepec. Such barometers of public opinion as *La Nación* and *El Mundo* of Buenos Aires commented favorably on both the Final Act and the Argentine resolution and pressed for Argentina's adherence.[108] Acting Foreign Minister César Ameghino congratulated the Mexico City meeting for its very important and necessary work. In keeping with Argentina's traditions, he declared in a March 7 press release, Argentina categorically rejected aggression as an instrument of national policy or of territorial expansion and reaffirmed its determination to maintain itself within the continental solidarity, repudiating any ideology that was foreign to republican and democratic traditions of the American nations.[109]

In the days following the Mexico City Conference it quickly became apparent that the chief obstacle to diplomatic recognition was Argentina's stubborn refusal to declare war. It was this issue that had prevented Perón from accepting the plan designed by Stettinius, Rockefeller, and Warren and approved by FDR. The Brazilians, who believed that Buenos Aires would never concede the issue, tried to force the State Department's hand. On March 10, two days after the close of the Chapultepec meeting, Foreign Minister Pedro Velloso announced to reporters that "adherence by Argentina to the Act of Chapultepec will result in reopening diplomatic relations with all American nations in the near future . . . a declaration of war will be unnecessary to gain this recognition."[110] Rockefeller, who had learned as much in his dealings with the American delegation at Mexico City, realized that a declaration of war was imperative if the American people were to accept a normalization of relations. Moreover, as the Latin Americanists subsequently informed their *latino* colleagues, under the Yalta accords a declaration was required for membership in the United Nations and for participation in the UNCIO. On March 26 Velloso, now in Washington, joined with Rockefeller in calling a meeting at Blair House of representatives of twelve "leading" American republics to work out "an exact formula for the de-isolation of Argentina."

After a brief period of deliberation the group decided that Argentina would have accepted the invitation and fulfilled the conditions proffered at Mexico City when she had (1) declared war on the Axis, (2) expressed conformity to and complied with the Final Act, and (3) signed the Final Act. The twelve decreed that after the Farrell government had taken these steps, the entire hemisphere would extend recognition and that the United States, as depository nation, would request that Argentina be invited to sign the United Nations Declaration.[111]

Meanwhile, in Buenos Aires, Colonel Perón, who had resigned himself to the necessity of such a move, was busy preparing military and civilian opinion for a declaration of war. While the public generally regarded belligerency as inevitable, the vice-president encountered a good deal of opposition from those younger nationalists in the army who were determined to brook no sniveling subservience to the United States and no alteration in Argentine foreign policy. In his search for concessions that might reconcile the integral nationalists to détente, the resourceful Perón turned to British and American circles in the Argentine capital and intimated that if he were going to participate in the war, someone would have to make up the nation's deficiencies in fuel, construction material, replacement parts, and armaments. After obtaining unofficial assurances that such aid would be forthcoming, he was able to erode opposition to rapprochement among his ultranationalist associates by holding out the promise of acquisition of all these materials, especially munitions.[112]

On March 27 Buenos Aires formally declared war on Germany, Italy, and Japan, and immediately thereafter Nelson Rockefeller called for consultation among the republics. Later in the day he held a press conference to announce that the signing of the Final Act by Argentina would not guarantee recognition but would be a significant move toward that goal. Leaving little doubt as to the final outcome, the assistant secretary expressed the view that the United States had never really broken relations with Argentina but had only withdrawn its ambassador.

Reactions in the United States to Argentina's declaration of war were mixed. Some hailed it as better late than never, but others, while calling the move a step in the right direction, proclaimed the announcement worthless since it was unaccompanied by additional measures. Official opinion in Latin America was overwhelmingly favorable, especially among Argentina's closest neighbors, who were obviously relieved at the development.[113]

The few remaining hard-liners within the department tried unsuccessfully to stem the tide. Eric Wendelin submitted a long memorandum to ARA, outlining the history of United States nonrecognition policy, repeating statements castigating Argentina that Stettinius had made in the past, reiterating Hull's views, and reaffirming his belief in unconditional nonrecognition. But like Bonsal and the ARA in 1943–44, Wendelin and Spaeth were well outside the decision-making circle of the State Department.[114]

On March 31 the Pan-American Union approved Argentina's request to sign the Final Act of Chapultepec. Simultaneously, in a meeting of the State Department's policy-planning staff, Dean Acheson certified that Argentina had declared war on the Axis, adhered to the Final Act, suspended pro-Axis newspapers, frozen Axis funds, and seized the assets of Axis firms. The department then decided that if all the nations of the hemisphere agreed, the American states would extend recognition on April 9.[115] On the evening of the thirty-first, Rockefeller and Warren went on the radio to explain the Argentine situation to the American public. Declaring that the ultranationalists in that country were on the run, Rockefeller announced that to date, Argentina had thoroughly mended her ways as far as the war and the Inter-American System were concerned. To those who believed in America's duty to rescue Argentina from totalitarianism he declared that the nature of the Argentine political system was not a proper matter of concern to the United States: "A policy of intervention may be necessary in war-torn Europe. . . . In the Western Hemisphere we have developed other methods of encouraging democracy . . . you can't superimpose democracy from the outside."[116]

From this point it was merely a matter of time. On April 4 Washington informed its envoys to the American republics of Acheson's report. On April 7 Stettinius received approval from FDR for recognition and for the appointment of Spruille Braden as ambassador to Argentina.[117] When on April 9 the twenty American republics simultaneously recognized the Farrell-Perón government, Argentina's year-old isolation within the hemisphere came to an end.

The extension of diplomatic recognition to the Farrell-Perón government was overshadowed by the death on April 12 of Franklin D. Roosevelt. His departure and Harry S. Truman's succession to the presidency, however, in no way altered the goals of American foreign policy. Like Roosevelt's, Truman's answer to the political and economic problems resulting from World War II, particularly the growing rivalry between members of the Big Three, was the creation of a viable international organization which could prevent aggression and facilitate material progress throughout the world. "The paramount significance for U.S. policy of Truman's accession to the presidency," wrote Thomas Campbell in *Masquerade Peace*, "was his decision to continue implementation of the UN policy. His first act was to announce that the San Francisco conference would meet on schedule. Through the next two months Truman constantly stressed avoiding any showdown with the Soviets until the Americans knew the outcome of the UN conference."[118] The Latin Americanists within the State Department, whose control over hemispheric affairs was not affected by the changing of the guard, were as intent as ever on reestablishing an inter-American community that would be united in its commitment to nonintervention, consultation, and commercial intercourse.[119]

The Latin Americanists and, to a certain extent, Stettinius were convinced that, given the identity of principles guiding each community, the two organizations, one global and one regional, could exist side by side. Indeed, like Welles, they believed that the two complemented rather than contradicted each other. Other State Department officials, led by Pasvolsky, continued to argue, as they had at Mexico City, that regionalism in the guise of an autonomous hemispheric organization made a viable world government impossible. They were originally opposed to American sponsorship of Argentine membership in the United Nations because they feared that such support would be interpreted by Russia and other powers as a vote by Washington for regionalism over internationalism. A series of events that transpired in April and May, however, served to convince the internationalists that Argentina's admission was essential to the very existence of the world organization. Thus, in the end, they joined forces with the Latin Americanists and worked to secure an invitation to the UNCIO for the Farrell-Perón regime.

In order to ensure that the Casa Rosada was eliminating the last vestiges of Axis influence from Argentine society, that the Farrell-Perón government was fully prepared to participate in the joint defense of the hemisphere, and that Argentina would not exclude United States businessmen from its postwar market, the Latin Americanists on April 17 sent to Buenos Aires a joint diplomatic-military mission headed by Avra Warren. Accompanying the chief of ARA were Generals G. H. Brett and I. H. Edwards of the Caribbean Defense Command, Brig. Gen. L. A. Walton of the War Department, and Adm. William Munroe, representing the navy. Thus did the Warren group represent four of the factions that were most ardently in favor of rapprochement: Warren, the old Latin Americanists; McClintock, the new Latin

Americanists and the business community; and Brett, Edwards, Walton, and Munroe, the military.[120]

Early reports to the State Department from the Warren Mission indicated that, above all else, the Casa Rosada wanted an invitation to the San Francisco Conference and would leave no stone unturned to obtain it. Perón decided to head the enthusiastic welcoming committee that greeted Warren and his colleagues at the airport. During the preliminary discussions that followed, the vice-president declared that his government was very desirous of working with Washington "in the interest of the Americas," and he requested that his guests frankly suggest the bases for such cooperation. Perón confided to Warren that he hoped rapprochement could proceed as rapidly as possible, and alluding to the question of Argentina's presence at the UNCIO, he declared that Buenos Aires understood clearly that there were "mutual commitments" as a result of Mexico City. When the chief of ARA suggested that anti-Argentine opinion in the United States placed certain limitations on what the State Department could do, Perón promised that his government was taking steps to win the North American press over to Argentina's side.[121]

After a huge memorial service for FDR, which was held in Metropolitan Cathedral on April 19, the Argentineans and their guests broke up into groups for talks on specific economic and military subjects. Elimination of pro-Axis activities and economic collaboration headed the list of topics. The Argentine secretary of commerce, Gen. Julio Cheici, assured Warren and McClintock that he was prepared to take whatever action was necessary to close down or establish governmental control over Axis firms. Moreover, he promised that rubber and other strategic materials would not be used to build up the army and navy but to facilitate production of materials essential to the Allied war effort. Later in the day, Warren and his military colleagues called at the Casa Rosada and, after exchanging pleasantries with Farrell, retired to the vice-president's offices and settled down to prolonged discussions. Perón immediately launched into an exposition of his political and social philosophy in which he emphasized the need to raise the Argentine standard of living through the development of industry, stimulation of agricultural production, and a more equitable distribution of wealth. The help of North American businessmen, he declared, would be essential to the fulfillment of these goals. With such aid, Argentina would be able to make available to the United Nations Relief and Rehabilitation Agency (UNRRA) "all materials necessary for relief and rehabilitation" in the war-devastated areas of the world.[122]

On April 21 the Argentine minister of marine accepted Admiral Munroe's proposal for collaboration between the Argentine and American navies, including the exchange of bases and technical information. The minister of war subsequently requested of Generals Brett and Edwards that they render all possible aid in instituting Argentine-American staff talks.[123]

There is no record of specific promises made by the Americans to the Argentineans concerning attendance at the UNCIO, but the State Department was obviously pleased with the Argentine position. When asked by Arnaldo Cortesi, veteran Latin American correspondent of the *New York Times*, to give his views on the state of Argentina, Warren replied that he had encountered a sincere public and official desire in Buenos Aires to fulfill the provisions of the Mexico City resolutions.[124] Upon his arrival in the United States on April 24, the head of ARA announced to newsmen that in view of the fact that Argentina had agreed to cooperate closely with the Allies in military, naval, and economic matters, Argentina might still have a chance to attend the San Francisco Conference after having signed the United Nations Declaration.[125]

Despite the Warren Mission, the Latin Americanists' ability to secure a place at the UNCIO for the Farrell-Perón government depended upon the belief by the internationalists and the White House that such a move would facilitate the establishment of the United Nations. To the distress of Rockefeller and his subordinates, the internationalists in mid April withdrew support from this the last step in rapprochement. Stettinius, at the direction of the White House, let it be known that diplomatic recognition of the Farrell-Perón government in no way committed the United States to sponsoring Argentina's adherence to the United Nations Declaration or its admittance to the UNCIO. There would be no commitment, the secretary proclaimed, until agreement was forthcoming "that from a world, as well as a hemispheric point of view, it was warranted."[126]

The reason for Truman's and Stettinius's change of heart surfaced during a meeting between the secretary of state and the British foreign secretary, Anthony Eden, in April. When, in the course of their discussions, Eden declared that Great Britain had no objection to Argentina's signing the United Nations Declaration and becoming a member of the United Nations, Stettinius replied that neither did the United States, but he was sure that Russia was adamantly opposed.[127] A new ingredient was thus added to an already complicated problem.

The Soviet Union not only vigorously objected to the inclusion of Argentina in the United Nations, but favored punishing the Argentineans for their "pro-Axis" stand during the war. In December 1944, in a violent front-page attack, *Pravda* had warned that after having supplied the Nazis with thousands of tons of war materials worth millions of dollars, Argentina was currently becoming an "asylum of Hitlerites."[128] In mid March the United States ambassador to Mexico, George Messersmith, began supplying Washington with lengthy reports that further clarified Soviet attitudes. The Russian chargé d'affaires in Mexico City began to leak stories to the local press to the effect that the Soviet Union would refuse to participate in the San Francisco Conference if the other powers permitted the Farrell-Perón government to attend. In April the Kremlin removed all doubt as to its position when *Red Star*, voice of the Soviet military establishment, warned that the USSR would boycott the San Francisco meeting if Argentina were included.[129]

In its attacks, the Soviet Union repeatedly emphasized Argentina's failure to sever relations with the Axis until 1944, its toleration of German espionage, and its domination since 1942 by two autocratic military governments. In a sense these self-righteous pronouncements (not unlike those of the United States through 1944) were disingenuous; Soviet opposition to Argentine membership was primarily motivated by a desire to weaken the Latin American bloc in the United Nations, a coalition that Moscow anticipated would be vehemently anti-Communist. At the Yalta Conference in February 1945, the Russians, concerned over their distinct numerical disadvantage in the proposed world organization, attempted to increase their membership while reducing the support of their two principal allies. Stalin initially insisted that all sixteen Soviet republics be accorded a vote as a means of balancing the British Commonwealth nations and Latin American support for the United States. In the end, Stalin, Churchill, and Roosevelt agreed to original membership for White Russia and the Ukraine. The Russians then pointed out that six Latin American states had not yet declared war on the Axis and hence would not be eligible to join the United Nations. The Big Three subsequently decided that all nonbelligerents would be allowed until March 1 to formalize hostilities.[130] Buenos Aires, however, did not declare war until March 28, and this fact, along with Argentina's wartime record, provided the Soviets with ample grounds for blocking the entrance into the UNCIO of a powerful and potentially hostile state.

On the eve of the San Francisco Conference, American policy-makers confronted an extremely delicate situation. Key states in the Latin American community had made it clear to the Latin Americanists that they would accept nothing less than original membership for the Argentineans.[131] At the same time, Stettinius, Pasvolsky, and their colleagues were fearful that if they forced Russia to accept Argentine participation in the UNCIO, the Soviets would boycott the meeting, thus destroying this new venture in collective security before it had been given a fair trial.[132] At that point neither group could have realized that an East-West split over multiple membership for the Soviet Union and the status of Poland would enable Latin America and its spokesmen in the State Department to secure an invitation for Argentina.

When the United States delegation—composed of Senators Tom Connally and Arthur Vandenberg, Congressmen Sol Bloom and Charles Eaton, Dr. Virginia Gildersleeve, Comdr. Harold Stassen, and Secretary Stettinius —met in San Francisco during the last week in April, one of the first questions they had to deal with concerned Russia's demand that the Ukraine and White Russia be seated at the conference. Speaking for the administration, Stettinius and Assistant Secretary James Dunn advised the group that at Yalta, Roosevelt had approved membership for the two Soviet republics. They strongly maintained that the United States should not antagonize the Soviet Union by failing to live up to this obligation. The United States ambassador to the Soviet Union, Averell Harriman, who was already consistently advocating a strong anti-Communist stand within administration councils, advised the delegates to support the seating of the Soviet republics in order to avoid providing Stalin with a pretext for evading his Yalta commitments regarding eastern Europe.[133] Already Washington and London were extremely concerned over what they considered to be Soviet subversion and encroachments in Poland and the Balkans.[134]

Latin America and the Latin Americanists within the State Department, meanwhile, had grasped the issue of membership for White Russia and the Ukraine as a lever to force the United States, and perhaps the Soviet Union, to support Argentine membership. On April 25 Nelson Rockefeller was instructed to "get your people [the American republics] lined up right away" in favor of multiple membership for the Soviet Union. He quickly returned and informed his colleagues that Latin Amercia would not vote for White Russia and the Ukraine unless the Big Three backed membership for Argentina. In the course of the ensuing discussion, Rockefeller took the position that at Mexico City the United States had assumed the responsibility for sponsoring the Farrell-Perón government and should now live up to its commitment.[135]

As it turned out, however, the United States delegation was as divided over the seating of Argentina as it was over the two Soviet republics. Arguing that the American people would be bitterly disillusioned if Argentina were allowed to sign the United Nations Declaration or to attend the San Francisco Conference, Senator Connally declared that he was definitely opposed to Argentine membership.[136] This view was enhanced by support from the White House. Truman had already informed Stettinius that, in his opinion, Argentina did not yet warrant the trust and support of the Allies. It was too soon, he argued, to say whether a "Johnny-come-lately" such as Argentina was in accord with Allied war aims or not.[137] Pasvolsky and his associates were certainly not anxious to take any action that would strengthen the hemispheric bloc. Not surprisingly, Cordell Hull, delegate *in absentia*, was at first adamantly opposed to admission.[138]

The danger was that if the United States did not back Argentine membership, the other nations of the Western Hemisphere might retaliate by blocking the seating of the Ukraine and White Russia. If they succeeded, then, as John Foster Dulles, the ranking Republican among the delegation's foreign-policy advisors, pointed out, the Russians could accuse the United States of using Latin American opposition as a stalking horse for Washington's attempts to limit Soviet influence in the United Nations. Moreover, Stalin, in the event that the two Russian states did not receive representation, could charge the United States and Great Britain with not having honored their Yalta pledges and thus furnish the Soviet Union with justification for not fulfilling its obligations in eastern Europe.[139] Tom Connally, Arthur Vandenberg, Averell Harriman, and James Dunn adopted this view and supported Argentine membership as a stratagem for preventing Russian domination in Poland and the Balkans.[140] In their minds, the overriding consideration was the hope that in arranging for the two extra votes for the

Soviet Union, the United States could induce Stalin to fulfill his pledges to broaden eastern European governments by holding free elections.[141]

At this point the task that faced American diplomats at San Francisco seemed impossible. At the risk of offending both public opinion and the president, they had to see the Farrell-Perón government seated in order to ensure that the western Hemisphere would support multiple membership for the Soviet Union. Given Latin America's pledge not to vote for admission of the two Soviet republics if Argentina were not seated, the UNCIO could conceivably reject the Ukraine and White Russia, possibly causing the Soviet Union to bolt the United Nations or, escaping that, providing it with an excuse for not honoring its Yalta pledges.

On April 26 the Latin Americanists, the internationalists, and the non–State Department representatives at San Francisco agreed upon a formula for compromise: Argentina could attend the United Nations Conference as an original member but would not be allowed to become a partner in the wartime alliance (i.e., not sign the United Nations Declaration). This approach would save appearances so far as the American public was concerned, while Argentina's presence at San Francisco would satisfy diplomatic requirements. The next step was to win Truman to the plan. On April 27 Stettinius phoned the White House to inform the president that the conference was on the verge of breaking up. Soviet Foreign Minister Molotov, the secretary reported, had delivered an ultimatum to the effect that the Russians would leave unless the Soviet republics were seated. He then offered the delegation's plan as the only solution. Truman still had serious misgivings, declaring that the steps that Argentina had taken seemed purely of the "bandwagon variety." Yet in the name of America's United Nations policy, he reluctantly acquiesced.[142]

With their schisms apparently healed, the United States delegates turned to the bizarre task of forcing Argentine membership on the Soviet Union in order that the two Soviet republics might be seated. Several members of the American delegation anticipated that Molotov would insist that the conference settle the matter of membership for White Russia and the Ukraine before turning to Argentina. The Russians, by separating the two problems, could possibly force the United States to align the other American nations behind multiple membership for the Soviet Union and then be free to obstruct the admission of Argentina. Consequently, James Dunn buttonholed Andrei Gromyko and informed him that the Argentine question was inseparably linked with the problem of the two Soviet republics.[143]

At a Big Four meeting called for the purpose of conferring with Latin American representatives, the Russians switched to a new approach. After Mexico's Ezequiel Padilla declared that Latin America would agree to membership for the Russian states only if the Big Four admitted Argentina, Molotov broke in and berated those present for daring to consider an invitation for Argentina while Poland remained outside the gate. Pointing out that Poland had been the first country invaded by the Nazi hordes and one of the hardest hit by the war, Molotov proclaimed that the Soviet Union would never stand by and see the UNCIO exclude Poland while it admitted a Fascist state such as Argentina.[144]

In a sentence the Russians had seized the initiative from the Anglo-Americans. With the Red Army in control of Poland, the Russians had transported the Polish Communist government-in-exile from Lublin to Warsaw and had proclaimed it as both the de facto and the de jure government. Inviting the Lublin regime to San Francisco would constitute tacit recognition by the Western powers, something that the United States and Great Britain were far from ready to grant. American and British diplomats at Yalta had insisted on the inclusion of "other Polish democratic leaders from within Poland and from abroad" in the Provisional (Lublin) Government, and they were not going to admit Poland until this had been accomplished.[145] The meeting ended with the Latin Americans threatening to withdraw support from White Russia and the Ukraine, the English warning that they would never agree to the seating of the Lublin government, and Molotov comparing the wartime records of Argentina and Poland.

In order for White Russia and the Ukraine to be admitted, and thus for the United States to live up to its Yalta commitment, the votes of the Latin American representatives were critical. But the price for gaining these votes was support for the admission of Argentina. Ironically, in order to bring pressure on Russia to fulfill its part of the Yalta bargain in regard to eastern Europe, the United States would have to guarantee Argentine membership over vociferous Soviet opposition. But in declaring that Russia would block Argentina's entry so long as Great Britain and the United States opposed the Polish Provisional Government, Molotov seemed to have undercut one of the reasons that the United States was urging the UNCIO to invite Argentina. Hard-line anti-Communists such as Vandenberg had agreed to the admission of Argentina primarily in order to curb Soviet influence in Europe. There was no question about Anglo-American opposition to the seating of Poland. When informed of the new Russian tactic, Truman instructed Stettinius to withdraw support from the Soviet republics if Molotov continued to insist on an invitation being issued to Poland.[146]

Meanwhile, the goals of the United States were advanced when the Latin American nations voted in the meeting of the Steering Committee on April 27 to seat the Soviet republics before they had received a commitment from Russia with regard to Argentina. After this display of Latin American good faith, Stettinius, Rockefeller, and Eden definitely decided that when the Executive Committee (composed of representatives of the Big Four and of delegates representing various global regions) met on April 30, the American and Commonwealth members, who together would constitute a majority, would seek to eliminate the Polish dimension from the White Russian–Ukranian–Argentinean matter by carefully separating the three issues. As they envisioned it, the meeting would (1) vote to seat the Soviet republics, (2) vote to invite Argentina to the UNCIO, and (3) defeat the Russians' proposal to seat the existing Polish government.[147]

The Anglo-American plan worked perfectly. The executive body quickly and unanimously voted to seat the Soviet republics. When the Argentine matter then came up, Molotov made good on his threat to break great-power unity. But the Commonwealth and Western Hemisphere nations were too numerous; Argentina was not to be denied. After the Russians decided not to bring up the Polish question, the only hurdle left for the three prospective new members was a final vote in the general meeting of the UNCIO.[148]

With Anthony Eden presiding, the plenary session convened on the following day and adopted a resolution that expanded the voting powers of the Soviet Union from one to three. When the Latin American delegates launched their drive in behalf of Argentina, Molotov rose to propose a postponement of the issue. To the extreme discomfort of the American republics, he pointed out that Argentina's past actions certainly had not conformed to the principles and objectives of the Grand Alliance. Had not "Secretary of State Hull yesterday branded Argentina as headquarters for a Fascist movement in this hemisphere and a potential source of infection for the rest of the Americas"? After making a case for Polish membership, he observed that thus far, unity had been preserved on all matters; it would be a shame to ruin this record because of a stampede on behalf of Argentina.[149]

Latin America was fully prepared. The republics were convinced that they had paid their dues to both Russia and the United States in voting for White Russia and the Ukraine, and they were determined to collect their reward. Colombia's Foreign Minister Alberto Lleras Camargo implored the delegates not to begin the United Nations experiment with an act that was in violation of the organization's basic principles by denying admission to a country because of disapproval of its internal affairs. Argentina's international conduct, which had been unswervingly correct, should be the only criterion for judging its admission. Latin American representatives again contended that because Argentina had declared war on the Axis, the Allies had an obligation to see that Argentina be seated. Glancing at the United States delegation, the Peruvian chairman asserted that the real questions involved in the Argentine matter were intervention in the affairs of a sovereign nation and, as he turned to look at the Russians, whether the American nations constituted a judicial and moral unity.[150]

For the United States the time had come to make its position absolutely clear. Stettinius took the floor to assert that the United States government was in entire accord with the view of the American republics that the Farrell-Perón regime had complied with the Mexico City Resolution and that therefore Argentina should be invited to San Francisco. After the Russians were able to muster only seven votes for postponement, the plenary session voted 31 to 4 to seat Argentina.[151]

The deterioration in Argentine-American relations and the concomitant decline of the Good Neighbor Policy that occurred from 1942 through 1944 had been the result in part of the bureaucratic conflict between the Welles Latin Americanists and the Hull internationalists. It was ironic, to say the least, that Argentina's reincorporation into the hemispheric fold and its admission into the United Nations were the product of cooperation between a new group of Latin Americanists and a new group of Wilsonian internationalists. For the new Latin American establishment in the State Department, the decision to invite the Farrell-Perón government to San Francisco marked the culmination of a campaign to alleviate apprehension south of the Rio Grande which had been caused by wartime intervention into Argentine affairs. Believing that the welfare of the United States and the entire hemisphere depended on the maintenance of an Inter-American System based on nonintervention, consultation, and economic interdependence, Rockefeller and his associates first secured Argentina's readmission to the American community and then maneuvered successfully to obtain a seat for it at the UNCIO. At the same time, the White House and many within the United States delegation, including Stettinius, Pasvolsky, and Hull, had accepted Argentina in order to maintain the integrity of the United Nations. Reflecting the widespread belief in America that an effective world organization was the only alternative to aggression and depression, these policy-makers had agreed to the seating of Argentina in order to prevent a bolt by the Communist bloc that would have destroyed the United Nations at its inception.

9

POSTSCRIPT TO DETENTE

Although Argentina's admission to the United Nations marked the successful culmination of an attempt by groups in the United States and various Latin American governments to normalize Argentine-American relations and to resurrect the Good Neighbor Policy, complete rapprochement and reestablishment of the principles of nonintervention and noninterference would require another two years. In many respects the period from 1945 through 1947 in Argentine-American relations was a replay of the 1941 through 1945 era. Continuing resentment in the United States over Buenos Aires' neutralist policies during the war, plus instability within the foreign-policy establishment, led to a brief revival of moral imperialism. In turn, essentially the same forces and groups that had been responsible for rapprochement in 1945 emerged in 1947 to force détente and the restoration of hemispheric solidarity.

The State Department's choice of an ambassador to restore formal diplomatic relations with Argentina was the veteran foreign-service officer and wartime ambassador to Colombia and Chile, Spruille Braden. As events were to reveal, Braden's views on the meaning of nonintervention and respect for the sovereignty of all nations differed drastically from those of Welles, Rockefeller, and Stettinius. With advocates of rapprochement neutralized by the flood tide of domestic criticism that came in the wake of Argentina's admission to the United Nations, Braden joined battle with the Farrell-Perón regime and worked openly for the return of democracy to Argentina.[1]

Braden's arrival in Buenos Aires coincided with a new wave of domestic repression. Using the recent declaration of war against the Axis as a pretext, Perón moved to end criticism of government policies and to hamstring his personal enemies. During the ensuing campaign to "preserve public order," federal police jailed Gen. Arturo Rawson and some seventy other anti-government figures, banned public meetings, and installed censorship of the press.[2] Indicating that he intended to be a positive force for democracy in Argentina, Braden attacked the Farrell-Perón government directly for not expelling Axis-controlled firms from the country and indirectly for blocking the nation's return to constitutionalism.[3]

The ambassador's criticism brought an immediate though rather paradoxical reaction from Farrell and Perón. On the one hand, Farrell announced that elections would be held by early 1946, and he lifted the state of siege for the first time in three years. On the other, Perón launched a carefully orchestrated attack on Braden, branding him as but another agent of North American imperialism.[4]

Meanwhile, in Washington, a shake-up in the State Department paved the way for the ascendancy of Braden and his policy of revolutionary democracy within the foreign-policy establishment. James Byrnes replaced Edward Stettinius, Jr., as secretary of state in July 1945. America's new chief diplomat immediately announced that in view of his ignorance of Latin American affairs, he was going to appoint an able subordinate to manage hemispheric problems. That subordinate was Spruille Braden.[5] In August, Nelson Rockefeller, openly confessing the failure of his soft-line policy toward Argentina, resigned to make way for Braden as assistant secretary of state for Latin American affairs.[6] Rockefeller, and to some extent Stettinius, had succumbed to public outrage over Argentina's being admitted to the United Nations, outrage that had only increased as the Farrell-Perón government continued to persecute its political opponents and suspend the right to free speech and assembly.

There were, however, those who dared to speak out against Braden and his attempt to return Argentina to the paths of constitutional democracy. Sumner Welles recited his Good Neighbor litany and blamed the State Department's hard-line policies on two groups: old Hull supporters within the department, who were intent on vindicating their mentor, and the Committee on Latin American Affairs within the CIO, which had called for Washington to prevent the spread of Argentine fascism to neighboring republics.[7] Joining Welles were Senators Tom Connally and Arthur Vandenberg, both of whom had been delegates to the Mexico City and the San Francisco conferences. During Senate confirmation hearings they repeatedly castigated Braden for endangering hemispheric solidarity. Connally and Vandenberg, like Welles, were committed to the concept of regional collective-security organizations working within the context of a world body, although the senators were concerned primarily with containing Soviet expansion, while Welles was preoccupied with preserving the Inter-American System.[8] Not surprisingly, this anti-Braden coalition represented some of the views and assumptions of those who had been responsible for Argentina's admission to the United Nations.

Despite this criticism, Braden was confirmed as assistant secretary, and from his new post he continued his war with Perón and Argentine fascism. In so doing, he shook the very foundations of inter-American solidarity. In early October, the State Department announced that because of the totalitarian and pro-Axis policies of the Farrell-Perón government, the United States could not conclude a treaty of military assistance with Argentina. In so doing, Washington scuttled the Foreign Ministers Meeting scheduled for October 20, which was to complete the work of the Chapultepec Conference by converting the Inter-American System into a collective-security organization. Even more damaging to Argentine-American relations and to the Good Neighbor Policy was the State Department's decision to publish its "Blue Book on Argentina," which claimed to prove conclusively that a tacit alliance had existed between the Farrell-Perón government and the Axis. What appalled so many *latinos* was the timing of the release. In October 1945 Perón had announced as a presidential candidate for the general elections to be held in February 1946. In an unmistakable effort to stop the Perón bandwagon, the United States published the Blue Book just one week prior to the election.[9]

To Braden's dismay, the Perónistas won a decisive victory. Washington's blatant attempt to influence the outcome of the presidential contest had no doubt helped, rather than hindered, Perón. Indeed, the outcome of the election, described by many Argentineans as the freest since 1916, constituted a repudiation of the Hull-Braden policy of revolutionary democracy and undercut the State Department's prime rationale for coercion of Argentina. At this point, Braden faced a choice of policies. The United States could acquiesce in its defeat gracefully, recognize the Perón regime as the legally constituted government, and proceed with the conclusion of a hemispheric mutual-defense pact, or it could, using the threat of Argentine expansion as a pretext, continue to try to isolate Argentina within the hemisphere. To the alarm of the Latin American republics and of various influential groups in the United States, Braden chose the latter course. Washington once again postponed the foreign ministers' meeting which had been scheduled for 1946 in Bogotá, and throughout the rest of the year called upon Buenos Aires to fulfill its commitments under the Act of Chapultepec.[10]

Just as in the spring of 1945, Perón, who had decided on a policy of reconciliation with the United States after his triumph in February, used the carrot and the stick in an effort to force Washington to end its coercive policies. On June 16 he opened diplomatic relations with the Soviet Union. By the end of the year he had nationalized several American-owned firms and was actively seeking to draw neighboring states into Argentina's economic sphere. At the same time he professed a desire for friendship with Washington and declared that in any future war, Argentina would be bound to fight with the United States and the rest of the American republics.[11]

Aiding Perón were the same forces and groups that had come forth in 1944–45 to press for an Argentine-American rapprochement. In the first place, there was no less a demand for Argentine food and fiber in Europe in 1946 than there had been in 1945. Indeed, the winter of 1946 was the worst that Europe had experienced in a generation. This, coupled with the economic chaos caused by World War II, made starvation a very real possibility in both occupied and nonoccupied areas, and caused those American policy-makers who were concerned primarily with the European situation to press for a normalization of relations with Argentina. Secondly, American exporters were just as anxious to sell Argentina the tires, tools, rolling stock, and heavy machinery that she so desperately needed as they had been in 1945. If Braden continued with his vendetta, American exporters believed that they would find the open door in Argentina shut firmly in their faces. In addition there were those, like Connally and Vandenberg, who believed that the United States had to be able to count on solid hemispheric support in the growing Soviet-American confrontation. Détente with Argentina, they believed, would restore inter-American solidarity, which in turn would protect the New World from Communist penetration. Many Latin American governments were themselves concerned about the threat of Soviet expansion, and they, no less than Connally and Vandenberg, viewed Washington's isolation of Argentina as an invitation to extrahemispheric intervention. Moreover, *latinos* had, since 1944, looked forward to the creation of a collective-security organization that would not only protect the Americas from any extrahemispheric threat but would also take the lead in solving socio-economic problems south of the Rio Grande.[12]

By early 1947 the Truman administration, which had become increasingly sensitive to criticism of Braden's hard-line policies, particularly by those who charged that these policies were hindering America's efforts to resist Soviet expansion, was ready to end the feud with Argentina and return once again to the principles of nonintervention and noninterference. When Gen. George C. Marshall, representing a group that had consistently urged cooperation rather than confrontation with Argentina, replaced Byrnes as secretary of state, the way was open for Braden's ouster and for détente with Buenos Aires. After a series of friendly gestures toward the Perón government, President Truman announced on June 3 that no obstacle remained to discussion looking toward the treaty of mutual assistance contemplated by the Treaty of Chapultepec.[13] Shortly thereafter Braden resigned. His replacement as assistant secretary was Norman Armour, who subsequently presided not only over normalization of relations with Argentina but over negotiation of the Pact of Rio in the fall of 1947. That agreement ended America's eleven-year campaign to erect a collective-security system that would include all the states of the hemisphere.[14]

In 1933 a small group of Latin American specialists within the State Department, building on initiatives begun by the Coolidge and Hoover administrations, set about to undo the damage to United States–Latin American relations that had been done by a generation of military and economic intervention into the affairs of various Central and South American republics. Invoking the principles of nonintervention and noninterference, they dismantled North America's system of protectorates south of the Rio Grande and refused to coerce Latin governments that threatened United States businesses with nationalization. Over a period of time the Latin Americanists within the State Department were able to dispel much of the mistrust and resentment that had characterized *latino* attitudes toward the United States since the turn of the century and, with varying degrees of success, to establish new relationships based on respect and mutuality of interest.

In part, the durability of the Good Neighbor Policy had depended upon the willingness of all American republics to join with the United States in resisting attempts by extrahemispheric sources to intervene in New World affairs and upon continuity within the United States foreign-policy establishment. During World War II, neither prerequisite was satisfied. Argentina chose to pursue a neutralist course, and the Latin American policy of the United States became the subject of a bitter bureaucratic struggle within the Roosevelt administration. Consequently, the principles of nonintervention and noninterference, together with "absolute respect for the sovereignty of all states," ceased to be the guideposts of Washington's hemispheric policy.

As has been noted, Argentina's decision to remain aloof from the struggle against the Axis was a product of Argentine geography, economics, culture, politics, and diplomatic tradition as well as of contemporary developments such as the Depression and the intensification of Argentine nationalism. Despite Argentina's political instability and despite intense pressure from the Allied community, Argentine attitudes toward World War II remained fairly constant from 1941 through 1945. The real variable in Argentine-American relations, and the key to understanding Washington's response to Argentine neutrality, was competition for control of policy between various individuals and agencies within the Roosevelt foreign-policy establishment.

The weeks immediately following the Japanese attack on Pearl Harbor witnessed an intense struggle within the State Department between two rival groups of diplomats for control of policy. The Welles Latin Americanists and the Hull internationalists, representing two different viewpoints on hemispheric affairs, fought both prior to and during the Rio Conference to have their policy recommendations endorsed by the chief executive. Because of direct access to the White House, exclusive control over certain vital information, proximity to the negotiating process, and a variety of other factors, the Latin Americanists succeeded in excluding their rivals from the decision-making process and, as a result, gained control over not only Argentine but also hemispheric policy.

The subtle coercive techniques pursued by the Latin Americanists throughout the remainder of 1942 were a reflection of their commitment to the Good Neighbor Policy (i.e., nonintervention, consultation, and overt respect for the sovereignty of each American state) and of pressure from the internationalists, the Treasury Department, and the Board of Economic Warfare. In order to advance a particular concept of the national interest, to wage economic warfare against the Axis more effectively, and to augment their power within the New Deal bureaucracy, the Treasury Department, under Morgenthau and White, and the Board of Economic Warfare, led by Wallace and Perkins, pressed the State Department for a hard-line posture toward Argentina. Pressure from these two sources drove the Latin Americanists and the internationalists into a momentary alliance during which Hull joined with the undersecretary in defending the Latin Americanists' policy of selective discrimination. The end result, however, was to undermine the Welles group and pave the way for the ascendancy of the internationalists within the State Department.

Welles's defection to the hard-liners in the fall of 1942, based in no small part on his desire to remain the arbiter of hemispheric policy, left the Latin Americanists leaderless and devoid of a conduit to the White House. Consequently, their power within the foreign-policy establishment gradually diminished until the summer of 1944, when Duggan and Bonsal were forced out of the State Department. The undersecretary's adoption of a hard-line attitude and the subsequent decline of the Latin Americanists destroyed the bureaucratic balance of power within the State Department and allowed Hull and his subordinates to dominate hemispheric policy throughout most of 1943 and all of 1944. As a result, the Wilsonian assumptions about the role of the United States in Latin America that underlay Hull's and Long's philosophy regarding foreign affairs began to come to the fore. After the revolution of June 1943, democratization of the Argentine political system became as important a goal to American policy-makers as elimination of the ties between Buenos Aires and the Axis capitals. Ironically, only continuing pressure from the Treasury Department and the Foreign Economic Administration, the successor agency to BEW, served to ameliorate (in the economic sphere at least) United States policy toward Argentina.

From mid 1943 until December 1944 the State Department employed every conceivable type of diplomatic weapon against Argentina in an attempt to compel it to abandon neutrality and return to constitutional government. Gradually these tactics—which included invoking the rest of the Latin American community against Argentina, upsetting the military balance of power in South America, contributing to the downfall of the Ramírez government, and, finally, instituting a policy of unilateral nonrecognition—created a reaction against the hard-liners within the foreign-policy establishment, the American business community, and the Inter-American System.

It was these factors, together with Roosevelt's decision to reorganize and streamline the State Department by installing new leadership, that made

211

possible a reversal of policy toward Argentina. The shake-up in the State Department in late 1944 introduced two additional groups of policy-makers into the Argentine-American equation. A new coterie of internationalists, headed by Edward Stettinius, Jr., and Leo Pasvolsky, assumed overall control of the State Department and devoted their efforts to implementing America's United Nations policy. At the same time, a new aggregation of Latin Americanists, headed by Nelson Rockefeller and his former subordinates in the Office of Coordinator of Inter-American Affairs, took charge of hemispheric matters. Sensitive to the demands of United States traders and investors who were then insisting on an end to coercion of Argentina, and at the same time convinced that the Good Neighbor Policy offered the best approach to safeguarding North America's strategic and economic interests south of the Rio Grande, the neo–Latin Americanists engineered a complete rapprochement with Argentina. The internationalists cooperated in the first phase of détente in order to gain general support among the Latin American republics for the United Nations concept and, during the second, to avoid an open split between East and West that might have destroyed the UNCIO at its inception.

As the principal participants in the decision-making process struggled to advance a concept of the national interest, to fulfill organizational goals, and to enhance their personal power, their efforts were dramatically affected by coalitions with other nations, agencies, and interest groups. For instance, the Argentine military profited from the fact that the Latin Americanists succeeded in controlling policy within the United States foreign-affairs establishment in 1942 and again in 1945. Neutrality, which was so important to the army's organizational goals of survival and aggrandizement, was a result, in part, of Washington's commitment to respect for the juridical equality of all states and for hemispheric solidarity. In turn, the United States' commitment to those principles was an outgrowth of the Latin Americanists' bureaucratic victory. There was, moreover, a tacit pact between Whitehall and the original group of Latin Americanists. This alliance at times became explicit, as in 1943, when Bonsal and Duggan joined with the British Foreign Office in attempting to restrain Hull and Long over the Transradio affair. The intimate relationship between the Justistas and Radicals on the one hand and the American embassy on the other clearly affected Armour's policy recommendations and, thus, United States policy toward Argentina. Finally, the fact that several leading Latin American nations and the Rockefeller Latin Americanists formed a coalition in the spring of 1945 had much to do with the seating of Argentina at San Francisco.

Something remains to be said about the policies themselves, the options that were thrust up through the bureaucratic structure to the chief decision-makers for their approval. In designing policy alternatives, officials are ever-mindful of the interests of their organization and of their personal power position, but for the substance of their recommendations they must draw on an aggregation of assumptions about the nature of the international community and the role that America should play in it. Consciously or unconsciously, virtually all of the diplomats and bureaucrats in charge of the "Argentine problem" during World War II relied on the Wilsonian tradition for their attitudes on foreign affairs. For those who chose to reject isolationism, there was hardly any other alternative.

Indeed, America's posture toward Argentina from 1942 through 1945 may be viewed as a conflict between two disparate strains contained in the Wilsonian philosophy. A determination to create an international community of sovereign nations pledged to observe in their dealings with each other the principles of self-determination and noncoercion is, of course, the best-known theme in the "New Diplomacy."[15] As Robert Divine has shown in *The Triumph of Internationalism,* the Roosevelt administration and a majority of Americans acknowledged the interdependence of nations during World War II and deliberately embraced world cooperation as an alternative to nationalism, expansionism, and war. This concept of community, clearly embodied in the Welles-Rockefeller approach to inter-American matters and in the Stettinius-Pasvolsky view of international affairs, prevailed in Argentine-American policy throughout much of 1942 and then again during the first half of 1945. The other theme in the Wilsonian approach is the belief that it is the duty of the United States to promote the spread of democratic institutions and processes and to use its might to compel other governments to pursue an enlightened course both in domestic and international affairs. This aspect of Wilsonianism, which was so apparent in the statements and policies of the Hull internationalists toward Argentina after June 1943, emerged triumphant when the Latin Americanists were eliminated from the decision-making process. Actually, Hull, Long, and their subordinates were committed to both goals. They believed, however, like Wilson, that not only were the two objectives compatible but that the democratization of the political systems of the nation-states of the world would facilitate the establishment of a viable collective-security organization.

As Laurence Duggan perceived all along, the two primary objectives of Wilsonian foreign policy are contradictory and at times mutually exclusive. America's attempts to export democracy have almost inevitably led to intervention in the affairs of other states, and as in late 1944, when the Hull group fought against the holding of an inter-American conference on the grounds that it might lead to the legitimization of the Farrell-Perón regime, they have undermined attempts to create an international concert of powers. Recognition of this contradiction is essential to an understanding of the diplomatic conflicts of the period. The Good Neighbor Policy, which was tested to the breaking point in Argentine-American relations during World War II, emerged as, among other things, an explicit rejection of revolutionary democracy and a reaffirmation of Wilsonian internationalism.

NOTES

PREFACE

1. Bryce Wood, *The Making of the Good Neighbor Policy* (New York,), pp. 309–12.
2. Ibid.
3. David Green, *The Containment of Latin America* (Chicago, 1971), pp. 85–136.
4. Edward O. Guerrant, *Roosevelt's Good Neighbor Policy* (Albuquerque, N.Mex., 1950), p. 212.
5. See, for example, John Morton Blum, ed., *The Price of Vision: The Diary of Henry A. Wallace, 1942–1946* (Boston, 1973), and *From the Morgenthau Diaries*, vol. 3 (Boston, 1967).
6. Richard E. Neustadt, *Presidential Power* (New York, 1960), p. 151;

Arthur M. Schlesinger, Jr., *The Age of Roosevelt*, vol. 2, *The Coming of the New Deal* (Boston, 1959), pp. 521–30; and Dean Acheson, *Present at the Creation* (New York, 1969), pp. 11–12.
7. For an extensive explanation of the decision-making process, see Graham T. Allison, *Essence of Decision* (Boston, 1971). Also helpful are "American Political and Bureaucratic Decision-Making," in Richard M. Pfeffer, ed., *No More Vietnams?* (New York, 1968), pp. 44–115, and Richard J. Barnet, *Roots of War* (New York, 1972).

CHAPTER 1

1. Among the most widely read and reliable accounts of United States policy toward Latin America are J. Lloyd Mecham, *A Survey of United States–Latin American Relations* (Boston, 1965); Samuel F. Bemis, *The Latin American Policy of the United States* (New

York, 1943); Edward Lieuwen, *U.S. Policy in Latin America* (New York, 1965); and Dexter Perkins, *A History of the Monroe Doctrine*, 3d ed. (Boston, 1963).
2. For a provocative interpretation of the New Manifest Destiny see Ernest R. May, *American Imperi-*

alism: A Speculative Essay (New York, 1968).

3. The two classic works on the forces responsible for American expansion at the turn of the century are Julius W. Pratt, *Expansionists of 1898* (Baltimore, 1951), and Walter LaFeber, *The New Empire* (Ithaca, N.Y., 1963). See also Albert K. Weinberg, *Manifest Destiny* (Baltimore, 1935), and Milton Plesur *America's Outward Thrust: Approaches to Foreign Affairs, 1865–1890* (De Kalb, Ill., 1971).

4. Quoted in Robert H. Ferrell, *American Diplomacy: A History* (rev. and enl. ed., New York, 1969), pp. 446–47.

5. The best general work on Roosevelt's foreign policy is Howard K. Beale, *Theodore Roosevelt and the Rise of America to World Power* (Baltimore, 1956). See, in addition, George E. Mowry, *The Era of Theodore Roosevelt, 1900–1912* New York, 1958); Raymond A. Esthus, *Theodore Roosevelt and the International Rivalries* (Waltham, Mass., 1970); David H. Burton, *Theodore Roosevelt: Confident Imperialist* (Philadelphia, 1968); and Richard D. Challener, *Admirals, Generals, and American Foreign Policy, 1898–1914* (Princeton, N.J., 1973).

6. See Doris A. Graber, *Crisis Diplomacy: A History of U.S. Intervention Policies and Practices* (Washington, D.C., 1959); Scott Nearing and Joseph Freeman, *Dollar Diplomacy* (New York, 1925); and Dana G. Munro, "Dollar Diplomacy in Nicaragua, 1909–1913," *Hispanic American Historical Review* 38 (1958): 209–38.

7. The most concise analysis of Wilson's foreign policy objectives is in Arthur S. Link, *Wilson the Diplomatist* (Chicago, 1965). For a detailed account of Wilson's policies see Link's *Woodrow Wilson and the Progressive Era, 1910–1917* (New York, 1954).

8. For Wilson's Mexican policy see Howard F. Cline, *The United States and Mexico* (Cambridge, Mass., 1953); Isidro Fabela, *Historia diplomática de la revolución mexicana, 1912–1917*, 2 vols. Mexico City, 1958–59); and Kenneth J. Grieb, *The United States and Huerta* (Lincoln, Nebr., 1969).

9. As quoted by Selig Adler, *The Uncertain Giant, 1921–1941: American Foreign Policy between the Wars* (New York, 1956), p. 95.

10. Ibid., pp. 96–97.

11. For the Latin American policy of the Harding-Coolidge era see L. Ethan Ellis, *Republican Foreign Policy, 1921–1933* (New Brunswick, N.J., 1968); Betty Glad, *Charles Evans Hughes and the Illusions of Innocence* (Urbana, Ill., 1966); Bryce Wood, *The Making of the Good Neighbor Policy* (New York, 1961); and Stanley Robert Ross, "Dwight Morrow and the Mexican Revolution," *Hispanic American Historical Review* 38 (1958): 515.

12. Alexander DeConde, *Herbert*

Hoover's Latin American Policy (Stanford, Calif., 1951), p. 51.

13. The literature on the New Deal phase of the Good Neighbor Policy is extensive. Heading the list is Wood's *Making of the Good Neighbor Policy*. See also Edward O. Guerrant, *Roosevelt's Good Neighbor Policy* (Albuquerque, N.Mex., 1950); Gordon Connell-Smith, *The Inter-American System* (London, 1966); David Green, *The Containment of Latin America* (Chicago, 1971); and numerous titles mentioned above.

14. See Donald M. Dozer, *Are We Good Neighbors? Three Decades of Inter-American Relations, 1930–1960* (Gainesville, Fla., 1961).

15. Anticipation of reciprocity is a concept developed by Wood in *The Making of the Good Neighbor Policy*, pp. 1–7.

16. Adler, *Uncertain Giant*, p. 113.

17. Edmund Smith, Jr., *Yankee Diplomacy: U.S. Intervention in Argentina* (Dallas, Tex., 1953), pp. 26–31, and Harold F. Peterson, *Argentina and the United States, 1810–1960* (Albany, N.Y., 1969), pp. 391–93.

18. Enrique Ruiz-Guiñazú, *La política argentina y el futuro de América* (Buenos Aires, 1944), p. 34.

19. Juan José Hernández Arregui, *La formación de la conciencia, nacional, 1930–1960* (Buenos Aires, 1960), pp. 64–68.

20. Arthur P. Whitaker, *The United States and Argentina* (Cambridge, Mass., 1954), pp. 5–7.

21. Marvin Goldwert, *Democracy, Militarism, and Nationalism in Argentina, 1930–1966* (Austin, Tex., and London, 1972), p. xi.

22. James R. Scobie, *Argentina: A City and a Nation* (New York, 1964), pp. 12–13.

23. Gustavo Gabriel Levene, *Historia argentina*, 3 vols. (Buenos Aires, 1964), 3:220–50.

24. Thomas F. McGann, *Argentina, the United States, and the Inter-American System, 1880–1914* (Cambridge, Mass., 1959), pp. 71–80.

25. Ibid., pp. 4–11.

26. Levene, *Historia*, 3:220–50; and Ruiz-Guiñazú, *La política*, pp. 39–48.

27. Hernández Arregui, *La formación*, pp. 262–64; and George I. Blanksten, *Perón's Argentina* (New York, 1967).

28. McGann, *Argentina*, pp. 77, 163–64.

29. José Luis Romero, *A History of Argentine Political Thought*, 3d ed., trans. and with an introduction by Thomas F. McGann (Stanford, Calif., 1963), pp. 227–28.

30. Scobie, *Argentina*, pp. 201–2.

31. For a view of the Socialist movement in particular and twentieth-century Argentine history in general see Juan José Real, *30 años de historia argentina* (Buenos Aires, 1962). Real was himself a prominent Socialist.

32. Carlos Ibarguren, *La historia que he vivido* (Buenos Aires, 1955), pp. 314–17; and Romero, *History of Argentine Political Thought*, pp. 367–79.

33. Ysabel F. Rennie, *The Argentine*

Republic (New York, 1945), pp. 268–74.

34. Romero, *History of Argentine Political Thought*, p. 235.

35. John C. Campbell, "Political Extremes in South America," *Foreign Affairs* 20:525–27.

36. Hernández Arregui, *La formación*, p. 392.

37. Nicolás Repetto, *Mi paso por la política* (Buenos Aires, 1957), p. 255; and Hernández Arregui, *La formación*, p. 252.

38. Romero, *History of Argentine Political Thought*, pp. 239–40; and Hernández Arregui, *La formación*, pp. 392, 352.

39. Goldwert, *Democracy, Militarism, and Nationalism*, p. 54; and Arthur P. Whitaker, *Argentina* (Englewood Cliffs, N.J., 1964), pp. 83–103.

40. Robert A. Potash, *The Army & Politics in Argentina, 1928–1945* (Stanford, Calif., 1969), pp. 107–8. For a somewhat biased history of the Justo administration see Ibarguren, *La historia*, pp. 440–69. See also Gustavo Gabriel Levene, ed., *Presidentes argentinos* (Buenos Aires, 1961), pp. 149–60, 228–30.

41. Potash, *Army & Politics*, pp. 117, 119; and Department of State, *Foreign Relations of the United States, 1942* (Washington, D.C., 1961), 5:12–26 (hereafter, volumes in this series will be referred to as *F.R.U.S.*)

42. Romero, *History of Argentine Political Thought*, p. 238; and

43. Real, *30 años*, pp. 56–57.

44. *F.R.U.S., 1941*, 6:330–33; Sumner Welles, *The Time for Decision* (New York, 1944), pp. 288–89; William L. Langer and S. Everett Gleason, *The Undeclared War, 1940–1941* (New York, 1953), p. 166; *F.R.U.S., 1942*, 5:379–85; "Export-Import Bank Loans to Latin America," *Foreign Policy Reports* 17 (June 1941): 89; and Rennie, *Argentine Republic*, pp. 247–48.

45. Bemis, *Latin American Policy*, pp. 290–93.

46. Whitaker, *United States and Argentina*, p. 106; and Smith, *Yankee Diplomacy*, pp. 28–31.

47. Smith, *Yankee Diplomacy*, p. 32.

48. Repetto, *Mi paso*, pp. 151–53.

49. Leandro P. Romero, "Relaciónes exterióres," in Jorge A. Paita, ed., *Argentina, 1930–1960* (Buenos Aires, 1961), p. 179; and Peterson, *Argentina and the United States*, pp. 393–95.

50. Bemis, *Latin American Policy*, pp. 355–60.

51. Rennie, *Argentine Republic*, pp. 266–68.

52. Ruiz-Guiñazú, *La política*, pp. 39–48; and Real, *30 años*, pp. 56–57.

53. Peterson, *Argentina and the United States*, pp. 399–402.

54. Smith, *Yankee Diplomacy*, pp. 47–49.

55. Romero, "Relaciónes exterióres," pp. 178–82.

56. Whitaker, *United States and Argentina*, pp. 109–11.

CHAPTER 2

1. Circular Telegram to All Diplomatic Missions in the Other American Republics, 9 December 1941, 710. consultation 3/16A, RG 59, Department of State, National Archives (hereafter referred to as DOS); and *F.R.U.S., 1941*, 6:118–19.

2. Richard E. Neustadt, *Presidential Power* (New York, 1960), p. 151; and Arthur M. Schlesinger, Jr., *The Age of Roosevelt*, vol. 2, *The Coming of the New Deal* (Boston, 1959), pp. 521–30. FDR's administrative techniques once led political boss Edward J. Flynn to remark: "The boss either appoints four men to do the job of one or one man to do the job of four." He added that none of the four knew what the other three were doing nor did the one know the scope of his authority. Arthur Krock, *Memoirs* (New York, 1968), p. 202.

3. The Diaries of Henry L. Stimson, 26 November 1942, 41:30, and 4 May 1943, 43:12, Sterling Library, Yale University; Conversation between Hull and Lord Halifax, 23 January 1944, boxes 59 and 60, folder 216, Papers of Cordell Hull, Library of Congress; Cordell Hull, *Memoirs of Cordell Hull*, 2 vols. (New York, 1948), 2:1145; Krock, *Memoirs*, p. 205; and Dean Acheson, *Present at the Creation* (New York, 1969), pp. 11–12. See also the Diaries of Adolf Berle, 18 December 1941, box 213, Franklin D. Roosevelt Library, Hyde Park, N.Y.

4. Dean Acheson describes the bureaucratic situation in the State Department in 1941 quite succinctly: "The heads of all these divisions [American Republics, European, etc.] like barons in a feudal system weakened at the top by mutual suspicion and jealousy between king [Hull] and prince [Welles], were constantly at odds, if not at war." Acheson, *Present at the Creation*, p. 15.

5. Radio Address by Welles, 24 January 1942, 710. conference 3/582, RG 59, DOS; *New York Times*, 25 September 1961, 14 June 1952, 21 December 1948; *Who's Who, 1942* (New York, 1942), p. 308; and Duggan to Rockefeller, 31 January 1944, RG 229, General Records of the Office of Coordinator of Inter-American Affairs (hereafter referred to as OCIAA), Washington Federal Records Center.

6. Sumner Welles, *The Time for Decision* (New York, 1944), p. 240.

7. Laurence Duggan, "Foundations of Inter-American Solidarity" (Address to the American Political Science Association, 29 December 1941), *Department of State Bulletin*, vol. 6, no. 132 (3 January 1942), pp. 8–11, quoted passage on p. 8.

8. Sumner Welles, *Seven Decisions That Shaped History* (New York, 1950), p. 100.

9. Ibid., pp. 105–19, quoted passage on p. 105.

10. Harold B. Hinton, *Cordell Hull:*

A Biography (Garden City, N.Y., 1942), pp. 129–30.

11. For the continuity between Hull's and Wilson's views on foreign affairs see Hull, *Memoirs*; and Julius W. Pratt, *The American Secretaries of States and Their Diplomacy*, vols. 12 and 13, *Cordell Hull, 1933–1944* (New York, 1964), 13:707.

12. *New York Times*, 27 September 1958. Long's intellectual ties with Wilson are apparent throughout his papers and diaries. See Papers of Breckinridge Long, in the Library of Congress; and Fred L. Israel, ed., *The War Diary of Breckinridge Long* (Lincoln, Nebr., 1966).

13. Hull, *Memoirs*, pp. 314–16.

14. Bryce Wood, *The Making of the Good Neighbor Policy* (New York, 1961), pp. 1–7; and Conversation between Hull and Lord Halifax, 23 January 1944, boxes 59 and 60, folder 216, Hull Papers.

15. John Morton Blum, *The Price of Vision: The Diary of Henry A. Wallace, 1942–1946* (Boston, 1973).

16. Berle Diaries, 25 July 1942, box 214, and Berle to Bankhead, 8 March 1940, box 55, Papers of Adolf Berle, Franklin D. Roosevelt Library, Hyde Park, N.Y.

17. Juan José Real, *30 años de historia argentina* (Buenos Aires, 1962), pp. 56–57; Ysabel F. Rennie, *The Argentine Republic* (New York, 1945), pp. 266–67; and Harold F. Peterson, *Argentina and the United States, 1810–1960* (Albany, N.Y., 1964), p. 399.

18. Hull, *Memoirs*, 2:1145.

19. Conversation between Hull and Maxim Litvinov, 2 January 1942, 710. consultation (3)/453, and Circular Telegram to All Diplomatic Missions in the Other American Republics, 9 December 1941, 710. consultation 3/16A, RG 59, DOS.

20. Hull, *Memoirs*, 2:1377.

21. Even the FBI, which always tended to see the worst in Argentina, admitted that this was the case. J. Edgar Hoover to Harry Hopkins, June 1943, box 140, Papers of Harry Hopkins, Franklin D. Roosevelt Library, Hyde Park, N.Y.

22. Gustavo Gabriel Levene, *Historia argentina*, 3 vols. (Buenos Aires, 1964), 3:243–45.

23. Carlos Ibarguren, *La historia que he vivido* (Buenos Aires, 1955), pp. 440–69.

24. Robert A. Potash, *The Army & Politics in Argentina, 1928–1945* (Stanford, Calif., 1969), p. 105. Argentine presidents were constitutionally forbidden from succeeding themselves.

25. Marvin Goldwert, *Democracy, Militarism, and Nationalism in Argentina, 1930–1966* (Austin, Tex., and London, 1972), p. 50.

26. Gustavo Gabriel Levene, ed., *Presidentes argentinos* (Buenos Aires, 1961), pp. 229–31.

27. Potash, *Army & Politics*, p. 143.

28. Ibid., p. 157; and Levene, *Historia Argentina*, 3:232.

29. *Noticias Gráficas*, 9 January 1942; and Potash, *Army & Politics*, p. 164.

30. Levene, *Presidentes argentinos*, pp. 149–60, 228–30, 232.

31. Potash, *Army & Politics*, p. 165.
32. Nicolás Repetto, *Mi paso por la política* (Buenos Aires, 1957), pp. 152, 202–13; and Goldwert, *Democracy, Militarism, and Nationalism*, p. 34.
33. Real, *30 años*, p. 56.
34. *F.R.U.S., 1942*, 5:17–18 and 373–75.
35. Real, *30 años*, pp. 56–57; Rennie, *Argentine Republic*, pp. 266–67; and Peterson, *Argentina and the United States*, p. 399.
36. Repetto, *Mi Paso*, p. 255.
37. *F.R.U.S., 1941*, 6:62–63.
38. Armour to Hull, 12 December 1941, 835.00/1099, RG 59, DOS.
39. "Export-Import Bank Loans to Latin America," *Foreign Policy Reports*, vol. 17, no. 7 (June 1941), pp. 84–89.
40. "Trade Agreement between Argentina and the United States," *Bulletin of the Pan-American Union* (December 1941), pp. 691–94.
41. J. C. deWilde and Bryce Wood, "U.S. Trade Ties with Argentina," *Foreign Policy Reports*, vol. 17, no. 18 (1 December 1941), p. 227.
42. Assistance Rendered to Argentina by the United States, 20 December 1941, Memoranda-Argentina, vol. 4, RG 59, Lot Files on Latin America, DOS.
43. *F.R.U.S., 1942*, 5:24–25.
44. Conversation between Berle, Dr. Cesar Varros Hurtado, and Dr. Aranjo, 13 January 1942, box 213, Berle Papers.
45. *F.R.U.S., 1941*, 6:66–67.
46. Frost (U.S. ambassador to Paraguay) to Welles, 26 December 1941, 710. consultation (3)/116,

and Welles to Frost, 29 December 1941, 710. consultation 3/124, RG 59, DOS.
47. Armour to Hull, 26 December 1941, 710. consultation 3/105, RG 59, DOS; Repetto, *Mi paso*, p. 255; and *Noticias Gráficas*, 9 January 1942.
48. Welles to Hull, 16 January 1942, 710. consultation (3)/344, RG 59, DOS; and *F.R.U.S., 1942*, 5:30–34.
49. Stimson Diaries, 10 November 1942, 41:30; 4 May 1943, 42:12; and 29 March 1945, 50:209–10.
50. William L. Langer and S. Everett Gleason, *The Underclared War, 1940–1941* (New York, 1953), p. 148; and Welles, *Seven Decisions*, pp. 105–6.
51. *F.R.U.S., 1942*, 5:379–81.
52. Department of the Army, "Relations of the Caribbean Defense Command with Argentina" (unpublished compilation), Military Records Division of National Archives.
53. Armour to Hull 9 January 1942, 710. consultations (3)/275 and (3)/278, and Welles to Hull, 24 January 1942, 710. consultation (3)/479, RG 59, DOS.
54. Laurence Duggan, *The Americas: The Search for Hemispheric Security* (New York, 1949), p. 87; and Welles, *Seven Decisions*, pp. 105–6.
55. Welles to Hull, 16 January 1942, 710. consultation (3)/344, RG 59, DOS; and *F.R.U.S., 1942*, 5:27.
56. Sumner Welles, "Address by the Under Secretary of State," *Department of State Bulletin*, vol. 6,

no. 134 (17 January 1942), pp. 57–58, 60.

57. Welles to Hull, 22 January 1942, 710. consultation 3/436, and Armour to Hull, 9 January 1942, 710. consultation (3)/275, RG 59, DOS.

58. Berle to Welles, 15 January, 1942, container 50, folder 148, Hull Papers.

59. Armour to Hull, 26 December 1941, 710. consultation 3/105, RG 59, DOS; Repetto, *Mi paso*, p. 255; *Noticias Gráficas*, 9 January 1942; and Potash, *Army & Politics*, p. 162.

60. Conversation re Aid to Chile, 21 January 1942, box 213, Berle Papers.

61. Welles, *Time for Decision*, p. 231.

62. Welles to Hull, 13 January 1942, container 50, folder 148, Hull Papers; and *F.R.U.S., 1942*, 5:26.

63. Argentina's position was aptly summed up by Foreign Minister Enrique Ruiz Guiñazú in a preconference interview with *La Nación* of Buenos Aires: "All international agreements must give primary consideration to the national interest in all its forms," he declared. Inter-American solidarity was an expression of "defensive cooperation and does not imply alliances, least of all military alliances. . . . The Rio meeting is a consultative assembly only." *La Nación*, 7 January 1942.

64. *F.R.U.S., 1942*, 5:27–28.

65. Ibid.

66. Welles to Hull, 19 January 1942, container 50, folder 148, Hull Papers; and *F.R.U.S., 1942*, 5:30–33.

67. Welles to Hull, 19 January 1942, container 50, folder 148, Hull Papers; and *F.R.U.S., 1942*, 5:30–33.

68. *F.R.U.S., 1942*, 5:33.

69. Welles to Hull, 22 January 1942, 710. consultation 3/436, RG 59, DOS.

70. *Wall Street Journal*, 23 January 1942.

71. Welles to Hull, 22 January 1942, 710. consultation 3/436, RG 59, DOS.

72. Ibid.

73. Welles, *Seven Decisions*, pp. 110–12.

74. *F.R.U.S., 1942*, 5:35.

75. Pratt, *Cordell Hull*, 13:707.

76. Berle Diaries, 12 January 1942, box 213.

77. Radio Address by Welles, 24 January 1942, 710. conference (3)/58b, RG 59, DOS; *F.R.U.S., 1942*, 5:36–39; and Welles, *Seven Decisions*, pp. 119–20.

78. Hull, *Memoirs*, 2:1149–50.

79. Welles to Hull and Roosevelt, 18 January 1942, box 7, South America Folder, President's Secretary's File, Papers of Franklin D. Roosevelt, Franklin D. Roosevelt Library, Hyde Park, N.Y.

80. Conversation between Morgenthau and Roosevelt, 7 March 1944, Presidential Diaries, 5:1341–43, Papers of Henry Morgenthau, Jr., Franklin D. Roosevelt Library, Hyde Park, N.Y.

CHAPTER 3

1. Berle Diaries, 1 and 2 February 1942, box 213.
2. For a history of World War II see Basil Collier, *The Second World War: A Military History* (New York, 1967).
3. Freda Kirchwey, "Unanimity at Any Price," *Nation*, 31 January 1942, p. 109.
4. Ibid., p. 116.
5. "Good Neighbors into Allies," *New Republic*, 26 January 1942, p. 103.
6. See, for example, *Nation*, 24 January 1942 and 27 December 1941.
7. *St. Louis Post-Dispatch*, 22 January 1942. In the aftermath of the Rio Conference, Chile, citing many of the same arguments put forth by Argentine diplomats, joined Argentina in refusing to sever relations with the Axis. Santiago finally declared war in January 1943. Gaddis Smith, *American Diplomacy during the Second World War, 1941–1945* (New York, 1965), p. 30.
8. *St. Louis Post-Dispatch*, 22 January 1942.
9. *Washington Post*, 30 January 1942.
10. See also David H. Popper, "Hemisphere Solidarity in the War Crisis," *Foreign Policy Reports*, vol. 18, no. 5 (15 May 1942), p. 51.
11. *F.R.U.S., 1942*, 5:38. On several occasions FDR gave the Latin Americanists reason to believe that he shared the internationalists' sense of urgency in regard to persuading Argentina to adopt a pro-Allied posture. On April 18 he declared to the Governing Board of the Pan-American Union: "My own thought is that perhaps there is one word that we could use for this war, the word 'survival'. . . . That is what it comes pretty close to being: the survival of our civilization, the survival of democracy, the survival of a hemisphere." "Informal Remarks of the President to Members of the Governing Board of the Pan American Union," *Department of State Bulletin*, vol. 6, no. 147 (18 April 1942), pp. 355–56.
12. Welles's Speech to Cuban Chamber of Commerce, 15 February 1942, 710. consultation (3)/644, RG 59, DOS. See also his remarks in *Commercial and Financial Chronicle*, 5 March 1942.
13. *F.R.U.S., 1942*, 5:354–56; and Armour to Welles, 835.00/1145, RG 59, DOS.
14. Raul Damonte Taborda, a prominent pro-Allied, anti-Castillo member of the Chamber of Deputies had approached several United States firms with branches in Buenos Aires for funds with which to overthrow the administration and had even discussed the proposed rebellion with Armour. Both Armour and Welles agreed that Castillo would like nothing better than to link Washington with a domestic revolution, and thus they acted to persuade Taborda to cease and desist at once. Armour to Welles, 23 February 1942, and Welles to Armour, 24

February 1942, 835.00/1145, RG 59, DOS.

15. See, for example, *F.R.U.S., 1943*, 5:422–23.

16. *F.R.U.S., 1942*, 5:402–3.

17. *F.R.U.S., 1943*, 5:407–8 and 422–23.

18. *Federal Records of World War II*, vol. 1, *Civilian Agencies* (Washington, 1950), pp. 226–27.

19. Rockefeller to Welles, 17 April 1942, box 500, RG 229, OCIAA; and Duggan to Hull, 18 December 1943, box 218, Secretary of State Hull Folder, Papers of Edward Stettinius, University of Virginia.

20. Conversation Between Duggan and Robert Wells (chairman of Coordination Committee for Argentina), 4 August 1942, Memoranda-Argentina, vol. 4, RG 59, DOS.

21. Welles to Bonsal, 6 February 1943, Memoranda-Argentina, vol. 3, RG 59, DOS.

22. Armour to Hull, 6 February 1943, 835.00/1358, RG 59, DOS.

23. Alberto Conil Paz and Gustavo Ferrari, *Argentina's Foreign Policy, 1930–1962*, trans. John J. Kennedy (Notre Dame, Ind., 1966), pp. 79–82; and Sumner Welles, *The Time for Decision* (New York, 1944), pp. 288–89.

24. Conil Paz and Ferrari, *Argentina's Foreign Policy*, pp. 83–87; and *F.R.U.S., 1942*, 5:379–85.

25. *F.R.U.S., 1942*, 5:387, 390; and Cordell Hull, *The Memoirs of Cordell Hull*, 2 vols. (New York, 1948), 2:1378.

26. *F.R.U.S., 1942*, 5:388–90.

27. Samuel W. Washington, "A Study in the Causes of Hostility toward the U.S. in Latin America: Argentina," External Research Paper no. 126.2, DOS (May 1957), p. 34.

28. Ibid.

29. Damonte Taborda to Welles, 6 February 1942, box 96, Welles Folder, President's Secretary's File, Roosevelt Papers.

30. Robert A. Potash, *The Army & Politics in Argentina, 1928–1945* (Stanford, Calif., 1969), pp. 172–73.

31. Armour to Hull, 18 February 1943, 835.00/1363, RG 59, DOS.

32. *F.R.U.S., 1941*, 6:384–86.

33. *F.R.U.S., 1942*, 5:307–8.

34. Ibid.

35. "Telling Argentina," *Business Week*, 4 April 1942, p. 37.

36. *F.R.U.S., 1942*, 5:21; and *F.R.U.S., 1943*, 5:483.

37. *F.R.U.S., 1942*, 5:342.

38. *F.R.U.S., 1943*, 5:314–24.

39. Potash, *Army & Politics*, pp. 167–70.

40. "Argentine Trade in 1942," *Bulletin of the Pan-American Union* (July 1943), p. 405; and Richard Pattee, "The Argentine Question: The War Stage," *Review of Politics*, vol. 8, no. 4 (October 1946), pp. 475–500.

41. *Department of State Bulletin*, vol. 7, no. 176 (7 November 1942), p. 897.

42. "Headaches on the Plata," *Business Week*, 5 December 1942, pp. 17–19; and White to Morgenthau, 19 February 1942, book 498, p. 288, Diaries of Henry Morgenthau, Franklin D. Roosevelt Library.

43. Armour to Hull, 6 December 1940, 685.414, RG 59, DOS.
44. British Aide-Memoir, container 59–60, folder 216, Hull Papers.
45. Sir David Kelly, *The Ruling Few* (London, 1952), p. 293.
46. Welles to FDR, 30 April 1943, box 96, Welles Folder, President's Secretary's File, Roosevelt Papers.
47. Berle Diaries, 24 January 1942, box 213.
48. For example see the *Times* (London), 10 June 1942.
49. Harrison to Bonsal, Duggan, and Welles, 10 June 1943, Memoranda-Argentina, vol. 3, RG 59, DOS.
50. Justo's efforts to identify himself with the Allied cause knew no bounds. After Brazil declared war on the Axis on 22 August 1942, Justo flew to Rio to offer his mili-

tary services to President Vargas. Marvin Goldwert, *Democracy, Militarism, and Nationalism in Argentina, 1930–1966* (Austin, Tex., and London, 1972), p. 55.
51. Report from Davies, 24 October 1942, O.S.S. 27124C; and Report on Political Situation in Argentina, 5 December 1941, O.S.S. 6589C, RG 226, General Records of the Office of Strategic Services (hereafter referred to as OSS), National Archives.
52. *New York Times*, 1 January 1943.
53. Welles to FDR, 6 February 1942, box 96, Welles Folder, President's Secretary's File, Roosevelt Papers.
54. Conversation between Blake-Tyler and Welles, 13 January 1943, Memoranda-Argentina, RG 59, DOS.

CHAPTER 4

1. Morgenthau was, of course, an ardent Germanophobe and an active Zionist. See, for example, Henry Morgenthau, Jr., *Germany Is Our Problem: A Plan for Germany* (New York, 1945), and his message to the National Conference for Palestine, quoted in *New York Times*, 19 January 1942.
2. Morgenthau unofficially appointed White as assistant secretary for "foreign relations" on 15 December 1941. Order no. 43, 15 December 1941, box 122, RG 56, General Records of the Department of Treasury (hereafter referred to as DOT), National Archives.
3. *New York Times*, 18 August 1948.
4. White to Morgenthau, 6 May 1942, book 524, p. 235, Morgenthau Diaries.
5. *New York Times*, 5 February 1944.
6. *Federal Records of World War II*, 1:771–72.
7. There was a Treasury Department representative on virtually every governmental entity concerned with Argentina.
8. John Morton Blum, ed., *The Price of Vision: The Diary of Henry A. Wallace, 1942–1946* (Boston, 1973), p. 24.
9. Jerry Greene to David Hulburd, 16 April 1942, box 5, notebook 13, Diaries of Henry A. Wallace, University of Iowa.
10. Blum, *Price of Vision*, pp. 67–68.

11. Greene to Hulburd, 16 April 1942, box 5, notebook 13, Wallace Diaries.

12. Greene to Hulburd, 17 April 1942, box 5, notebook 13, Wallace Diaries.

13. Ibid.

14. Greene to Hulburd, 16 April 1942, box 5, notebook 13, Wallace Diaries.

15. Ibid.

16. Wallace Diaries, 8 April 1942, box 5, notebook 13.

17. Blum, *Price of Vision*, pp. 67–68.

18. Ibid., pp. 78–79.

19. Berle Diaries, 2 February 1943, box 214. See also Berle to Hull, 14 May 1942, box 55, Berle Papers.

20. Wallace Diaries, 20 May 1942, box 5, notebook 14.

21. Blum, *Price of Vision*, p. 51.

22. Ibid., p. 24.

23. Ibid., p. 77.

24. Greene to Hulburd, 16 April 1942, box 5, notebook 13, Wallace Papers.

25. *New York Times*, 18 August 1948.

26. Blum, *Price of Vision*, pp. 67, 68, 77, 91, 99–100. See also Frank Coe to Milo Perkins, 1 June 1942, box 40, RG 169, General Records of the Foreign Economic Administration (hereafter referred to as FEA), Washington Federal Records Center. The spring of 1942 was a particularly tumultuous period for the Roosevelt foreign-policy establishment. While BEW, Treasury, and State fought "tooth and nail," and the feud between Welles and Hull continued to simmer, Felix Frankfurter and a "pro-British" coterie in Washington were plotting to have Hull removed as secretary of state and to supplant him with Dean Acheson. Berle Diaries, 10 March and 25 April 1942, box 213.

27. "Procedure for Exports to Argentina," in *Documents on American Foreign Relations*, ed. Leland M. Goodrich and Marie J. Carroll, vol. 5, *1942–1943* (Boston, 1944), p. 143.

28. The board had no doubt as to its supremacy in the area of export-import policy toward Argentina. In December 1942 Perkins informed Dean Acheson that "it is understood that the final export licensing authority is vested in and must remain with BEW. . . . Further, it is essential to the most efficient conduct of our foreign relations that the Mission in Buenos Aires not be exposed to the criticism which might attend the exercise by it of final authority regarding export control." Perkins to Acheson, 17 December 1942, box 40, RG 169, FEA. See also *F.R.U.S., 1942*, 5:506.

29. Armour, in conformity with the undersecretary's determination to avoid the appearance of blatant coercion, attempted to deal with Axis financial activities in Argentina by working through the Central Bank, many of whose officials were pro-American. In November the ambassador notified the State Department that both the Treasury Department's demand that various financial institutions suspected of transacting business with Axis firms be frozen and its over-

all operation in Argentina were jeopardizing his liaison with the Central Bank. *F.R.U.S., 1942,* 5: 506–8.

30. *New York Times,* 14 November 1942.

31. Conversation between Morgenthau and Hoover, 7 May 1942, book 525, p. 13, Morgenthau Diaries.

32. In late February, Treasury Department representatives testified before the Senate Internal Subcommittee that officials in charge of Foreign Funds Control and the Proclaimed List had to assume more direct control over the Allied economic-warfare activities in Latin America if they were to be effective. "A preliminary sounding out to the State Department," they complained, "indicates an unsympathetic attitude . . . apparently based on the fear that Treasury and the Board of Economic Warfare would be moving in on a field that the State Department wishes to keep exclusively under its own jurisdiction, even though it were to mean a much less efficient administration." White to Morgenthau, 24 February 1942, book 500, p. 265, Morgenthau Diaries.

33. Morgenthau to FDR, 15 May 1942, book 528, p. 300, Morgenthau Diaries.

34. Meeting of Sub-Committee of the Board of Economic Warfare, 14 May 1942, book 528, p. 217, Morgenthau Diaries.

35. Ibid.

36. Ibid.

37. Morgenthau to FDR, 15 May 1942, book 528, p. 300, Morgenthau Diaries.

38. John Morton Blum, *From the Morgenthau Diaries,* vol. 3, *Years of War, 1941–1945* (Boston, 1967), p. 195; and Hull, *Memoirs,* 2:1379.

39. *F.R.U.S., 1942,* 5:471–74.

40. Ibid., p. 471 n.58.

41. Blum, *Morgenthau Diaries,* pp. 196–97.

42. Conversation between White and Long, 23 May 1942, book 531, p. 165, Morgenthau Diaries.

43. Conversation between Long and White, 23 May 1942, book 531, p. 166, Morgenthau Diaries.

44. Hull to Morgenthau, 30 May, 1942, book 534, p. 176, Morgenthau Diaries.

45. Acheson to Armour, 25 May, 1942, box 40, RG 169, FEA.

46. White to Hull, 10 November, 1942, book 578, p. 139, Morgenthau Diaries.

47. Paul to Morgenthau, 6 November 1942, book 582, p. 72, Morgenthau Diaries.

48. Ibid.

49. Philip Wright to Bonsal, 14 November 1942, Memoranda-Argentina, vol. 3, RG 59, DOS.

50. Meeting on Argentina, 15 July 1942, RG 56, DOT; Philip Wright to Bonsal, 14 November 1942, Memoranda-Argentina, vol. 3, RG 59, DOS; *F.R.U.S., 1942,* 5:506–8; and Paul to Morgenthau, 23 November 1942, book 588, p. 177, Morgenthau Diaries.

51. Berle Diaries, 20 and 24 June 1942, box 214.

52. Clarence H. Haring, *Argentina*

and the United States (Boston, 1941), p. 58.

53. Ysabel F. Rennie, *The Argentine Republic* (New York, 1945), pp. 275–79.

54. Harold F. Peterson, *Argentina and the United States, 1810–1960* (Albany, N.Y., 1964), pp. 407–9.

55. *New York Times*, 12 April 1942.

56. *New York Times*, 6 June 1942.

57. *F.R.U.S., 1942*, 5:201–4.

58. Ibid., 5:205–8.

59. Ibid.

60. Biddle to Hull, 17 August 1942, container 50, folder 150, Hull Papers.

61. Reed to Hull, 29 September 1942, 835.00/1280, RG 59, DOS.

62. *New York Times*, 9 October 1942.

63. Robert A. Potash, *The Army & Politics in Argentina, 1928–1945* (Stanford, Calif., 1969), pp. 174–76.

64. Marvin Goldwert, *Democracy, Miltarism, and Nationalism in Argentina, 1930–1966* (Austin, Tex., and London, 1972), p. 57.

65. Reed to Hull, 29 September 1942, 835.00/1280, RG 59, DOS; and David H. Popper, "U.S. Presses Hemispheric Solidarity Program," *Foreign Policy Bulletin*, vol. 21, no. 21 (13 March 1942), pp. 3–4.

66. *New York Times*, 9 October 1942.

67. *Washington Post*, 13 October 1942.

68. *F.R.U.S., 1942*, 5:210–11.

CHAPTER 5

1. *F.R.U.S., 1942*, 5:76–77; and "In Defense of the Americas against Axis Political Aggression: The Emergency Advisory Committee for Political Defense," *Department of State Bulletin*, vol. 12, no. 289 (7 January 1945). See also Berle to Hull, Duggan, and Bonsal, 17 December 1943, and Berle to Hull, 14 July 1942, box 58, Berle Papers.

2. Ibid.

3. *F.R.U.S., 1942*, 5:79–84.

4. Spaeth to Hull, 27 December 1941, 710. consultation (3)/142, RG 59, DOS.

5. Wallace Diaries, 19 August 1943, box 8, notebook 23.

6. *F.R.U.S., 1942*, 5:218–24.

7. Ibid., pp. 225–30.

8. Ibid., pp. 228–30.

9. Ibid., pp. 233–34.

10. Ibid., pp. 236–37, 240.

11. Bonsal to Welles, 11 November 1942, Memoranda-Argentina, vol. 3, RG 59, DOS; and *F.R.U.S., 1942*, 5:250–51.

12. Welles to Bonsal, 6 February 1943, Memoranda-Argentina, vol. 3, RG 59, DOS; and Armour to Hull, 6 February 1943, 835.00/1358, RG 59, DOS.

13. *F.R.U.S., 1943*, 5:7–9.

14. Drier to OCIAA, 21 January 1943, Memoranda-Argentina, vol. 3, RG 59, DOS.

15. Bonsal to Duggan, 29 May 1942, Memoranda-Argentina, vol. 3, RG 59, DOS; and *F.R.U.S., 1942*, 5: 229, 234.

16. *F.R.U.S., 1942*, 5:39, 247; and Bonsal to Duggan, 20 July 1942, Memoranda-Argentina, vol. 3, RG 59, DOS.

17. *F.R.U.S., 1942*, 5:110–16.
18. Ibid., pp. 115, 119, 134, 140, 153.
19. Ibid.
20. Bonsal to Long and Duggan, 2 October 1942, Memoranda-Argentina, vol. 3, RG 59, DOS.
21. Meeting between ARA, Long, Duggan, and Berle, 22 January 1943, Memoranda-Argentina, vol. 3, RG 59, DOS.
22. *F.R.U.S., 1942*, 5:163, 176–78.
23. Ibid., pp. 178–79.
24. Meeting between ARA, Long, Duggan, and Berle, 22 January 1943, Memoranda-Argentina, vol. 3, RG 59, DOS.
25. Robert A. Potash, *The Army & Politics in Argentina, 1928–1945* (Stanford, Calif., 1969), pp. 179–94. See also Conversation between Welles and Jose W. Agusti, 30 April 1943, box 96, President's Secretary's File, Roosevelt Papers.
26. Conversation between White and Morgenthau, 21 December 1943, book 686, p. 35, Morgenthau Diaries.
27. Potash, *Army & Politics*, pp. 179–94.
28. For a sympathetic treatment of the formation and objectives of the GOU see Carlos Ibarguren, *La historia que he vivido* (Buenos Aires, 1955), pp. 497–98.
29. Felix Luna, *El 45* (Buenos Aires, 1969), pp. 31–32. Marvin Goldwert argues that the Radical party, "the major vehicle of the middle-class struggle against the oligarchy," played a key role in the rise of the integral nationalists in 1943. An all-consuming desire for power caused them to reject a popular front with the Socialists and Pro-gressive Democrats and to offer the Radical presidential nomination to Ramírez. Marvin Goldwert, *Democracy, Militarism, and Nationalism in Argentina, 1930–1966* (Austin, Tex., and London, 1972), pp. 77–78.
30. Juan José Real, *30 años de historia argentina* (Buenos Aires, 1962), p. 64.
31. For a recitation of the events surrounding the June coup see Bartolomé Galíndez, *Apuntes de tres revoluciones* (Buenos Aires, 1956).
32. Ibid.
33. *F.R.U.S., 1943*, 5:369.
34. Ibid., pp. 365–66.
35. Armour to Hull, 9 June 1943, 835.00/1501, RG 59, DOS.
36. Conversation between Jack Camp and Allan Dawson, 6 July 1943, Memoranda-Argentina, vol. 3, RG 59, DOS.
37. Caffery to Hull, 9 June 1943, 835.00/1517, RG 59, DOS; and Armour to Hull, 6 June 1943, 835.00/1455, RG 59, DOS.
38. *F.R.U.S., 1943*, 5:371; and Conversation between Duggan and Armour, 7 June 1943, 835.00/1482, RG 59, DOS.
39. Armour to Hull, 9 June 1943, 835.00/1509, RG 59, DOS.
40. Armour to Hull, 14 June 1943, 835.00/1564, RG 59, DOS.
41. Armour to Hull, 13 July 1943, 835.00/1690, RG 59, DOS. At one point Armour even threatened to resign if Washington did not sign a pending petroleum agreement and make other concessions to the Ramírez government. Conversation between Jack Camp, Bonsal,

and Duggan, 6 July 1943, 835.00/ 1644, RG 59, DOS.

42. *F.R.U.S., 1943*, 5:430–34, 436.
43. Bonsal to Duggan, 26 June 1943, Memoranda-Argentina, vol. 3, RG 59, DOS.
44. John Morton Blum, *The Price of Vision: The Diary of Henry A. Wallace, 1942–1946* (Boston, 1973), pp. 649–59.
45. Wallace Diaries, 9 July 1943, box 8, notebook 23.
46. Blum, *Price of Vision*, p. 78.
47. Wallace Diaries, 27 September 1943, box 8, notebook 23.
48. Wallace Diaries, 27 August 1943, box 8, notebook 23.
49. Crowley to Acheson, 21 April 1943, box 40, RG 169, FEA.
50. Ogden White to James McCamey, 3 June 1943; Objectives of the BEW in Argentina, 5 July 1943; and Arthur Paul to Lauchlin Currie, 30 November 1943, box 40, RG 169, FEA.
51. Dawson to Duggan et al., 5 June 1943, Memoranda-Argentina, vol. 3, RG 59, DOS.
52. Dawson to Bonsal et al., 15 July 1943, Memoranda-Argentina, vol. 3, RG 59, DOS.
53. According to Sir David Kelly, British ambassador to Argentina, United States news correspondents and government officials constantly misjudged the Argentine situation. A prime example was the June revolution—essentially a coup carried off by a group of army officers—which they hailed as a popular uprising by the Radicals. Sir David Kelly, *The Ruling Few* (London, 1952), p. 295.
54. *New York Times*, 5 June 1943.
55. *St. Louis Post-Dispatch*, 5 June 1943.
56. José Luis Romero, *A History of Argentine Political Thought*, 3d ed., trans. and with an introduction by Thomas F. McGann (Stanford, Calif., 1963), p. 244.
57. Hoover to Hopkins, 8 and 12 June 1943, box 140, FBI Reports—Argentina, Hopkins Papers. Hoover and the FBI not only enjoyed direct access to the White House but even retained control over information transmitted to the Oval Office. In October 1943, Hopkins wrote to Hoover, assuring the director that he never passed on FBI intelligence to the State Department or any other agency: "I have never passed on anything you have given me to the Department because I assumed you would send them whatever you wanted to send them." Hopkins to Hoover, 23 October 1943, box 140, FBI Reports—Argentina, Hopkins Papers.
58. For a discussion of the origins of *Acción Argentina* see Nicolás Repetto, *Mi paso por la política* Buenos Aires, 1957), pp. 205–8.
59. Armour to Hull, 13 July 1943, 835.00/1580, and Hull to Armour, 16 July 1943, 835.00/1643, RG 59, DOS.
60. *New York Times*, 8 June 1943.
61. "Revolution in the Argentine," *New Republic*, 14 June 1943.
62. Freda Kirchwey, "Expediency in Argentina," *Nation*, 26 June 1943, p. 881.
63. Hull to Armour, 16 June 1943, 835.00/1485, RG 59, DOS.
64. Duggan to Welles, 24 June 1943,

835.00/1582, RG 59, DOS. According to some accounts, Storni, who was a liberal nationalist, had originally written a very conciliatory note. The aggressive passages and the demand for arms aid were inserted by Ramírez and the integral nationalists. Alberto Conil Paz and Gustavo Ferrari, *Argentina's Foreign Policy, 1930–1962*, trans. John J. Kennedy (Notre Dame, Ind., 1966), p. 107.

65. *F.R.U.S., 1943*, 5:419–22.

66. Hull to Armour, 16 July 1943, 835.00/1643, RG 59, DOS; and *F.R.U.S., 1943*, 5:417.

67. *New York Times*, 28 July 1943; and Hull to Armour, 27 July 1943, 835.00/1689A, RG 59, DOS.

68. Conil Paz and Ferrari, *Argentina's Foreign Policy*, pp. 111–12.

69. *F.R.U.S., 1943*, 5:450.

70. *F.R.U.S., 1943*, 5:419–22. See also Berle to Hull, 27 August 1943, box 58, Berle Papers.

71. Hull's Reply to Storni, *Department of State Bulletin*, vol. 9, no. 220 (11 September 1943), pp. 162–66.

72. Reed to Hull, 23 September 1943, 835.00/1900 and 835.00/1901, RG 59, DOS.

73. *F.R.U.S., 1943*, 5:460–61.

74. Conil Paz and Ferrari, *Argentina's Foreign Policy*, p. 111.

75. *La Hora*, 7 September 1943; and *La Nación*, 8 September 1943.

76. Corrigan to Hull, 16 September 1943, 835.00/1902, RG 59, DOS.

77. Wilson to Hull, 9 September 1943, 835.00/1809, RG 59, DOS.

78. *New York Times*, 29 August 1943.

79. *Washington Post*, 8 September 1943.

80. Military Intelligence Report on Argentina, 10 July 1943, 835.00/2134, RG 59, DOS.

81. Hoover to Hopkins, 12 June 1943, box 140, FBI Reports—Argentina, Hopkins Papers.

82. The ultranationalists were, to say the least, enraged by the outcome of the Hull-Storni affair and attempted to blame the whole thing on Washington. See Enrique Ruiz-Guiñazú, *La política argentina y el futuro de América* (Buenos Aires, 1944).

83. *Documents on American Foreign Relations*, 6:190–91.

84. *New York Times*, 3 December 1943.

85. *El Mercurio*, 12 November 1943.

86. Cordell Hull, *The Memoirs of Cordell Hull* (New York, 1948), 2:1227–30.

87. Blum, *Price of Vision*, p. 61.

88. Wallace Diaries, 30 and 31 March 1943, box 5, notebook 13. Bullitt received certain "incriminating" documents pertaining to Welles from R. Walton Moore, whom Welles had edged out for the undersecretaryship. Moore, determined to have revenge on his rival, passed on the material and enlisted Bullitt's aid as he, Moore, lay on his deathbed. Orville H. Bullitt, ed., *For the President: Personal and Secret* (Boston, 1972).

89. Wallace Diaries, 21 December 1944, box 11, notebook 13.

90. Bullitt, ed., *For the President*, pp. 512–16.

91. Fred L. Israel, ed., *The War Diary*

of Breckinridge Long (Lincoln, Nebr., 1966), p. 324.

92. Wallace Diaries, 21 August 1943, box 8, notebook 23; and Conversation between Morgenthau and Wallace, 26 August 1943, Presidential Diaries, vol. 5, p. 1274, Morgenthau Papers.

93. Israel, *War Diary*, p. 324.

94. Welles to FDR, 16 August 1943, box 95, Welles Folder, President's Secretary's File, Roosevelt Papers; and Conversation between Morgenthau and FDR, 7 March 1944, Presidential Diaries, vol. 5, pp. 1341–43, Morgenthau Papers.

95. Welles to FDR, 21 September 1943, box 95, Welles Folder, President's Secretary's File, Roosevelt Papers.

96. Berle Diaries, 1 September 1943, box 215.

97. Blum, *Price of Vision*, p. 238.

98. Stimson Diaries, 7 September 1943, vol. 44, p. 101.

99. Berle Diaries, 19 June 1943, box 215.

100. Wallace Diaries, 24 August 1943, box 8, notebook 23; and Berle Diaries, 1 September 1943, box 215.

101. Blum, *Price of Vision*, p. 91.

102. Ibid., p. 288.

103. "Stettinius Linked to New Diplomacy," *New York Times*, 27 September 1943; and Stettinius to Hull, 3 March 1944, box 218, Stettinius Papers.

104. E. Willard Jensen to Hopkins, 4 February 1939, box 109, Business Administration Council Folder, Hopkins Papers.

105. Thomas M. Campbell, *Masquerade Peace: America's U.N. Policy, 1944–1945* (Tallahassee, Fla., 1973).

106. Conversation between Hull and Stettinius, 4 October 1943, box 237, Stettinius Papers.

107. Conversation between Stettinius and Duggan, 8 and 13 October 1943, and Berle to Stettinius, 22 October 1943, 835.00/2183, RG 59, DOS.

108. Memo on Economic Policy toward Argentina, 3 February 1943, Memoranda-Argentina, vol. 3, RG 59, DOS.

109. Drier to Bonsal, 22 May 1943, Memoranda-Argentina, vol. 4, RG 59, DOS.

CHAPTER 6

1. Quoted in José Luis Romero, *A History of Argentine Political Thought*, 3d ed., trans. and with an introduction by Thomas F. McGann (Stanford, Calif., 1963), p. 244.

2. Juan José Real, *30 años de historia argentina* (Buenos Aires, 1962), p. 63.

3. Ysabel F. Rennie, *The Argentine Republic* (New York, 1945), pp. 274–75; and Robert J. Alexander, *The Perón Era* (New York, 1951), pp. 12–13.

4. Armour to Hull, 19 October 1943, 835.00/2026, RG 59, DOS.

5. Gustavo Gabriel Levene, ed., *Presidentes argentinos* (Buenos Aires, 1961), pp. 238–39.

6. Deerwester to Col. William Ad-

ams, 24 September 1943, box 8, notebook 23, Wallace Diaries.

7. Biddle to Hull, 1 October 1943, 800.20210/1460, RG 59, DOS.

8. Relations between the State and Treasury departments had become so strained by the summer of 1943 that Assistant to the President James F. Byrnes was prompted to suggest the establishment of a formal set of ground rules regulating the foreign operations of both agencies.

9. Paul to Morgenthau, 23 October 1943, book 672, p. 22, Morgenthau Diaries.

10. Minutes of Meeting between Treasury and State, 26 October 1943, box 84, folder 376, Stettinius Papers.

11. Berle Diary, 7 September 1943, box 215.

12. Ibid.

13. Conversation between Morgenthau and Stettinius, 21 December 1943, book 686, p. 45, Morgenthau Diaries.

14. *F.R.U.S., 1943,* 5:496.

15. FDR to Stettinius, 25 October 1943, box 54, folder 376, Stettinius Papers.

16. John Morton Blum, ed., *From the Morgenthau Diaries,* vol. 3 (Boston, 1976), pp. 197–98.

17. *New York Times,* 7 November 1943.

18. Hector Lazo to Leo Crowley, 29 September 1943, box 40, RG 169, FEA. The American embassy was profoundly disturbed by recent changes in the Ramírez cabinet. It was also being subjected to heavy pressure from FEA representatives in Buenos Aires to turn to finan-

cial coercion as a means for solving both economic and political problems in Argentina. The same day the public was "informed" that financial controls were being considered, the ambassador cabled Washington and once again urged immediate freezing on the grounds that it would only add to the unpopularity of the Ramírez government and contribute to its downfall. *F.R.U.S., 1943,* 5:493–95.

19. Treasury Group Discussion, 1 November 1943, book 762, pp. 6–7, Morgenthau Diaries.

20. Stettinius to Hull, undated, box 218, Stettinius Papers.

21. Meeting on Freezing of Argentine Funds, 2 November 1943, book 672, p. 142, Morgenthau Diaries.

22. Morgenthau to Stettinius, 2 November 1943, book 672, pp. 166–72, Morgenthau Diaries.

23. Conversation between Hull and Paraguayan Ambassador, 20 November 1943, boxes 59 and 60, folder 243, Hull Papers.

24. "Argentina and Paraguay Sign Trade Treaty," *Commercial and Financial Chronicle,* 16 December 1943, p. 2453.

25. Armour to Hull, 18 December 1943, 835.00/2234, RG 59, DOS.

26. *El Mercurio,* 8 November 1943; and Armour to Hull, 9 November 1943, 835.00/2157, RG 59, DOS.

27. Wallace Diaries, 21 January 1944, box 9, notebook 26.

28. David Green, *The Containment of Latin America* (Chicago 1971), pp. 142–43.

29. Berle Diaries, 6 January 1944, box 215.

30. Manuel Seoane, "The South American Conspiracy," *Nation*, 15 January 1944, p. 66. In the wake of the Bolivian uprising the *New York Times* urged the use of non-recognition to force the Ramírez administration to cease its machinations, explaining that "we have a right to do what we can to encourage a trend toward democracy anywhere in Latin America and discourage trends away from it." *New York Times*, 26 January 1944, p. 18.

31. Wallace Diaries, 21 January 1944, box 9, notebook 26.

32. Ibid.

33. As early as 2 November 1943, Randolph Paul reported Duggan as having said that the overthrow of the Argentine government was in accordance with United States foreign policy. Paul to Morgenthau, 2 November 1943, book 672, p. 164, Morgenthau Diaries.

34. *Washington Post*, 26 January 1944; and *New York Times*, 4 January 1944.

35. Berle Diaries, 5 September 1943 and 22 February 1944, box 215; and Wallace Diaries, 27 January 1944, box 9, notebook 26.

36. Wallace Diaries, 20 January 1944, box 9, notebook 26.

37. Berle Diaries, 5 September 1943 and 2 February 1944, box 215; and Wallace Diaries, 21 January 1944, box 9, notebook 26.

38. Stimson Diaries, 4 January 1944, vol. 46, pp. 8–9.

39. *F.R.U.S., 1943*, 5:509–10.

40. Inter-American Conference on War and Post-War Problems: Memo on Estrada Doctrine, 2 February 1945, box 9, Papers of Leo Pasvolsky, Library of Congress.

41. *F.R.U.S., 1943*, 5:34.

42. *New York Times*, 26 December 1943.

43. Conversation between Hull and Brazilian Ambassador, 3 January 1944, boxes 57 and 58, folder 192, Hull Papers.

44. Conversation between Hull and Peruvian Ambassador, 12 January 1944, 835.00/2305, RG 59, DOS; and Hull, *Memoirs*, 2:1390.

45. Alusna (Buenos Aires) to FDR, 24 January 1944, Map Room Files, box 18, folder 1, Roosevelt Papers.

46. Berle Diaries, 6 January 1944, box 215.

47. Bonsal, Duggan, and Collado to Stettinius, 13 November 1943, Memoranda-Argentina, vol. 4, RG 59, DOS.

48. Collado to Hull, 5 January 1944, box 53, folder 165, Hull Papers.

49. There are those who feel that this would indeed have been the case. Louise Peffer has written that Ramírez would not have dared risk even a brief stoppage of meat exports. An embargo would have hurt all major branches of Argentine industry. Even if Argentina had been able to find markets on the spur of the moment, it lacked adequate refrigerated shipping. E. Louise Peffer, "Cordell Hull's Argentine Policy and Britain's Meat Supply," *Inter-American Economic Affairs* 10 (Autumn, 1956): 5–13.

50. *F.R.U.S., 1944*, 7:288–89.

51. Conversation between Bonsal,

Blake-Tyler, and G. F. Theobald, 1 November 1943, Memoranda-Argentina, vol. 4, RG 59, DOS.

52. Conversation between Hull and Halifax, 27 December 1943, boxes 59 and 60, folder 216, Hull Papers.

53. Sir David Kelly, *The Ruling Few* (London, 1952), pp. 287–303.

54. Conversation between Hull and Halifax, 5 January 1944, 711.35/222, RG 59, DOS.

55. Percy W. Bidwell, "Good Neighbors in the War, and After," *Foreign Affairs* 21 (April 1943): 529.

56. Conversation between Hull and Campbell, 10 January 1944, and Blake-Tyler, 9 August 1943, 835.00/2285, RG 59, DOS.

57. *F.R.U.S., 1944*, 7:87–92.

58. Bryce Wood, *The Making of the Good Neighbor Policy* (New York, 1961), pp. 1–7; and Conversation between Hull and Espil, 21 October 1942, boxes 57 and 58, folder 187, Hull Papers.

59. Conversation between Hull and Peruvian Ambassador, 12 January 1944, 835.00/2305, RG 59, DOS.

60. Conversation between Hull and Halifax, 23 January 1944, boxes 59 and 60, folder 216, Hull Papers.

61. Blum, *Morgenthau Diaries*, 3:200.

62. Conversation between Paul and Morgenthau, 21 December 1943, book 695, Morgenthau Diaries.

63. Berle Diaries, 10 January 1944, box 215.

64. Ibid.

65. Berle to FDR, 8 January 1944, box 32, Argentina Folder, President's Secretary's File, Roosevelt Papers.

66. *F.R.U.S., 1944*, 7:228–29.

67. Memo on Argentine Statement, 24 January 1944, Memoranda-Argentina, RG 59, DOS.

68. Ibid.

69. Conversation between Paul and Morgenthau, 24 January 1944, book 696, p. 21, Morgenthau Diaries.

70. Levene, *Presidentes argentinos*, p. 240.

71. Conversation between Duggan and Armour, 26 January 1944, and Duggan to Hull, 27 January 1944, Memoranda-Argentina, vol. 4, RG 59, DOS; and *F.R.U.S., 1944*, 7:241.

72. *F.R.U.S., 1944*, 7:238–39. In reality the resolutions passed at the Rio de Janeiro and Washington conferences in 1942 recommended certain courses of action to the American republics. None of the delegations had committed their home governments to anything. See *F.R.U.S., 1942*, 5:32–35, and Pan American Union, Congress and Conference Series no. 39: Financial Control (Washington, 1942).

73. Conversation between Hull and Adrian Escobar, 2 February 1944, boxes 57 and 58, folder 187, Hull Papers.

74. Levene, *Presidentes argentinos*, p. 240; and Potash, *Army & Politics*, pp. 237–40. Aside from considerations of ideology and national interest, a number of generals and colonels violently opposed a severance because Germany was blackmailing them. According to one FBI report, the German embassy

had financed frolics at fashionable resorts and gambling casinos for members of Ramírez's staff and other high-ranking officers. Berlin let it be known that the day Buenos Aires broke relations, Germany would publish a complete list of those Argentine officers who were on the take. Hoover to Hopkins, 9 December 1943, box 140, FBI Reports—Argentina, Hopkins Papers.

75. Ibid.
76. *F.R.U.S., 1944*, 7:248–49.
77. Ibid., pp. 386–87.
78. Ibid., p. 382.
79. Levene, *Presidentes argentinos*, pp. 244–45.

CHAPTER 7

1. Gustavo Gabriel Levene, ed., *Presidentes argentinos* (Buenos Aires, 1961), p. 239.
2. Ibid. Actually the integral nationalists were, as a group, very antilabor. Equating unions with socialism and/or communism, they jailed labor leaders and intervened in unions. Only with Perón's accession to the position of secretary of labor and social security did the government's antilabor campaign subside. He was to use this position to fashion a unique alliance between labor and the military. Marvin Goldwert's *Democracy, Militarism, and Nationalism in Argentina, 1930–1966* (Austin, Tex., and London, 1972), pp. 86–88.
3. Levene, *Presidentes argentinos*, p. 240.
4. For an account of Ramírez's last months in office and an analysis of the factors responsible for his loss of power see Felix Luna, *El 45* (Buenos Aires, 1969), pp. 26–35.
5. Robert A. Potash, *The Army & Politics in Argentina, 1928–1945* (Stanford, Calif., 1969), pp. 232–37.
6. *F.R.U.S., 1944*, 7:252–53.
7. Potash, *Army & Politics*, pp. 238–39.
8. Ibid., pp. 232–37.
9. Joseph R. Barager, *Why Perón Came to Power* (New York, 1968), p. 25.
10. For a discussion of Perón's relations with organized labor see Carlos S. Fayt, *Naturaleza del peronismo* (Buenos Aires, 1967), pp. 86–96.
11. In 1967 Fayt published the results of a study about the nature of Perónism, which was conducted under the auspices of the faculty of political law at the University of Buenos Aires. After an exhaustive investigation, they concluded first that Perónism was simply Perón. His will to power and his extreme, almost physical sense of reality prompted him to begin developing his own governmental and political structures while he was war minister, secretary of labor and social services, and vice-president during the Ramírez interlude. Perónism was a national movement with a popular base. For the middle and lower classes, Perón represented social and economic fulfillment

and participation by them in the political process. He used simple images that the people could understand, repetition of ideas to keep them in the public mind, and paternalism as tools to dominate and manipulate the masses. Moreover, this study asserts that Perónism was the Argentinean version of Italian fascism, its major characteristics being (1) the belief that action must precede doctrine; (2) the value of order, hierarchy, and discipline; (3) the negation of liberalism and Marxism; (4) the concept that the nation and the government must be dedicated to a single doctrine and a single will; and (5) advocacy of the corporate state. Finally, Fayt contends that Perónism was a product of the social and economic discontent that had been accumulating in Argentina since 1930; it was the political answer to the social and economic conditions of Argentina in 1943. Fayt, *Naturaleza*, pp. 28–41.

12. *F.R.U.S., 1944*, 7:255.

13. Ibid.

15. *New York Times*, 25 February 1944.

16. See, for example, *Los Angeles Times*, 26 February 1944.

17. U.S., Congress, House, "Cuba Opposes Spanish and Argentine Fascism," 78th Cong., 2d sess., 14 January 1944, *Congressional Record*, 90:A235–36.

18. U.S., Congress, House, "Franco, Farrell, and De Gaulle," 78th Cong., 2d sess., 1 August 1944, *Congressional Record*, 90:A3497–98.

19. *Washington Post*, 26 February 1944.

20. *F.R.U.S., 1944*, 7:252–53.

21. Ibid., pp. 294–95.

22. Ibid.

23. Ibid., pp. 259–60.

24. Stettinius to Hull, 4 March 1944, box 218, Stettinius Papers.

25. Hoover to Hopkins, 4 February 1944, box 140, FBI Reports—Argentina, Hopkins Papers. See also Stettinius to FDR, 15 February 1944, box 32, Stettinius Folder, President's Secretary's File, Roosevelt Papers.

26. Berle Diaries, 10 January 1944, box 215.

27. See, for example, Statement of Policy by Hull, 21 June 1944, container 53, folder 168, Hull Papers.

28. *F.R.U.S., 1944*, 7:260–62.

29. Conversation between Hull and Morgenthau, 8 September 1944, book 77, p. 120, Morgenthau Diaries.

30. Stimson Diaries, 11 January 1944, vol. 46, p. 12.

31. Bonsal to Duggan, 22 March 1944, Memoranda-Argentina, vol. 4, RG 59, DOS.

32. Bonsal to Stettinius, 1 March 1944, and Bonsal to Duggan, 4 March 1944, Memoranda-Argentina, vol. 4, RG 59, DOS.

33. Duggan to Hull, 26 June 1944, Memoranda-Argentina, vol. 4, RG 59, DOS.

34. *F.R.U.S., 1944*, 7:325.

35. Conversation between Hull and Chilean Ambassador, 20 March 1944, boxes 57 and 58, folder 195, Hull Papers.

36. Draft of Speech on Argentine Sit-

uation, 19 June 1944, container 53, folder 168, Hull Papers.

37. For RPA recommendations on the course to be pursued toward Argentina see Wendelin to Duggan, 2 March 1944, 835.00/2645, RG 59, DOS.

38. So great was Wendelin's animus toward Argentina that at one point he refused to approve the passports of a group of Seventh Day Adventist missionaries who wanted to travel to Africa via Argentina. He feared that the Latin community might view such fraternization as indicative of a thaw in Argentine-American relations. Wendelin to Shipley, 8 September 1944, Memoranda-Argentina, vol. 4, RG 59, DOS.

39. See Pierre Boal to Hull, 27 March 1944, container 53, folder 166, Hull Papers.

40. *New York Times*, 19 July 1944.

41. J. K. Bacon to Bonsal and Duggan, 2 February 1944, Memoranda-Argentina, vol. 4, RG 59, DOS.

42. Memorandum for the President, 30 March 1944, book 716, p. 254, Morgenthau Diaries.

43. Meeting re Freezing of Argentina, 3 March 1944, book 706, p. 54, and Meeting on Freezing of Argentine, 6 March 1944, book 706, p. 214, Morgenthau Diaries.

44. Conversation between Morgenthau and FDR, 7 March 1944, Presidential Diaries, 5:1341–43, Morgenthau Papers.

45. Meeting on State Department's policy toward Argentina, 9 March 1944, book 708, p. 8, Morgenthau Diaries.

46. Throughout late 1943 and early 1944 the FEA continued to advocate the most stringent action toward Argentina. "You are right: Action—and tough action—should be taken on the Argentine," FEA counsel Oscar Cox wrote to Hopkins on 16 January 1944. "That's the only language those fellows will understand. The only trouble with babying them is that it just doesn't work. If we don't act we stand a good chance that a lot of South America will be badly affected before the war is over." Oscar Cox to Hopkins, 16 January 1944, box 148, Papers of Oscar Cox, Franklin D. Roosevelt Library, Hyde Park, N.Y.

47. Conversation between Morgenthau and Acheson, 27 April 1944, book 724, p. 256, Morgenthau Diaries.

48. Memorandum for the President, 30 March 1944, book 716, p. 254, Morgenthau Diaries.

49. Morgenthau to Hull, 27 April 1944, book 724, p. 268, Morgenthau Diaries.

50. John Morton Blum, ed., *The Price of Vision: The Diary of Henry A. Wallace, 1942–1946* (Boston, 1973), p. 301.

51. Wallace Diaries, 4 April 1944, box 10, notebook 28.

52. Blum, *Price of Vision*, p. 300.

53. Ibid., pp. 290, 291, 318.

54. Conversation between Acheson and Morgenthau, 4 May 1944, book 727, p. 123, Morgenthau Diaries.

55. *F.R.U.S., 1944*, 7:269.

56. John Morton Blum, ed., *From the Morgenthau Diaries*, vol. 3. (Boston, 1967), p. 205.

57. Meeting on Freezing of Argen-

tina, 10 May 1944, book 730, p. 134, Morgenthau Diaries.

58. Ibid.

59. Morgenthau to FDR, 10 May 1944, book 730, p. 143, Morgenthau Diaries.

60. Stettinius to Acheson, 27 March 1944, box 215, Stettinius Papers; and Meeting on Freezing of Argentina, 27 April 1944, book 724, p. 244, Morgenthau Diaries.

61. When the Argentine matter came up at Quebec, Morgenthau said nothing. "I simply felt," he later told his staff, "I was doing more than I should and I just had my eye on the bull's eye, which was what is the future of Germany." Report on Quebec Conference, October 1944, book 772, p. 219, Morgenthau Diaries.

62. Spaeth to Armour, 28 August 1944, Memoranda-Argentina, vol. 4, RG 59, DOS.

63. Memorandum for the Secretary, 24 March 1944, book 713, p. 308, Morgenthau Diaries.

64. Meeting between Wallace, Jones, and Morgenthau, 29 March 1944, book 716, p. 65, Morgenthau Diaries.

65. Conversation between Wallace and Morgenthau, 4 April 1944, book 717, p. 129-B, Morgenthau Diaries.

66. Conversation between Morgenthau and Wallace, 27 April 1944, book 724, p. 239, Morgenthau Diaries. See also Wallace Diaries, 3 April 1944, box 10, notebook 28.

67. Hull and the internationalists were warmed in late May by a show of grass-roots support in the nation's capital. After the Argentine ambassador attempted to crash the Argentine Independence Day festivities of McKinley High School, the students boycotted the celebration. Said Barbara Benedict, president of the Spanish Club, "We thought we would be demonstrating friendship with the Argentine people and not with the Argentine Government until that Ambassador stuck his nose into the picture." The House of Representatives subsequently passed a resolution praising the "principal, teachers, and pupils of McKinley High School" for their stand. "The viciousness and hypocricy of the dictatorship in Argentina," proclaimed a legislator, "has once again been exposed by courageous educators and the free American press." U.S., Congress, House, Argentine Fascist Intervention in American Affairs, 78th Cong., 2d sess., 26 May 1944, *Congressional Record*, 90:5037–38. See the *Congressional Record* for 1 August 1944, 90:A3497, for Celler's remarks; and *New York Times*, 25 May 1944.

68. Duggan to Hull, 1 February 1944, Memoranda-Argentina, vol. 4, RG 59, DOS.

69. Questions the British May Raise, 11 March 1944, box 249, and State Department to Combined Food Board, 13 January 1944, box 250, Stettinius Papers.

70. Combined Food Board to Acheson and Campbell, 17 January 1945, box 250, Stettinius Papers.

71. Combined Food Board to Acheson and Hadow, 15 April 1944, box 250, Stettinius Papers.

72. Combined Raw Materials Board

to Acheson and Hadow, 17 January 1944, box 250, Stettinius Papers.

73. Combined Shipping Adjustment Board to Acheson and Campbell, 17 January 1944, box 250, Stettinius Papers.

74. Conversation between Member of London Embassy and Neville Butler, 23 September 1944, 835.00/9-2344, RG 59, DOS.

75. Reed to Armour, 17 July 1944, 835.00/7-1744, RG 59, DOS.

76. FDR to Joint Chiefs of Staff, 24 January 1944, 091.3 Argentina, RG 218, General Records of the Combined Chiefs of Staff (hereafter referred to as COC).

77. E. Louise Peffer, "Cordell Hull's Argentine Policy and Britain's Meat Supply," *Inter-American Economic Affairs* 10 (Autumn, 1956): 14, 16; Cordell Hull, *The Memoirs of Cordell Hull* (New York, 1948), 2:1414; and Conversation between Stettinius and Morgenthau, 5 March 1944, book 706, pp. 168–69, Morgenthau Diaries.

78. Conversation between Stettinius and Morgenthau, 5 March 1944, book 707, p. 168, Morgenthau Diaries.

79. Memo on Stettinius-Eden Conversations, 15 April 1944, box 225, Stettinius Papers; and Hull to FDR, 12 September 1944, President's Secretary's File, Roosevelt Papers.

80. Meeting on Cabinet Meeting, 18 May 1944, book 733, pp. 30–31, Morgenthau Diaries.

81. Berle to Hull, 12 June 1944, box 58, Berle Papers.

82. FDR to Hull, 15 July 1944, Map Room Files, box 19, Roosevelt Papers.

83. Ibid.

84. In an effort to placate Hull, Roosevelt cabled Churchill and urged the "Former Naval Person" to let Argentina know, without endangering the meat contract, that "we are fed up with her pro-Axis sentiments and practices." Churchill subsequently replied that he and his colleagues wanted to do everything possible to help the president and Mr. Hull with their South American problems, but the one point to remember was that whereas the United Kingdom had imported more than sixty-six million tons of beef in 1938, she was currently subsisting on twenty-five million. *F.R.U.S., 1944,* 7:333.

85. Ibid., pp. 102, 337; and Department of the Army, "Relations of the Caribbean Defense Command with Argentina" (unpublished compilation), Military Records Division of National Archives, pp. 11–12.

86. See also Hull to Stettinius, 5 August 1944, container 62, folder 261, Hull Papers.

87. Spaeth to Long, 25 August 1944, container 188, Long Papers.

88. Conversation between Hull and Halifax, 16 September 1944, 835.00/9-1644, RG 59, DOS.

89. *F.R.U.S., 1944,* 7:366 n.13.

90. Ibid., pp. 361–63.

91. Ibid., p. 360.

92. Conversation between D. F. Christy (Wilson and Co.) and E. A. Gilmore (RPA), 11 January 1945, Memoranda-Argentina, vol. 5, RG 59, DOS.

93. "Argentine Appraisal," *Wall Street Journal*, 23 February 1945.
94. Duggan to Hull, 9 March 1944, 835.00/2669, RG 59, DOS.
95. Ibid.
96. J. F. Simmons to Hull, 11 March 1944, 835.00/2577, RG 59 DOS.
97. Conversation between Bonsal and Messersmith, 7 March 1944, Memoranda-Argentina, vol. 4, RG 59, DOS.
98. Conversation between Berle and Dr. Carlos Martins, 6 January 1944, box 215, Berle Diaries.
99. Memo on Estrada Doctrine, 2 February 1945, box 9, Pasvolsky Papers.
100. Ibid.
101. See, for example, Conversation between Hull and Gajardo, 20 July 1944, boxes 57 and 58, folder 195, Hull Papers; and Conversation between Hull and Brazilian Ambassador, 16 August 1944, Memoranda-Argentina, vol. 4, RG 59, DOS.
102. *F.R.U.S., 1944*, 7:395–96.
103. *New York Times*, 29 March 1944.
104. Ibid.
105. Joseph Newman, "Latin American Republics Eager to Renew Argentine Ties," *New York Herald Tribune*, 15 May 1944; and *F.R.U.S., 1944*, 7:14–15.
106. *F.R.U.S., 1944*, 7:271.
107. Armour to Hull, 5 June 1944, 835.00/2868, RG 59, DOS.
108. *F.R.U.S., 1944*, 7:276.
109. Ibid.
110. "Argentine Threat: Colonel Perón's Speech," *Washington Post*, 3 July 1945.
111. Ibid.
112. Significance of Perón's Speech of 10 June 1944, 4 July 1944, R and A 2304, RG 226, OSS.
113. Ibid.
114. See, for example, Spaeth to Hull, 19 June 1944, container 188, Folder-Argentina, 1944, Papers of Breckinridge Long, Library of Congress.
115. In late June, Hull advised FDR that the attitude of several Latin American states, including Brazil, toward nonrecognition depended on the position assumed by the United Kingdom. If the British followed an independent course in the matter, he declared, then not only would Washington's policy of nonrecognition be endangered, but the American people would be thoroughly aroused against the United States' chief wartime ally. On July 13 FDR cabled Churchill that Armour was being recalled for consultation. Though "nearly all" the other American states were going to follow suit, the collective withdrawal would go largely for nought if Ambassador Kelly remained in Buenos Aires. Churchill reluctantly acquiesced in the president's request. Winant to Hull, 17 July 1944, Memoranda-Argentina, vol. 4, RG 59, DOS; Hull to FDR, 30 June 1944, Map Room Files, box 19, Roosevelt Papers; *F.R.U.S., 1944*, 7:298; and Churchill to FDR, 1 July 1944, container 53, folder 169, Hull Papers.
116. *F.R.U.S., 1944*, 7:317–20.
117. President's Naval Aide to Secretary, Joint Chiefs, 29 June 1944, May Room Files, box 101, Roosevelt Papers.

118. "Non-recognition of Argentine Regime," *Department of State Bulletin*, vol. 11, no. 266 (30 July 1944), pp. 107–9.
119. Ibid.
120. *La Nación* and *El Mundo*, 27 June 1944.
121. *New York Times*, 10 September 1944.
122. Conversation between Armour and Uruguayan Ambassador, 28 August 1944, Memoranda-Argentina, vol. 4, RG 59, DOS.
123. Conversation between Hull and Peruvian Ambassador, 17 August 1944, Memoranda-Argentina, vol. 4, RG 59, DOS.
124. Conversation between Long and Foreign Minister of the Dominican Republic, 8 September 1944, container 188, folder Argentina 1944, Long Papers.
125. Churchill to FDR, 1 July 1944, container 53, folder 169, Hull Papers.
126. Robert Welles (chairman, Coordinating Committee for Argentina) to Rockefeller, 13 January 1944, box 50, RG 229, OCIAA.
127. *New York Times*, 21 July 1944.
128. Ibid.
129. Meeting between Hull, Stimson, and Morgenthau, 20 September 1944, book 773, p. 4, Morgenthau Diaries.
130. On March 4, according to Morgenthau, the secretary of state launched into his "usual tirade" declaring that everyone in the country was for him except Drew Pearson and Sumner Welles. The latter, said Hull, was telling everyone to disregard Cordell Hull, for he, Welles, would be "in the saddle" after the election. Conversation between Hull and Morgenthau, 4 May 1944, book 727, p. 204, Morgenthau Diaries. Support for Welles's point of view both in Latin America and the United States became so alarming to Hull that he asked FDR to make a forceful statement in support of current American policy toward Argentina. The secretary complained that the "chief disseminator of pro-Argentine propaganda" was leaving the impression not only that FDR was his closest personal friend but also that the president was in full agreement with the critics of U.S. policy. The president complied with a press release that spoke vaguely about the need to honor international commitments. Hull to FDR, 26 September 1944, container 54, folder 170, Hull Papers; and *F.R.U.S., 1944*, 7:356–57.
131. Conversation between Hull and Chilean Ambassador, 22 March 1944, boxes 57 and 58, folder 195, Hull Papers; and *F.R.U.S., 1944*, 7:306.
132. Conversation between Hull and Bolivian Chargé d'Affaires, 12 July 1944, boxes 57 and 58, folder 191, Hull Papers.
133. Conversation between Hull and Chilean Chargé d'Affaires, 1 July 1944, Memoranda-Argentina, vol. 4, RG 59, DOS.
134. *F.R.U.S., 1944*, 7:346–47. See also Statement of Policy by Hull, 21 June 1944, container 53, folder 168, Hull Papers.
135. See, for example, Berle Diaries, 12 December 1944, box 216.

136. Armour to Hull, 18 September 1944, container 54, folder 170, Hull Papers; and Duggan to Hull, March 1944, box 218, Stettinius Papers.

137. Conversation between Armour and MacIntosh, 27 October 1944, 835.00/2744, RG 59, DOS.

138. Lane (American ambassador to Colombia) to Hull, 26 October 1943, box 496, RG 229, OCIAA.

139. *F.R.U.S., 1944*, 7:31–33.

140. Ibid., pp. 34–37.

141. Ibid., pp. 29–30.

142. Ibid., pp. 28–29.

143. Inter-American Reactions to the Argentine Proposal for a Conference of Foreign Ministers, 20 November 1944, R and A 2714, RG 226, OSS.

144. *F.R.U.S., 1944*, 7:43–45; Hull, *Memoirs*, 2:1404; and Conversation between Armour and Chilean Ambassador, 7 November 1944, Memoranda-Argentina, vol. 4, RG 59, DOS. See also Berle to Hull, 10 January 1944, box 58, Berle Papers.

145. *F.R.U.S., 1945*, 9:57–62.

146. See, for example, Conversation between Hull and Colombian Ambassador, 20 June 1944, 711.35/252, RG 59, DOS.

147. Hull, *Memoirs*, 2:1404.

148. *F.R.U.S., 1944*, 7:27–28.

149. Wendelin to Armour, 20 November 1944, Memoranda-Argentina, vol. 4, RG 59, DOS; and Stettinius to U.S. Chargé d'Affaires in Mexico City, 2 November 1944, 710. consultation (4)10-3044, RG 59, DOS.

150. Wendelin to Armour, 20 November 1944, Memoranda-Argentina, vol. 4, RG 59, DOS. Eric Wendelin continued to be the driving force behind opposition to détente. On November 7 he wrote to Frank Johnston, publisher of the *American Exporter*, that in coercing Argentina, Washington was simply trying to apply the lessons learned from its bitter experience with the Nazis in the 1930s and trying to prevent the continuing existence of this "festering sore" in the Americas. Wendelin to Johnston, 7 November 1944, found with 835.00/10-2544, RG 59, DOS.

151. Long to FDR, 11 November 1944, container 188, folder Argentina 1944, Long Papers.

152. *F.R.U.S., 1944*, 7:43–45.

153. Report by Foreign Activity Correlation, 14 November 1944, 835.00/11-1444, RG 59, DOS.

154. *F.R.U.S., 1944*, 7:47–51.

155. Ibid., pp. 25–26.

156. Ibid., pp. 54–55.

157. Stettinius to FDR, 21 November 1944, Memoranda-Argentina, vol. 5, RG 59, DOS.

158. *F.R.U.S., 1944*, 7:81–83; and Colombian Embassy to State Department, 8 January 1945, and U.S. Ambassador to Ecuador to Stettinius, 12 January 1945, 710. Conference War and Postwar 1–1245, RG 59, DOS.

159. *F.R.U.S., 1945*, 9:3–4.

160. *F.R.U.S., 1944*, 7:28–29.

161. Ibid., pp. 75, 80.

162. *F.R.U.S., 1945*, 9:1–3.

CHAPTER 8

1. See, for example, Gaddis Smith, *American Diplomacy during the Second World War, 1941–1945* (New York, 1965).

2. Conversation between Hull and Morgenthau, 8 September 1944, book 770, p. 120, Morgenthau Diaries.

3. Conversation between Hull and Morgenthau, undated, book 763, p. 204, Morgenthau Diaries.

4. Thomas M. Campbell, *Masquerade Peace: America's U.N. Policy, 1944–1945* (Tallahassee, Fla., 1973), p. 67.

5. "Resignation of Cordell Hull as Secretary of State," *Department of State Bulletin*, vol. 11, no. 284 (3 December 1944), pp. 649–53.

6. For Morgenthau's attitude toward the Coordinator's Office see Conversation between Morgenthau and Rockefeller, 12 January 1942, book 485, p. 116, Morgenthau Diaries.

7. On the OCIAA's struggle to survive into the postwar era see, for example, Rockefeller to Stettinius, 7 January 1944, box 499, RG 229, OCIAA.

8. *New York Times*, 7 June 1944.

9. *F.R.U.S., 1945*, 9:50.

10. Welles to Rockefeller, 26 March 1942, box 500, RG 229, OCIAA; *F.R.U.S., 1945*, 9:9; and Duggan to Rockefeller, 28 October 1943 and 31 January 1944, RG 229, OCIAA.

11. Rockefeller to Duggan, 29 March 1944, box 496, RG 229, OCIAA.

12. Nelson A. Rockefeller, "Will We Remain Good Neighbors after the War?" *Saturday Evening Post*, 6 November 1943, p. 74.

13. Conversation between Morgenthau and FDR, 7 March 1944, Presidential Diaries, book 5, pp. 1341–43, Morgenthau Papers.

14. Lockwood to Johnstone, 28 October 1942, box 143, RG 229, OCIAA.

15. Rockefeller to Stettinius, 11 November 1943, box 499, and Duggan to Rockefeller, 31 January 1944, box 496, RG 229, OCIAA.

16. David Green, *The Containment of Latin America* (Chicago, 1971), p. 142.

17. Duggan to Rockefeller, 28 October 1943, box 496, and Rockefeller to FDR, 1 May 1944, box 510, RG 229, OCIAA.

18. Rockefeller to E. B. Mann, 9 December 1949, Rockefeller Family Archives, Rockefeller Center, New York, N.Y.

19. Memoranda on Supply of Replacement Parts to Argentine Army and Navy, 1 March 1943, Memoranda-Argentina, vol. 3, RG 59, DOS.

20. See, for example, J. K. Bacon to Bonsal, 23 October 1943, Memoranda-Argentina, vol. 4, RG 59, DOS. In February 1945 Wendelin observed to Warren that the activities of Colonel Cavenah, head of the United States Air Mission in Buenos Aires, "had been a source of continuing embarrassment to us." Wendelin to Warren, 2 February 1945, Memoranda-Argentina, vol. 5, RG 59, DOS.

21. *F.R.U.S., 1942*, 5:371–72.

22. Department of the Army, "Relations of the Caribbean Defense Command with Argentina" (unpublished compilation), Military Division of National Archives, pp. 19, 24; and Bonsal to Hull, 30 December 1943, Memoranda-Argentina, vol. 4, RG 59, DOS.
23. "Relations of the Caribbean Defense Command," pp. 2, 23–25.
24. Proposed Economic Sanctions with Respect to Argentina, 19 January 1944, 91.3, boxes 252–56, RG 218, COC. See also Stimson Diaries, 24 May 1943, vol. 42, p. 66.
25. Secretary of War Stimson was an ardent supporter of hemispheric solidarity and a long-time disciple of the Monroe Doctrine. Stimson Diaries, 26 April 1945, vol. 51, p. 75, and 10 May 1945, vol. 51, p. 116.
26. Wallace Diaries, 7 January 1945, box 9, notebook 26.
27. There was more than just a tacit alliance between the United States military and the American trading community. On 24 October 1944 Gen. George Brett wrote to Eric Johnston, president of the United States Chamber of Commerce: "The U.S. can establish itself on a basic business-like footing . . . there will be an increased solidarity among the American republics. Any military or commercial enterprise in any one of these countries must clearly indicate that the major benefit is for the country concerned, this benefit to create stability both politically and economically within that country." He went on to say that the future of the world depended on the Western Hemisphere and that of the hemisphere, on the United States. "Relations of the Caribbean Defense Command," pp. 21–22.
28. "America's Corporate Stake Abroad—$7,000,000,000," *Business Week*, 22 August 1942; and Memo on Value of U.S. Investments in Argentina, 18 January 1944, Memoranda-Argentina, vol. 4, RG 59, DOS.
29. *New York Times*, 23 July 1944. Some businessmen were not willing to wait for the State Department to act. According to *El Popular* of Mexico City, officials of DuPont and Imperial Chemicals held a series of talks with Perón in Buenos Aires, looking toward a settlement of the Argentine question. Messersmith to Stettinius, 19 December 1944, 835.00/12-1944, RG 59, DOS.
30. Armand May to Hull, 13 April 1942, 835.00/1175, RG 59, DOS.
31. "Tune in on Export," *American Exporter*, 19 October 1944.
32. Alfred H. Benjamin to FDR, 12 May 1942, 835.00/1184, RG 59, DOS.
33. Conversation between Bonsal and Attorney for National City Bank of New York, 29 October 1943, Memoranda-Argentina, vol. 4, RG 59, DOS.
34. For reports on official and semi-official British activities designed to facilitate postwar trade with Argentina, see Armour to Hull, 13 April 1944, Memoranda-Argentina, vol. 4, RG 59, DOS. For Britain's view of the wartime conduct and objectives of United

States traders in Argentina see Sir David Kelly, *The Ruling Few* (London, 1952), p. 293. United States exporters were particularly upset at rumors that Great Britain was reexporting lend-lease goods to Argentina in order to gain a trade advantage. Alleged Misuse of Lend-Lease by Great Britain, 7 July 1941, box 123, Papers of Harry Hopkins, Franklin D. Roosevelt Library.

35. Armour to Hull, 20 January 1944, 835.00/2298, RG 59, DOS; and Report on Argentine Export-Import Programs, 29 June 1944, box 218, Stettinius Papers.

36. Conversation between Wendelin and I. C. Jacobs, 28 July 1944, Memoranda-Argentina, vol. 4, RG 59, DOS.

37. "Tune in on Export."

38. "The War and Business Abroad," *Business Week*, 13 January 1945.

39. For an idea of the respect with which the United States business community viewed Argentina's credit record see Frederick Stern, "Prospects for Argentine Bonds," *Barron's*, 2 February 1942.

40. *Wall Street Journal*, 14 March 1945. See also the issue of 2 March 1945.

41. Edward Reed (U.S. chargé d'affaires in Buenos Aires) to Stettinius, 2 March 1945, 835.00/3-245, RG 59, DOS.

42. Conversation between Armour and Shaw, 24 November 1944, box 19, Memoranda-Argentina, vol. 5, RG 59, DOS.

43. "The War and Business Abroad," *Business Week*, 3 February 1945.

44. "One Good Neighbor Blunders,"

Wall Street Journal, 14 March 1945.

45. John Lear, "The Truth about Argentina," *Saturday Evening Post*, 25 November 1944.

46. See, for example, address by Eric Johnston to Economic Club of New York, quoted in *New York Times*, 2 April 1943; and "Abroad," *Barron's*, 25 January 1943.

47. See address by Robert J. Watt to Economic Club of New York, quoted in *New York Times*, 2 April 1942.

48. John Morton Blum, ed., *The Price of Vision: The Diary of Henry A. Wallace, 1942–1946* (Boston, 1973), p. 318.

49. Stimson Diaries, 27 April 1945, vol. 51, p. 79; and Campbell, *Masquerade Peace*, p. 128.

50. Press Report of "Softening in United States Attitude toward Argentina," 7 December 1944; Wendelin to Lockwood, 3 January 1945; and Spaeth to Armour, 13 December 1944, Memoranda-Argentina, vol. 5, RG 59, DOS.

51. *F.R.U.S., 1944*, 7:287–99.

52. Ibid.

53. Stettinius to Armour and Rockefeller, 11 December 1944, Memoranda-Argentina, vol. 5, RG 59, DOS.

54. Memo for the President on U.S. Policy toward Argentina, 2 January 1945, 711.35/1-245, RG 59, DOS.

55. Division of River Plata Affairs to Lockwood, 3 January 1945, Memoranda-Argentina, vol. 5, RG 59, DOS.

56. Warren to Stettinius, 28 February

1945, box 285, Stettinius Papers; and *F.R.U.S., 1945,* 9:100–101. See also President's Work Sheet, 21 November 1944, box 95, Stettinius Folder, Roosevelt Papers.

57. *F.R.U.S., 1945,* 9:368–70.

58. Luis Fiore, the individual in charge of intervention of Axis firms in Argentina, assured American embassy officials that all firms with any Axis ties at all would be intervened and that the government was planning to call elections in the very near future. David Berger to Stettinius, 16 December 1944, file no. XL-9031, RG 226, OSS; and Division of River Plata Affairs to Division of American Republics Affairs, 10 March 1945, Memoranda-Argentina, vol. 5, RG 59, DOS.

59. *F.R.U.S., 1945,* 9:368–70.

60. Ibid., p. 505.

61. Hoover to Hopkins, 18 January 1945, box 140, FBI Reports—Argentina, Hopkins Papers.

62. Berle Diaries, 23 December 1944, box 216.

63. Ibid., 7 February 1945, box 216.

64. Ibid.

65. *New York Times,* 12 January 1945.

66. U.S., Congress, House, Remarks of Congressman Jack Z. Anderson pertaining to Argentina, 79th Cong., 1st sess., 23 February 1945, *Congressional Record,* 91:1397–98.

67. *La Noche,* 4 January 1945.

68. *La Razón,* 4 January 1945; and *El Tiempo,* 4 January 1945.

69. Caffery to Stettinius, 16 January 1945, 710. Conference War and Postwar/2-145, RG 59, DOS.

70. *El Mercurio,* 15 January 1945.

71. *La Noche,* 15 January 1945.

72. Campbell, *Masquerade Peace,* pp. 122–25.

73. Washington increased Latin America discontent in February 1945 by informing the six Latin American nations who had not declared war on the Axis that if they did not do so, they would be excluded from the UNCIO. Having received invitations to previous United Nations meetings without question, the nonbelligerent were surprised and angered by this last-minute demand that they declare war on the nearly defeated Axis countries. Laurence Duggan, *The Americas: The Search for Hemispheric Security* (New York, 1949), pp. 107–8.

74. Campbell, *Masquerade Peace,* pp. 114–15.

75. *F.R.U.S., 1945,* 9:20–21.

76. Ibid., 9:24–25.

77. Stettinius to Joseph Grew (acting secretary of state), 18 February 1945, 711.32/2-1845, RG 59, DOS.

78. Meeting between Santos and FDR, 8 March 1945, box 285, Stettinius Papers.

79. *F.R.U.S., 1944,* 7:27–86; and Wire Service Reports Received by State Department, 10 March 1945, RG 59, DOS.

80. On the Latin Americanists' awareness of the need for caution in dealing with Argentina see Warren to Stettinius, 28 February 1945, box 285, Stettinius Papers; and *F.R.U.S., 1945,* 9:100–101.

81. See Main Objectives of U.S. Delegation, 2 February 1945, box 10, Pasvolsky Papers.

82. New Left historians argue that

this was simply a stratagem to facilitate United States economic exploitation of Latin America. In his *Containment of Latin America*, David Green writes, in connection with the Chapultepec Conference: "From its low-tariff position to its attempted ban on state-run trading enterprises, the United States' position was an effort to make sure that the power of government would not be used in the postwar period to close off any bloc area, regional or national, to United States economic expansion." David Green, *The Containment of Latin America* (Chicago, 1971), pp. 178, 167.

83. Meeting between Santos and FDR, 8 March 1945, box 285, Stettinius Papers.

84. Campbell, *Masquerade Peace*, pp. 114–15.

85. *F.R.U.S., 1945*, 7:81; and Draft of a Telegram on Argentina to President, 20 February 1945, box 285, Stettinius Papers.

86. Meeting of United States Delegation, 20 February 1945, box 285, Stettinius Papers.

87. Conversation between U.S. Ambassador to Colombia and Foreign Minister, 21 February 1945, and Stettinius Record of Proceedings, 23 February 1945, box 285, Stettinius Papers.

88. Stettinius to Grew for FDR, 22 February 1945, 835.00/2-2245, RG 59, DOS; and Memo on Political and Economic Relations with Argentina, 20 April 1946, box 62, folder 261, Hull Papers.

89. FDR to Stettinius, 24 February 1945, 835.00/2-2445, RG 59, DOS.

90. Stettinius Record of Proceedings, 21 February 1945, box 285, Stettinius Papers.

91. The secretary had made it plain to the numerous and very active Argentine agents in Mexico City that if their country took certain steps, "the door would not be slammed in her face." Minutes of the Steering Committee Meeting, 5 March 1945, box 286, Stettinius Papers.

92. "It is evident that there are two groups in the American Delegation: the group that thinks entirely globally and knows little about the hemisphere, and the group that thinks about the hemisphere first, and global matters second," Berle recorded in his diary on February 20. "I do not know whether they will come in contact or not." Berle Diaries, 20 February 1945, box 216.

93. Berle Diaries, 20 and 27 February 1945, box 216.

94. Ibid., 20 February and 1 March 1945, box 216.

95. Ibid., 6 March 1945, box 216.

96. Ibid., 27 February and 6 March 1945, box 216.

97. Grew to FDR, 1 March 1945, box 95, Stettinius Folder, President's Secretary's File, Roosevelt Papers; and Berle Diaries, 1 March 1945, box 216.

98. Berle Diaries, 6 March 1945, box 216; and *New York Times*, 1 March 1945.

99. "Act of Chapultepec," *Department of State Bulletin*, vol. 12, no. 297 (4 March 1945), pp. 339–40.

100. Campbell, *Masquerade Peace*, pp. 118–20.

101. Stettinius Record of Proceedings, 21 February 1945, box 285, Stettinius Papers.

102. "Inter-American Conference on Problems of War and Peace: Resolution Concerning Argentina," *Department of State Bulletin*, vol. 12, no. 299 (18 March 1945).

103. Minutes of Steering Committee Meeting, 5 March 1945; Handwritten Report of High-level United States Meeting, 7 March 1945; and Daily Record of Stettinius, 5 March 1945, box 286, Stettinius Papers.

104. Handwritten Report of High-level United States Meeting, 5 March 1945, box 286, Stettinius Papers; and "Statement by the Secretary of State on the Conclusion of the Conference," *Department of State Bulletin*, vol. 12, no. 298 (8 March 1945), p. 400.

105. Opinion in the United States was generally favorable both toward the Act of Chapultepec and the Argentine resolution. See, for example, *Washington Post*, 5 March 1945; and *Chicago Tribune*, 9 March 1945.

106. *El Mercurio*, 8 March 1945; and *La Nación*, 8 March 1945.

107. U.S. Ambassador to Panama to Stettinius, 8 March 1945, 710. Conference War and Postwar/3-845, RG 59, DOS.

108. *La Nación*, 8 March 1945; and *El Mundo*, 8 March 1945.

109. *F.R.U.S., 1945*, 9:147. Quote from State Department summary.

110. Wire Service Reports Received by State Department, 10 March 1945, 835.00/3-1045, RG 59, DOS.

111. *F.R.U.S., 1945*, 1:362–69.

112. Reed to Stettinius, 17 March 1945, 835.00/3-1745, RG 59, DOS.

113. See, for example, *New York Times*, 28 March 1945; and *St. Louis Post-Dispatch*, 28 March 1945. For *latino* reaction see U.S. Ambassador to Paraguay to Stettinius, 29 March 1945, 835.00/3-2945, RG 59, DOS.

114. For example, Lockwood curtly informed RPA on April 10 that Argentina, by signing the Final Act, had virtually ended any possibility that Axis agents would be able to use Argentina as a base of operations. Lockwood to Division of River Plata Affairs, 10 April 1945, Memoranda-Argentina, vol. 5, RG 59, DOS.

115. *F.R.U.S., 1945*, 1:200; and *F.R.U.S., 1945*, 9:372–73.

116. Statement of Events on Argentina, undated, container 54, folder 172, Hull Papers.

117. FDR to Stettinius, 7 April 1945, Map Room Files, box 23, Roosevelt Papers.

118. Campbell, *Masquerade Peace*, p. 145.

119. By March 1945 Rockefeller and his colleagues were convinced that only by working both to reincorporate the errant state into the hemispheric family of nations and to secure an invitation for Argentina to join the United Nations could Washington prove that it had returned to its prewar concept of community. Statement of Events in Argentina since October 1944, undated, box 54, folder 172, Hull Papers; and Conversation between Martin Popper (National Lawyers Guild) and Lockwood, 4

April 1945, Memoranda-Argentina, vol. 5, RG 59, DOS.

120. Warren to Stettinius, 18 April 1945, 711.35/4-1845, RG 59, DOS; and Juan Perón, *Tres revolucións militares* (Buenos Aires, 1963), p. 96.

121. Warren to Stettinius, 18 April 1945, 711.35/4-1845, RG 59, DOS; and Juan Perón, *Tres revolucións militares*, p. 96.

122. Reed to Stettinius, 19 April 1945, 711.35/4-1945, RG 59, DOS.

123. Warren to Stettinius, 21 April 1945, 711.35/4-2145, RG 59, DOS.

124. *New York Times*, 21 April, 1945.

125. *New York Times*, 24 April 1945; and Berle Diaries, 5 April 1945, box 216.

126. *F.R.U.S., 1945*, 9:372–73.

127. *F.R.U.S.*, 1945, 1:329.

128. *New York Times*, 20 December 1944.

129. Messersmith to Stettinius and Rockefeller, 19 March 1945, 500.cc/3-1345; and Messersmith to Stettinius, 19 March 1945, 835.00/3-1545, RG 59, DOS. See also Berle Diaries, 20 March 1945, box 216.

130. *F.R.U.S., Diplomatic Papers: The Conference at Malta and Yalta, 1945*, p. 773.

131. The Colombian foreign minister had told newsmen that Secretary Stettinius had promised at the Chapultepec Conference that if Argentina "behaved really well," he would use his good offices to see that it was invited to the San Francsico meeting. U.S. Ambassador to Colombia to Stettinius, 14 April 1945, 500.cc/4-445, RG 59, DOS.

132. See Campbell, *Masquerade Peace*; and *F.R.U.S., 1945*, 1:397.

133. *F.R.U.S., 1945*, 1:395–96, 398, 417; and Arthur H. Vandenberg, Jr., ed., *The Private Papers of Senator Vandenberg* (Boston, 1952), p. 182.

134. See, for example, Berle Diaries, 5 April 1945, box 216. Fearful of the wave of adverse opinion that would engulf the State Department in the wake of the seating of the two republics, Stettinius had tried in late March to deny to the Russians that a commitment had been made at Yalta. His efforts came to nought. Campbell, *Masquerade Peace*, p. 149.

135. Tom Connally, *My Name Is Tom Connally* (New York, 1954), p. 279; and *F.R.U.S., 1945*, 1:401.

136. *F.R.U.S., 1945*, 1:397.

137. Conversation between Stettinius and Anthony Eden, 21 April 1945, box 250, Stettinius Papers.

138. The hard-liners on the Argentine question were strengthened in their arguments by news received on April 23 that the Farrell-Perón government had ordered the arrest of over sixty officers and civilians for allegedly conspiring against the government. Included in their number were such ardent supporters of the Allies as Rawson, Tonazzi, and Santamarina. Wendelin to E. B. Butler and Dana Munro, 23 April 1945, Memoranda-Argentina, vol. 5, RG 59, DOS. Hull, *Memoirs*, 2:1405–7. During an interview with Stettinius shortly before the admission of Argentina, Hull agreed to United States support of Argen-

tine membership on the grounds that such a move would ensure the seating of the Ukraine and White Russia and thus prevent the Soviet Union from disrupting the meeting. Conversation between Hull and Stettinius, 27 April 1945, box 245, Stettinius Papers. See also Conversation between Hopkins and Morgenthau, 20 June 1945, Presidential Diaries, 7:1670–71, Morgenthau Papers.

139. *F.R.U.S., 1945*, 1:398, 417.

140. Ibid., pp. 410–23, 417–18. Green writes that Vandenberg was at first adamantly opposed to an invitation for Argentina and to an invitation to the Soviet republics, but by April 30 he had dropped his opposition to the seating of Byelorussia and the Ukraine because Latin American opinion had become strongly anti-Soviet as a result of the episode. Green, *Containment of Latin America*, pp. 220, 222. It may be argued, however, that Vandenberg, undeniably a hard-line anti-Communist, reversed himself on the question both of the Argentine and of Soviet republics because he thought that such a change would compel the Kremlin to live up to its Yalta agreements.

141. *F.R.U.S., 1945*, 1:395, 398, 417. Green maintains that the United States delegation at San Francisco agreed to link the issue of the Argentine and the Soviet republics because "most of the delegates were coming to see hemispheric solidarity as a tool to be used against Russia in the conference." Green, *Containment of Latin*

America, p. 217. If one recognizes that fulfillment of the Yalta pledges ("free" elections in Poland and east Europe) was the goal of America's "anti-Russian" policy, this was, in a sense, true.

142. Stettinius to Joseph Grew, 27 April 1945, 500.cc/4-2745, RG 59, DOS; and Conversation between Stettinius and Truman, 26 April 1945, box 245, Stettinius Papers. Even though Truman had been in the White House for only a matter of days, he sensed that the admission of Argentina would produce a tidal wave of public outrage. Events proved him correct. The trickle of critical mail that began in late April turned into a mighty flood as Washington's support of Argentine membership became apparent in early May. See, for example, Harold G. Cutwright to Truman, 27 April 1945; Maurice A. Hanline to Truman, 1 May 1945; B. C. Baxter et al. to Truman, 6 May 1945; and Frank E. Brennan to Truman, 15 May 1945, Department of State, folder 20, Papers of Harry S. Truman, Truman Library, Independence, Mo.

143. *F.R.U.S., 1945*, 1:485.

144. Ibid., pp. 486–87.

145. Lloyd C. Gardner, *Architects of Illusion* (Chicago, 1970), p. 52.

146. Conversation between Stettinius and Truman, 28 April 1945, box 245, Stettinius Papers.

147. Conversation between Eden and Stettinius, 29 April 1945, box 245, Stettinius Papers.

148. "Verbatim Minutes of the First

Plenary Session," *Documents of the United Nations Conference on International Organization*, vol. 1 (London and New York, 1945), p. 148.

149. "Verbatim Minutes of the Fifth Plenary Session," *Documents of the United Nations Conference on International Organization*, pp. 344–72.

150. Ibid.

151. Ibid.

CHAPTER 9

1. For public reaction to Argentina's admission to the United Nations see Harold G. Cutwight to Harry S. Truman, 27 April 1945; Maurice A. Hanline to Harry S. Truman, 1 May 1945; B. C. Baxter et al. to Harry S. Truman, 6 May 1945; and Frank E. Brennan to Harry S. Truman, 15 May 1945, DOS, folder 20, Papers of Harry S. Truman. See also "Pandora's Box at the U.N.C.I.O.," in *Report on San Francisco*, pamphlet published by the *Washington Post* (Washington, D.C., 1945), pp. 10–11.

2. Joseph Grew to Edward Stettinius, 27 April 1945, 500.cc/4-2745, RG 59, DOS.

3. Harold F. Peterson, *Argentina and the United States, 1810–1960* (New York, 1964), pp. 446–47.

4. Ibid., p. 448.

5. Ibid.

6. "The Good-Neighbor Policy," *Department of State Bulletin*, vol. 13, no. 323 (2 September 1945), pp. 327–32.

7. Peterson, *Argentina and the United States*, p. 451.

8. David Green, *The Containment of Latin America* (Chicago, 1971), pp. 253–54; and John Morton Blum, ed., *The Price of Vision: The Diary of Henry A. Wallace, 1942–1946* (Boston, 1973), pp. 295–96.

9. Peterson, *Argentina and the United States*, p. 452.

10. Ibid., pp. 454–55.

11. Ibid., pp. 455–56.

12. Ibid.

13. "Argentina Urges Mutual Assistance," *Department of State Bulletin*, vol. 16, no. 415 (15 June 1947), p. 1177.

14. Green, *Containment of Latin America*, p. 254.

15. Robert A. Divine, *Second Chance: The Triumph of Internationalism in America during World War II* (New York, 1967).

BIBLIOGRAPHIC ESSAY

SECONDARY WORKS

Among the most widely read and reliable accounts of United States policy toward Latin America are John Lloyd Mecham, *A Survey of United States–Latin American Relations* (Boston, 1965); Samuel F. Bemis, *The Latin American Policy of the United States* (New York, 1943); Edward Lieuwen, *U.S. Policy in Latin America* (New York, 1965); and Dexter Perkins, *A History of the Monroe Doctrine*, 3d ed. (Boston, 1963). Other general works are Doris A. Graber, *Crisis Diplomacy: A History of U.S. Intervention Policies and Practices* (Washington, D.C., 1959); and Donald M. Dozer, *Are We Good Neighbors? Three Decades of Inter-American Relations, 1930–1960* (Gainesville, Fla., 1961). A more recent survey is Wilfrid H. Callcott's *The Western Hemisphere: Its Influence on United States Policies to the End of World War II* (Austin, Tex., 1968).

The two standard works on the forces responsible for American expansion at the turn of the century are Julius W. Pratt, *Expansionists of 1898* (Baltimore, 1951); and Walter LaFeber, *The New Empire* (Ithaca, N.Y., 1963). See also Albert K. Weinberg, *Manifest Destiny* (Baltimore, 1935); and Milton Plesur, *America's Outward Thrust: Approaches to Foreign Affairs, 1865–1890* (DeKalb, Ill., 1971). For a provocative interpretation of the new manifest destiny see Ernest R. May, *American Imperialism: A Speculative Essay* (New York, 1968).

The leading account of United States policy toward Latin America during the Progressive Era and World War I is Dana G. Munro's *Intervention and Dollar Diplomacy in the Caribbean: 1900–1921* (Princeton, N.J., 1964). The best general work on Theodore Roosevelt's foreign policy is Howard K. Beale's *Theodore Roosevelt and the Rise of America to World Power* (Baltimore, 1956). See in addition George E. Mowry, *The Era of Theodore Roosevelt, 1900–1912* (New York, 1958); Raymond A. Esthus, *Theodore Roosevelt and the International Rivalries* (Waltham, Mass., 1970); David H. Burton, *Theodore Roosevelt: Con-*

253

fident Imperialist (Philadelphia, 1968); and Richard D. Challener, *Admirals, Generals, and American Foreign Policy, 1898–1914* (Princton, N.J., 1973).

For a dated discussion of Taft's policies toward Latin America see Scott Nearing and Joseph Freeman, *Dollar Diplomacy* (New York, 1925). A more recent study is Walter V. Scholes and Marie V. Scholes, *The Foreign Policies of the Taft Administration* (Columbia, Mo., 1970). Also valuable is Dana G. Munro, "Dollar Diplomacy in Nicaragua, 1909–1913," *Hispanic American Historical Review*, vol. 38 (1958).

The most concise analysis of Wilson's foreign-policy objectives appears in Arthur S. Link's *Wilson the Diplomatist* (Chicago, 1965). For a detailed account see Link's *Woodrow Wilson and the Progressive Era, 1910–1917* (New York, 1954). Wilson's near disastrous dealings with Mexico are described in Howard F. Cline, *The United States and Mexico* (Cambridge, Mass., 1953); Isidro Fabela, *Historia diplomática de la revolución mexicana, 1912–1917*, 2 vols. (Mexico City, 1958–59); and Kenneth J. Grieb, *The United States and Huerta* (Lincoln, Nebr., 1969).

Selig Adler's *The Uncertain Giant, 1921–1941: American Foreign Policy between the Wars* (New York, 1965) offers the best survey of United States diplomacy during the 1920s and 1930s. For Latin American policy during the Harding-Coolidge era see Lewis Ethan Ellis, *Republican Foreign Policy, 1921–1933* (New Brunswick, N.J., 1968); Betty Glad, *Charles Evans Hughes and the Illusions of Innocence* (Urbana, Ill., 1966); Bryce Wood, *The Making of the Good Neighbor Policy* (New York, 1961); and Stanley Robert Ross, "Dwight Morrow and the Mexican Revolution," *Hispanic American Historical Review*, vol. 38 (1958). Alexander DeConde's *Herbert Hoover's Latin American Policy* (Stanford, Calif., 1951) presents a detailed study of United States–hemispheric relations from 1929 to 1932. An excellent recent study is Robert F. Smith, *The United States and Revolutionary Nationalism in Mexico, 1916–1932* (Chicago, 1972).

Literature on the New Deal phase of the Good Neighbor Policy is extensive. Heading the list is Wood's *Making of the Good Neighbor Policy*. His delineation of the concept of the anticipation of reciprocity is particularly important. Edward O. Guerrant's *Roosevelt's Good Neighbor Policy* (Albuquerque, N.Mex., 1950) gives a basic history of the implementation of FDR's Latin American programs. Gordon Connell-Smith, *The Inter-American System* (London, 1966), and David Green, *The Containment of Latin America* (Chicago, 1971), are also pertinent.

For United States–Latin America relations during World War II see Green's *Containment of Latin America*. A New Left historian, Green argues that existing inter-American ties were altered during World War II because United States policy-makers were convinced that the trend toward revolutionary nationalism posed a threat to North American markets and investments. More balanced is Frank D. McCann, Jr., *The Brazilian-American Alliance, 1937–1945* (Princeton, N.J., 1973).

The best general works on Argentina are James R. Scobie's *Argentina: A City and Nation* (New York, 1964); Gustavo Gabriel Levene, *Historia argentina*, 3 vols. (Buenos Aires, 1964); and Arthur P. Whitaker's *The United States and Argentina* (Cambridge, Mass., 1954). Ysabel F. Rennie's *The Argentine Republic* (New York, 1945) is dated but includes helpful information on Argentine politics and nationalism. Harold F. Peterson provides a rather superficial account of Argentine-American relations in his *Argentina and the United States, 1810–1960* (Albany, N.Y., 1964), but this book is useful for its basic narrative structure. Thomas F. McGann's *Argentina, the United States, and the Inter-American System, 1880–1914* (Cambridge, Mass., 1957); Juan José Hernandez Arregui, *La formación de la conciencia nacional, 1930–1960* (Buenos Aires, 1960); and José Luis Romero, *A History of Argentine Political Thought*, 3d ed., trans. and with an introduction by Thomas F. McGann (Stanford, Calif., 1963), describe the forces and factors responsible for the development of the Argentine national character and provide valuable insights into Argentine attitudes toward the nation's proper role in world affairs. There are two excellent English-language studies of Argentine politics during the 1930s and 1940s: Robert A. Potash, *The Army & Politics in Argentina, 1928–1945* (Stanford, Calif., 1969); and Marvin Goldwert, *Democracy, Militarism, and Nationalism in Argentina, 1930–1966* (Austin, Tex., and London, 1972). Goldwert and Potash are particularly adept at explaining the relationship between the army, Argentine nationalism, and politics. A valuable source of biographical data on Argentina's chief executives and of basic information on each president's administration is Gustavo Gabriel Levene, ed., *Presidentes argentinos* (Buenos Aires, 1961). For a view of the socialist movement in particular and twentieth-century Argentine history in general see Juan José Real, *30 años de historia argentina* (Buenos Aires, 1962). *La historia que he vivido* (Buenos Aires, 1955), by Carlos Ibarguren, is a first-person account of political developments in Argentina during the 1930s and 1940s by a prominent Argentine nationalist. A valuable if biased commentray on Argentine foreign policy and inter-American relations during the initial stages of World War II is Enrique Ruiz-Guiñazú's *La política argentina y el futuro de América* (Buenos Aires, 1944). Ruiz Guiñazú was Ramón Castillo's foreign minister. For a good treatment of the Storni affair see Alberto Conil Paz and Gustavo Ferrari, *Argentina's Foreign Policy, 1930–1962*, trans. John. J. Kennedy (Notre Dame, Ind., 1966). Bartolomé Galíndez's *Apuntes de tres revoluciones* (Buenos Aires, 1956) contains an excellent analysis of the revolution of June 1943. For an account of Ramirez's last months in office and a discussion of the factors responsible for his loss of power see Felix Luna's *El 45* (Buenos Aires, 1969). There are, of course, a number of works on the Perón era. Among the best in English are George I. Blanksten's *Perón's Argentina* (New York, 1967); Robert J. Alexander's *The Perón Era* (New York, 1951); and Joseph R. Barager, ed., *Why Perón Came to Power* (New York, 1968). The best study of the man and the historical phenomenon is Carlos S. Fayt's *Naturaleza del peronismo* (Buenos Aires, 1967). For Perón's own description of his goals and policies at the close of World War II see Juan Perón, *Tres revoluciones militares* (Buenos Aires, 1963).

For detailed background information on the Argentine economy and United States–Argentine economic relations from 1939 through 1945 see "Trade Agreement between Argentina and the United States" (December 1941) and "Argentine Trade in 1942" (July 1942), in the *Bulletin of the Pan American Union*. On the crucial meat question, E. Louise Peffer, "Cordell Hull's Argentine Policy and Britain's Meat Supply," *Inter-American Economic Affairs* (Autumn, 1956), is quite useful. This piece neglects, however, wider British economic interests in Argentina and the factors behind Hull's economic policy.

One of the few scholarly works dealing with the American republics and the United Nations is John A. Houston's *Latin America in the United Nations* (New York, 1956). This work details Latin America's objectives and attitudes at the San Francisco Conference and after. In addition, a number of analyses published at the time helped to clarify Latin America's position at the close of the war. Among the best are Samuel Guy Inman, "Some Latin American Views on Post-War Reconstruction," *Foreign Policy Reports* (15 March 1944); and William Fox, "The Super Powers at San Francisco," *Review of Politics* (January 1946).

For an excellent analysis of decision-making in diplomacy see Graham T. Allison, *Essence of Decision* (Boston, 1971). Also helpful are "American Political and Bureaucratic Decision-Making," in Richard M. Pfeffer, ed., *No More Vietnams?* (New York, 1968); and Richard J. Barnet, *Roots of War* (New York, 1972). Barnet is particularly adept at identifying the various kinds of interest groups that have affected policy formulation during the twentieth century. For Franklin Roosevelt's unique approach to administration and decision-making see Richard E. Neustadt, *Presidential Power* (New York, 1960); Arthur M. Schlesinger, Jr., *The Age of Roosevelt*, vol. 2, *The Coming of the New Deal* (Boston, 1959); and two books by James MacGregor Burns: *Roosevelt: The Lion and the Fox* (New York, 1956) and *Roosevelt: The Soldier of Freedom* (New York, 1970).

As far as postwar planning within the Roosevelt and Truman administrations is concerned, the two most helpful studies were John Lewis Gaddis, *The United States and the Origins of the Cold War, 1941–1947* (New York, 1972); and

Thomas M. Campbell, *Masquerade Peace: America's UN Policy, 1944–1945* (Tallahassee, Fla., 1973).

MEMOIRS AND PUBLISHED DIARIES

The two volumes of *The Memoirs of Cordell Hull* (New York, 1948) provide detailed accounts of specific events relating to the Argentine question. Hull's recollections are not always invalidated by the numerous axes he had to grind. This source is invaluable for Hull's attitudes and rationalizations during the Argentine affair. Sumner Welles has written two books, *The Time For Decision* (New York and London, 1944) and *Seven Decisions That Shaped History* (New York, 1950, 1951), which are simultaneously commentaries on American foreign policy during the New Deal period and indirect accounts of the undersecretary's years in the State Department. As unbiased guides to an understanding of the sources of American policy, they leave much to be desired. Hull's role, for example, is almost completely neglected. Dean Acheson, in *Present at the Creation* (New York, 1969), alludes to the infighting in the State Department during Hull's tenure as secretary of state, while *The Americas: The Search for Hemispheric Security* (New York, 1949), by Lawrence Duggan, discusses United States–Argentine policy from the point of view of one who violently disagreed with Hull's get-tough policy. For an account of the Welles-Hull dispute from the perspective of a Hull supporter see Fred L. Israel, ed., *The War Diary of Breckinridge Long* (Lincoln, Nebr., 1966). The roles played by Henry Morgenthau and the Treasury Department in the formulation of Argentine policy is delineated in John Morton Blum, ed., *From the Morgenthau Diaries*, 3 vols. (Boston, 1959–1967). Blum's equally superb *The Price of Vision: The Diary of Henry A. Wallace, 1942–1946* (Boston, 1973) outlines the position taken by Henry Wallace and the Board of Economic Warfare toward both Argentina and various bureaucratic rivals. These two books are invaluable for understanding interpersonal and interagency conflicts in the upper echelons of the federal bureaucracy during World War II. For a description of the scandal that helped to bring about Sumner Welles's downfall see Orville H. Bullitt, ed., *For the President: Personal and Secret* (Boston, 1972). A helpful Argentine memoir is Nicolás Repetto's *Mi paso por la política* (Buenos Aires, 1957). See Tom Connally, *My Name Is Tom Connally* (New York, 1954), and Arthur H. Vandenberg, Jr., ed., *The Private Papers of Senator Vandenberg* (Boston, 1952), for the views of two of the principal participants in the San Francisco Conference. President Truman's *Memoirs* (New York, 1955–56) include a brief rationale for his approval of the seating of the Argentine delegation at the UNCIO. The recollections of the British ambassador to Argentina, Sir David Kelly, *The Ruling*

Few (London, 1952), constitute an invaluable description of Argentine society and politics, and of Anglo-American policy as seen from the British point of view.

PERIODICALS

In attempting to gauge the temper of American public opinion toward Argentina and its impact on United States policy, I selected a group of newspapers and journals that was small enough in number to permit in-depth investigation but large enough to allow for geographical and philosophical differences. The *New York Times* and the *New York Herald Tribune* both provided useful detailed coverage of the Argentine-American feud, while the *Times* editorialized frequently on relations between the two countries from a moderately liberal point of view. Two pro–New Deal papers that were continually concerned with developments in Argentina were the *St. Louis Post-Dispatch* and the *Washington Post*. After the Stettinius-Rockefeller group succeeded to power in the State Department, the *Post-Dispatch* reluctantly stuck with the administration, while the *Post* became vehemently critical of United States policy. The American Left is represented in this work chiefly by the *Nation* and the *New Republic*, both ardent advocates of friendship with Russia and staunch foes of Argentina's various wartime governments. The *Chicago Tribune*, the *Los Angeles Times*, and the *Saturday Evening Post* speak for those Americans who admired the Liberty League, opposed the New Deal, and abhorred the Soviet Union. These oracles tended to be more understanding of the policies, both domestic and foreign, that were pursued by Argentina during World War II. *Business Week*, the *Wall Street Journal*, the *Commercial and Financial Chronicle*, *Barron's*, the *American Exporter*, and *Export Trade and Shipper* proved to be valuable sources of information on the state of the Argentine economy and trade relations between Argentina and the United Nations. They were, as well, excellent spokesmen for the American business and financial community.

This study does not pretend to include an in-depth analysis of either Argentine or Latin American public opinion. Selected editorials from *La Nación*, *Noticias Gráficas*, and *La Hora*—all of Buenos Aires—were used to indicate popular revulsion at certain policies pursued by the United States. *El Mercurio* of Santiago, *El Popular* of Mexico City, *O Globo* of Rio de Janeiro, and *La Noche* of La Paz, among others, were cited to show that in 1944–45, various Latin American nations took essentially similar positions on the rehabilitation of Argentina, postwar planning, and the future of the Good Neighbor Policy.

OFFICIAL AND SEMIOFFICIAL PUBLICATIONS

Like all studies dealing with twentieth-century American foreign policy, this project began with the Department of State's *Foreign Relations of the United States, 1940–1945*. These volumes contain telegrams, memoranda, and dispatches selected from the files of relevant governmental agencies and presidential libraries. The documents furnish a basic narrative of Argentine-American relations for the period under investigation. For insights into the motives and goals of the policy-makers, particularly where interpersonal and interagency rivalries are concerned, the scholar must look elsewhere. The *Department of State Bulletin*, published by the State Department, and *Documents on American Foreign Relations*, published by the World Peace Foundation, furnished the texts of important statements, press releases, and speeches on Argentina during the war years. *External Research Papers*, studies of specific diplomatic problems by State Department analysts which were published by the department, were useful for background data. For a semiofficial but surprisingly impartial narrative of events relating to the Argentine affair see the *Foreign Policy Bulletin*, published by the Foreign Policy Association. *Foreign Policy Reports*, published by the same group, contains a series of articles on Argentine-American wartime relations by various members of the foreign-policy establishment. For a verbatim account of all official meetings held at the San Francisco Conference see *Documents of the U.N.C.I.O., San Francisco, 1945* (London and New York, 1945), published by the United Nations Information Organization. "Relations of the Caribbean Defense Command with Argentina," an unpublished compilation by the Historical Section of the Caribbean Defense Command, includes intelligence reports on developments within Argentina, a description of CDC actions toward various Argentina wartime governments, and an explanation of the motives underlying those actions. Although it did produce a few letters and speeches on legislative attitudes toward the Argentine problem, the *Congressional Record* proved to be a remarkably barren source for this study.

UNPUBLISHED SOURCES

The two sources that are basic to understanding both the decision-making process and Argentine-American wartime relations are the State Department decimal files and lot files on Latin America housed in the National Archives in Washington, D.C. The decimal file consists of incoming and outgoing diplomatic communiques, letters from public officials and private citizens, foreign press clippings, and intelligence reports. The lot files contain copies of intradepartmental memoranda concerning Argentina, arranged by date. This source was particularly helpful in enabling me to trace the continuing debate on policy formulation and to define the various cliques that developed within the department.

The archives also contain the records of other agencies with input into the decision-making process. The General Records of the Office of Strategic Services are massive. OSS officers submitted literally thousands of reports on Argentine affairs and Axis activities within Argentina to the State Department and other government agencies. By cross checking with the records of other agencies and with the private papers of the key participants, I was able to discover which organizations and individuals had access to OSS reports and which reports were most influential in shaping their policy recommendations. The General Records of the Department of the Treasury were not at all helpful, primarily because nearly all significant memoranda had been removed from the material turned over to the archives and had been retained by the department. Treasury Department officials proved to be most uncooperative about allowing me access to these records. Fortunately, Henry Morgenthau made copies of virtually all inter- and extra-office memoranda and took them with him when he left. The General Records of the Combined Chiefs of Staff, which are lodged in the military division of the archives, were useful in determining the military's attitude toward Argentina. Also administered by the National Archives but housed in the Federal Records Center at Suitland, Maryland, are the general Records of the Foreign Economic Administration and the General Records of the Office of Coordinator of Inter-American Affairs. The FEA files contain memos that indicate the attitude of the agency's leadership toward Argentina and, to a certain extent, the considerations that helped to shape these attitudes. There is also valuable information on the conflict in Buenos Aires between representatives of the FEA and officials of the United States embassy. The coordinator's files were helpful primarily in defining the views and motives of the coordinator, Nelson Rockefeller. These records contain detailed information on the activities of the OCIAA committees in each Latin American country. Because of Argentina's challenge to United States policy and the significance of that challenge to the bureaucratic struggle in Washington, however, the local committee in Argentina did not possess enough clout to influence United States policy. Moreover, to my disappointment, I discovered few comments by OCIAA field officers on the evolution of United States policy toward Argentina and the assumptions that underlay it.

In the Library of Congress the pertinent private collections to see are the papers of Cordell Hull, Breckinridge Long, and Leo Pasvolsky. The Hull Papers, although disappointing, contain information on the secretary's attempts to coerce various Latin American states into supporting United States policy toward Argentina during 1944. Long's correspondence supplied additional data on the Hull-Welles dispute. As special advisor to the State Department, Leo Pasvolsky played a significant role in the development of United States policy for the Chapultepec and San Francisco conferences. His papers were especially helpful in shedding light on the postwar planning process within the State Department during 1944 and 1945.

The Diaries and Papers of Henry Stimson are located in Sterling Library, Yale University. The letters, notes, and transcripts of telephone conversations that are contained in this well indexed collection clearly reveal the secretary of war's views on Argentina, hemispheric security, the Monroe Doctrine, and the Good Neighbor Policy.

The papers of Edward Stettinius, Jr., at the University of Virginia contain 750,000 items relating in one way or another to the secretary of state's public life. The vast majority of letters and memos deal with trivial matters, and as of 1974 the collection was virtually unorganized. There are, nonetheless, several memos in the Stettinius Papers that are essential to an understanding of his relationships to FDR, Nelson Rockefeller, and the decision-making process. They also provide several valuable insights into the reasoning behind the State Department's decision in 1945 to reverse its policy toward Argentina.

Although much of the material in the diaries of Henry A. Wallace has been duplicated in Blum's *Price of Vision*, this collection at the University of Iowa contains vital information on the Board of Economic Warfare and its head, Milo Perkins. In addition, Wallace's notebooks include memos and transcripts that help to clarify the vice-president's views on postwar planning and Argentina; particularly useful are the not always uncritical comments of Wallace's and Perkin's subordinates on the motives and goals of their superiors.

The papers of Harry S. Truman were disappointing. The Argentine folder adds little to existing knowledge on the president's role in the decision to admit Argentina to the United Nations in 1945. The collection does, however, contain a sizable body of material dealing with popular reaction to the admission of Argentina and to the Argentine-American rapprochement in general.

The Franklin D. Roosevelt Library at Hyde Park includes the papers of a number of individuals who were intimately associated with the making of hemispheric policy during World War II. Perhaps the least helpful were the papers of the president. The President's Secretary's File and the Map Room File yielded material pertaining to United States policy during both the Rio Conference and the Bolivian Coup. Perhaps the single most valuable collection was the diary and papers of Henry Morgenthau, Jr. The diary detailed the Treasury Department's position on the Argentine question; the motives of Morgenthau and his chief assistant, Harry Dexter White; and the Treasury Department's relationship with other governmental agencies. The Presidential Diaries, which are records of Morgenthau's meetings with FDR, did more to clarify both the president's attitude toward Argentina and the struggle within his administration for control of Argentine policy than did any other single source that I consulted. In the Papers of Harry Hopkins there is a good bit of material on the Argentine question as discussed at the London, Moscow, and Yalta conferences. Most valuable was a collection of letters, telegrams, and reports in the Hopkins Papers entitled "FBI Reports on Argentina." J. Edgar Hoover periodically supplied Roosevelt and Hopkins with intelligence on developments in Argentina that were replete with his own personal observations. Evidently, the White House relied on this source more heavily than on any other. The diaries of Adolf Berle were a gold mine of information with regard to the evolution of hemispheric policy as a whole during World War II, the emergence of various cliques within the State Department, and the Warren mission in 1945.

There were, of course, unpublished sources that I did not consult but that might seem pertinent to scholars interested in the field—the papers of Spruille Braden, United States ambassador to Argentina from 1945 to 1946, and George Messersmith, ambassador to Mexico and later to Argentina, for example. During the latter stages of my research I rarely encountered a letter or memo that I had not previously seen. The papers of all of the principal participants, with the exception of Sumner Welles, whose papers are still closed to the public, have been consulted; I simply saw no need to seek additional comments by those who were not directly involved.

INDEX

Acción Argentina, 95–97

Acheson, Dean, 70, 142, 192, 226 n.26; and bureaucratic situation in State Department, 219 n.4; and internationalists, Latin Americanists, 25; opposes freezing of Argentine assets, 69, 114–17; as peacemaker in State Department, 43; and State Department rivalry with BEW, 66

Act of Chapultepec, 187–92, 202, 208–9; Latin American reaction to, 189–90; U.S. opinion toward, 249 n.105

Act of Havana, 19

Adams, John Quincy, 2

Alianza de la Nacionalista, 12

Allies (World War I), 10

Allies (World War II), 26, 41, 52, 55, 69, 75, 79–80, 91, 96, 100–102, 124, 126, 137, 146–47, 167, 188, 201; depend on Argentine foodstuffs, 146–47; raw material stockpiles of, 122

Ameghino, Cesár, 190

America. *See* United States

American and Foreign Power Company, 103–54

American Associated Company, 74

American Factors Company, 174

American Republic Affairs Division, United States State Department (ARA), 68, 84, 86, 140–41, 167, 191–93; new leadership in, 169–70

Anderson, Jack Z., 181

Anglo-American Trading Corporation, 174

appeasement, 79

Aranha, Oswaldo, 34, 36, 152

Argentina, 44–45, 77–81, 84–85, 89, 97, 99, 108, 112, 118, 124, 130, 137–38, 141, 156, 174, 205; and Act of Havana, 19; American journalists on, 176–77; Axis declares war on, 190–92; Axis espionage and subversion in, 73–76; Axis severs relations with, 127; and Buenos Aires Conference, 15; collective-security system in, fears domination by U.S., 7; and Connally's statement, 38; continuing prosperity in, 55, 151; and Declaration of Lima, 17; distribution of newsprint in, 47; establishes relations with Soviet Union, 268; Europe's economic dependence on, 8, 96; foreign-policy establishment in, 111–12; geographic characteristics of, 9; Great Britain concludes military-aid agreement with, 58; Great Britain's economic ties with, 56; and Havana Conference, 18; and Hull-Storni affair, 99–103; internationalists on, 26–27; lacks industrial resources, 9; Latin American attitudes toward, 182–83; Latin Americanists on, 24; and Lima Conference, 17; and Mexico City Conference, 185–90; and military balance of power in South America, 91; and Montevideo Committee, 81; national characteristics of, 8–10; neo-internationalists on, 178; neo–Latin Americanists on, 172; and OCIAA propaganda, 49; and Panama Conference, 18; and Pearl Harbor, 29–30; and Proclaimed List, 54–55; as producer of raw materials, 9; renounces aggression, 190; So-

Index

Hoover, J. Edgar, 95, 102, 104, 230 n.57; has negative view of Argentina, 69

Hoover administration, 209

Hopkins, Harry, 95, 102, 146, 177, 230 n.57; and formation of FEA, 93; and Stettinius, 108

Hora, La, 101, 117

Huerta, Victoriano, 120

Hulburd, David, 65

Hull, Cordell, 6, 27, 31, 33, 35, 40, 45, 55, 60, 62, 68, 70–71, 79–81, 97, 108, 112–13, 130, 132, 141, 146, 150, 177, 181–82, 201, 206, 211–12, 226 n.26, 241 n.115; agrees to secret talks between Armour and Farrell government, 115; and Anglo-Argentine meat contract, 150–51; and Argentine membership in U.N., 198, 250–51 n.138; and Buenos Aires Conference, 15; determined to democratize Argentine political system, 96; and economic sanctions against Argentina, 123–27; excluded from decision-making process, 137, 168–69; and freezing of Japanese assets, 144; and Havana Conference, 19–21; and Hull-Storni affair, 99–103; in internationalist "organization," 24; and left-wing conspiracy, 66; and Montevideo Committee report, 82–83; presses Argentina to become nonbelligerent ally, 128–30; and Ramírez government, 124; and recognition of Farrell government, 136–37; and recognition of Rawson and Ramírez governments, 91–92; refuses Argentina intelligence on Axis espionage, 129; resigns, 168–69; and Rio Conference, 39–40, 43; in Roosevelt foreign-policy establishment, 40; sends severance ultimatum to Argentina, 98; sensitive to charges of appeasement, 79; and telecommunications between Argentina and Axis, 85–87; and U.S. economic concessions to Argentina, 30; and Wallace, BEW, 66–67; and Welles, 72–73, 103–7, 138, 159; and Wilson, 25; and Wilsonian internationalism, 113. *See also* internationalists

Hull-Storni affair, 99–103

Iceland, 154

Ickes, Harold, 61

immigration, European, 8

Industrias Metalurgicas, 58

Ingram, Jonas, 121, 137, 155

"integral nationalism," 13

integral nationalists, 55, 178; ally with Castillo, 28; antilabor feeling among, 236 n.2; ascendancy of, in Argentina, 112; on declaration of war against Axis, 191–92; foreign and domestic goals of, in 1943, 88–89; and Radical party, 229 n.29

Inter-American Conference on Problems of War and Peace, 165. *See also* Mexico City Conference

Inter-American System, 78, 126, 138, 150, 153–54, 160, 162–64, 178, 182, 192, 207, 211; Argentine-American debate over, 7; attitude of Latin Americanists toward, 25–26; defined by Welles, 23–24; discussed at Buenos Aires Conference, 15; Duggan's attitude toward, 23–24; and Rio resolutions, 41

International Conference of American States, 16–17. *See also* Lima Conference

International Harvester, 173

internationalism: attitude of Latin America toward, 182; use of, by Argentineans at Buenos Aires Conference, 15

internationalists, 42, 43, 60, 73, 76, 81, 127–31, 159, 168–69; and Anglo-Argentine meat contract, 148–49; Argentine attitude toward, after Pearl Harbor, 26–27; and Argentine revolution of June, 1943, 89; determined to overthrow Ramírez government, 96–97, 121–22; and freezing of Argentine assets, 70; and Good Neighbor Policy, 24–26; and inter-American meeting on Argentina, 161–62; and Latin Americanists, 210–12; and nonrecognition of Farrell government, 137–40; and overthrow of Farrell-Perón government, 164; and Perón's speech of June 10, 156–57; and publication of FBI reports on Argentina, 126–27; question integrity of Argentine severance resolution, 128; and Roosevelt foreign-policy establishment, 25–26; and Stettinius, 108; and trade sanctions against Argentina, 122–24, 150–52; and U.S. business interests in Argentina, 150; want to democratize Argentine political system, 112, 138–39; and Wilsonian internationalism, 111–13, 213–14; and World War II, 87

International Monetary Fund, 184

International Telephone and Telegraph Company, 173

intervention, 5, 16, 209; declining need for, after World War I, 4; Latin Americanists try to eradicate, 23; nonrecognition as form of, 120; and "no transfer principle," 18–19; Rockefeller's denunciation of, 192; Wallace on, 67

Irigoyen, Hipólito, 10

isolationism, 15

Italy, 6–7, 21, 29, 36–37, 39, 50, 52, 56, 66, 79, 86, 95, 97, 100, 114, 128, 133, 143, 150; Argentina declares war on, 191; attempts to penetrate South America, 16

Japan, 6–7, 16, 29, 36–37, 39, 50, 52, 56, 79, 86, 97, 100, 128–29, 133, 167; Argentina declares war on, 191; Argentina severs ties with, 127; its military gains in 1942, 43–44

Jews, 75, 121

Johnston, Eric, 245 n.27

Johnstone, D. B., 171

Joint Army and Navy Advisory Board, 124, 130, 157

Joint Chiefs of Staff, United States, 172–173. *See also* military, the United States

Jones, Jesse, 61, 64–65, 93

Jones, Marvin, 145

journalists, Latin American, 182

journalists, U.S.: and Argentine revolution of June, 1943, 94–95; and Castillo government, 45; criticize U.S. policy on Argentina, 176–77; and Farrell government, 134–36; and Hull-Storni affair, 102; and Rio Conference, 44–45

Justistas, 212

Justo, Augustín, 31–32; champions Allied-Argentine solidarity, 76; forms alliance with liberal nationalists, 28; opposed by British in Argentina, 59; and sources of power, 27-29

Kelly, Sir David, 57, 158

Kirchwey, Freda, 44

Knox, Philander, 3

Krock, Arthur, 104, 106

LaFollette Progressives, 5

Latin America, 1–2, 5–7, 23, 41, 57, 98, 140, 145, 179, 205; and Argentina's admission to UNCIO, 197–202; and Argentina's call for an inter-American conference, 161; countries in, to be excluded from UNCIO, 247 n.73; desires Argentine-American rapprochement, 153–54, 208–9; and dollar diplomacy, 3; fears Argentine aggression, 183; fears domination of world affairs by Big Four, 160–61; fears Soviet expansion, 160–61, 208–9; fears World War II would revive U.S. imperialism, 7; German and Italian penetration of, 16; and Good Neighbor Policy, 6; and Mexico City Conference, 182–84, 189–90; and Pearl Harbor, 29; recognizes Ramírez government, 91; and Rio Conference, 40–41; seen by U.S. as object of British imperialism, 149; supports nonrecognition of Bolivian government, 119–21; U.S. goals in, 1; vulnerable to Axis attack, 36; Wallace on, 67; wants postwar economic aid from U.S., 160; and Wilsonian internationalism, 4

Latin Americanists, 60, 74, 76, 112, 131, 152, 162, 168, 209; anticipate spontaneous revolution in Argentina, 121–22; and Bolivian revolution of 1943, 119–21; composition of, and their attitude on inter-American relations, 23–24; deprive Argentina of military aid, 49–52; desire to protect Argentine sovereignty, 19; and freezing of Argentine assets, 115–16; impact of Welles's resignation on, 106; and internationalists, 70–71, 140–41, 210–12; need to secure Argentine cooperation in war effort, 44–46; oppose Crowley's appointment, 94; oppose hard-line policy, 84; and policy of selective economic deprivation, 52–53; and Proclaimed List, 54; and propaganda in Argentina, 47–48; reject unilateral coercion, 46–47, 138–40; and relationship of nonintervention to Good

Index